Praise for
VIPER PILOT

"Dan Hampton's *Viper Pilot* truly impressed me—if you're a combat vet, it's sweaty palms again; if not, strap in and get ready. Filled with lots of action, here's a real and up-close look at modern fighter combat, told straight from the cockpit. It's an enjoyable read that's good all the way through."

—Colonel Jacksel Broughton (USAF, Ret.),
recipient of the Air Force Cross for extraordinary
heroism and author of *Rupert Red Two: A Fighter Pilot's Life*

"An instant aviation classic, Dan Hampton's *Viper Pilot* captures the essence of Wild Weasel fighter operations. His recollections and thrilling portrayals of combat missions kept me glued to the story. I am proud to have fought with 'Two Dogs': he is a courageous, talented, smart fighter pilot—always the consummate warrior."

—Brigadier General David L. Moody (USAF, Ret.)

"*Viper Pilot* is fantastic. Lt. Col. Dan Hampton offers a personal, irreverent, no-holds-barred look into the life of an Air Force fighter pilot. A great read!"

—Dale Brown, former USAF captain and
New York Times bestselling author of *A Time for Patriots*

"A rare riveting memoir of a highly decorated fighter pilot that's packed with grit, swagger, and great humor. Do not miss this one!"

—W. E. B. Griffin and William E. Butterworth

About the Author

The *New York Times* bestselling author of *Viper Pilot*, U.S. Air Force Lieutenant Colonel (Ret.) Dan Hampton flew 151 combat missions during his twenty years in the USAF (1986–2006). For his service in the Iraq War, Kosovo conflict, and first Gulf War, Col. Hampton received four Distinguished Flying Crosses with Valor, a Purple Heart, eight Air Medals with Valor, five Meritorious Service Medals, and numerous other citations. He is a graduate of the elite USAF Fighter Weapons School, USN Top Gun School, and USAF Special Operations School. Hampton was named his squadron's Instructor Pilot of the Year six times and pioneered air-combat tactics that are now standard. A graduate of Texas A&M University, he has published articles in the *Journal of Electronic Defense, Air Force Magazine, Airpower* magazine, and several classified tactical works for the *USAF Fighter Weapons Review*.

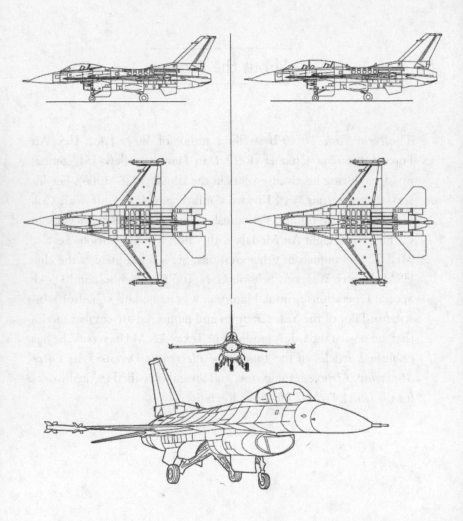

VIPER PILOT

A MEMOIR OF AIR COMBAT

DAN HAMPTON

wm
WILLIAM MORROW
An Imprint of HarperCollins*Publishers*

Map courtesy of the UN Cartographic Section. All other images courtesy of the author.

A hardcover edition of this book was published in 2012 by William Morrow, an imprint of HarperCollins Publishers.

FIRST WILLIAM MORROW PAPERBACK EDITION PUBLISHED 2013.

Designed by Jamie Lynn Kerner

The Library of Congress has cataloged the hardcover edition as follows:

Hampton, Dan.
  Viper pilot : a memoir of air combat / Dan Hampton.
    p. cm.
Includes index.
ISBN 978-0-06-213035-8 1. Fighter pilots—United States—Biography. 2. F-16 (Jet fighter plane). 3. United States. Air Force—Biography. 4. Persian Gulf War, 1991—Aerial operations, American. 5. Persian Gulf War, 1991—Personal narratives, American. 6. Iraq War, 2003–2011—Aerial operations, American. 7. Iraq War, 2003–2011—Personal narratives, American. 8. Electronic warfare aircraft—United States. I. Title.
  UG626.2.H335A3 2012
  358.40092—dc23
  [B]
                                    2012016117

ISBN 978-0-06-213034-1

23 24 25 26 27 LBC 20 19 18 17 16

To *my brother fighter pilots—and all who have seen The Elephant.*

Nothing can compensate my family for the constant worry and sleepless nights my profession caused them; but I thank them all, especially my parents and beautiful wife, Beth, for their patience and forbearance.

There are only two types of aircraft—fighters and targets.
—DOYLE "WAHOO" NICHOLSON, USMC

CONTENTS

AUTHOR'S NOTE

I WROTE THIS BOOK MYSELF. RECONSTRUCTING THE COMBAT scenes in *Viper Pilot* wasn't difficult—they are forever etched in my memory. However, I confirmed every date, time, and call sign against actual flight data cards, mission reports, and intelligence summaries. These events have all been declassified and can usually be found, in one form or another, in open sources.

Classified information is not directly discussed, for obvious security reasons. This includes technical specifications about weapon systems, tactics, and aircraft capabilities. Where essential, real names of pilots do appear, always with the express permission of the individuals involved. Otherwise, pseudonyms or call signs are utilized.

Lastly, the Office of the Secretary of the Air Force has conducted its own independent review of this book and approved it for publication as originally written.

—D.H.

VIPER PILOT

PROLOGUE

ANGEL OF DEATH

March 24, 2003
Nasiriyah, Iraq

"C'MON . . . C'MON . . ." I GRITTED MY TEETH. FORCING MY aching jaws to relax, I pulled the throttle back further and dropped the F-16's nose a few degrees toward the ground. As the Viper slid down into the dusty brown mess below us, I felt unaccustomed anxious twinges jab through my gut.

"All Players, all Players . . . this is LUGER on Guard for Emergency Close Air-Support. Any CAS-capable flights report to LUGER on Indigo Seven . . . repeat—any CAS-capable flights report to LUGER on Indigo Seven. Emergency CAS in progress. LUGER out."

I stared at the stack of mission materials on my knee. I'd never heard of Indigo Seven, but I had a comm card that was supposed to have every frequency in the galaxy on it for a given mission.

Fuck it.

Another fucking freq I don't have. I swore at the idiots who'd done the mission planning in the *six* months before the war. They drank coffee, sat on their butts, and generated an enormous amount of material, 90 percent of which was useless.

I knew some of them. Smart guys, but so utterly convinced they were correct that they'd failed to heed anyone else's suggestions. The results spoke for themselves. I didn't even have a decent large-scale map of Iraq, and no provision had been made at all for Close Air-Support missions (CAS).* I was a Wild Weasel, a surface-to-air missile killer—close air-support wasn't our primary mission. But those of us who'd fought the First Gulf War or Kosovo knew better. When troops on the ground needed help, any fighter available was supposed to be there—fast.

FUEL . . . FUEL . . . the green symbology flashed in the center of my Heads Up Display (HUD). Toggling it off, I quickly typed in a new minimum fuel number. A much lower number. It might keep the warning signal from bothering me, but it wouldn't put another pound of JP-8 in my fuel tanks. It was also a cardinal sin. If you didn't have enough fuel to finish your mission, then you returned to base. Simple.

Or not.

The Second Gulf War was in its fifth day, and a unit of the Third Battalion Second Marines had gotten cut off north of Nasiriyah in southern Iraq. They'd called for Emergency Close Air-Support, which meant any fighters able to respond were to scratch their existing missions and race to the scene. It was literally life or death.

Operating under the call sign ROMAN 75, my four-ship (a flight of four fighters) had been immediately rerolled to try and save the Marines. Unfortunately, the biggest sandstorm in recent

---

*For help along the way with acronyms and aviation jargon, please see the glossary at the end of the book. A map of Iraq follows the glossary.

history was headed this way, and two other flights of fighters had been unable to get down through the stuff and find the grunts.

So I wasn't optimistic.

But this was war, and you did what you had to do.

"ROMAN . . . ROMAN . . . this is CHIEFTAIN . . . say . . ." CHIEFTAIN was the Marine unit that called for close air-support. The crackling radio erupted with the unmistakable popping of automatic weapons in the background.

I swallowed, hard. I knew what he was asking. *Where the hell are you? What's taking so long? You've got to get here NOW or we're all dead.*

I licked my lips, feeling my tongue rasp over cracked skin that hadn't tasted water in nearly eight hours. "CHIEFTAIN . . . CHIEFTAIN . . . ROMAN 75 is attacking from the south . . . sixty seconds."

Southern Iraq is ugly. No two ways about it. As I stared out over the vast Mesopotamian plain, I wondered, not for the first time, why we never seemed to go to war in pretty places. Lichtenstein or Ireland maybe. Bermuda.

Today it was just a tan mess. The jagged blue-green scar of the Euphrates River was muted, like someone had thrown a sheer brown cloth over it. Usually the earth east of the river, toward the Iranian border, looked green and relatively fertile. Now it was blanketed in shades of mud. The horizon worried me, since it had disappeared into a dirty-brown wall boiling up from the southwest, covering Iraq in an ominous shadow. Farther west, the sky had turned a dull black from the ground up to 50,000 feet. The sun was a faded orange smear, barely visible through the curtain of sand.

I glanced around the cockpit again. Adjusting a setting here, rechecking one there. Along the right console, way in the back, I had a canvas bag about the size of a shoebox. This held the aircraft's data cartridge and classified tapes. Once they were loaded, I used the bag for my water bottle, extra piddle packs, and some food. I unzipped it so, hours later, I could get inside with one hand. I always looked forward to snack time. Sort of a reward for surviving.

My fighter dropped through 7,000 feet, and I stole one more look at the ominous sky around me. The sandstorm was almost here. The front edge of it had rolled up from the southwest, obscuring everything in a tan haze. I'd split off my Number Three and Four aircraft and just kept my wingman orbiting above the target area. There was no need for both of us to be down here.

"ROMAN . . . RO . . ."

There was panic in the Forward Air Controller's voice, and I fought back the nearly overwhelming urge to shove the nose forward and dive into the fight. I wouldn't help them by getting myself killed. If I could see the ground, it would be different, but the dust made an immediate attack impossible.

I keyed the mike and spoke clearly and unemotionally. I hoped a calm, confident voice would do them good, even if I hardly felt that way myself. Fighter pilots are great actors.

"CHIEFTAIN . . . confirm no friendlies are on the road. Repeat . . . confirm no friendlies are on the road."

"Affirmative! Affirmative . . . all friendlies . . . road . . . west of the road . . ."

I zippered in reply, and as the dust swallowed the jet, I called up my Air-to-Ground weapons display and selected one of the two AGM-65G infrared Maverick missiles slung beneath my wings.

They were big. About 600 pounds each and able to precisely guide by tracking contrasts in the heat, or lack of heat, around a target.

"Sonofabitch . . ."

I was staring at my display, seeing what the Maverick saw, and it was crap. Completely washed out, like a TV station that had gone off the air in a cloud of brown static.

Four thousand feet . . . and five miles to the target. Not much time.

I quickly switched to the other missile. Same thing. "Bastard . . ."

The blowing sand wasn't helping, but it wouldn't do this much damage, and I thumped the glare shield in frustration. I'd been so busy that I'd forgotten that the sun was going down. IR missiles worked fine at night, because they basically tracked contrasts, not a visual picture. But for a few hours on either side of sunset or sunrise, everything was the same temperature unless it was heated internally. Called diurnal crossover, it was unavoidable, and it nearly always destroyed the infrared picture. This was exactly why we used other weapons during those times. But the only other tool I had was my cannon. That meant getting very low and very close.

But men were dying. Our men.

I strained forward against the ejection-seat harness and continued down.

Three thousand feet. Four hundred eighty knots and descending. I was riveted to my radar altimeter, which gave me a digital readout of my actual height above the ground. A lifesaver at night or in bad weather. Like now.

Maybe the dust will thin out lower down. I took a breath and ignored my thumping heart. It truly was hammering against my chest. No kidding.

"ROMAN . . . ROMAN . . . the Rags have crossed the road . . . they're . . . they're . . . *stand by!*"

"Rags" was politically incorrect shorthand for *raghead*. Meaning the Iraqi Army, in this case. I tried to lick my lips again but gave up. Pulling the throttle farther back, I fanned my speed brakes to slow the F-16 down as it passed 2,000 feet.

There!

I blinked several times to make sure I wasn't hallucinating.

Darker brown. Rocks and the ugly, stunted green bushes that dotted Iraq. Ground!

Immediately staring forward through the HUD, I centered the steering cues toward the only position I'd been given.

3.3 miles.

I quickly glanced at the Radar Warning Receiver. Happily, it was empty of any signals from radar-guided missiles or antiaircraft artillery. Of course, it wouldn't pick up infrared missiles or the few hundred AK-47s down there, but I'd take what good news I could find.

Leveling the fighter at a thousand feet, I closed the speed brakes and pushed the throttle enough to hold 400 knots. This gave me speed to maneuver without sucking down what little gas remained.

"ROMAN . . . they . . . position . . . between the road and the hill . . ." The transmission was garbled and riddled with static.

Hill? What hill?

His radio was breaking up badly. Something else to blame on the approaching sandstorm.

" . . . anything on the road . . . repeat . . . kill anything on the road!"

"ROMAN 75 copies." So, nothing friendly was on the road, and I had a license to kill.

And there it was.

A winding gray ribbon running north to south. The edges were irregular and dust swirled over most of it as I angled in from the southeast. Cranking the jet over, I lined up the steering line on the target. Staring down at the display above my left knee, I was seeing what the Maverick missile saw.

Nothing. Not a fucking thing.

As I raised my eyes, the Iraqi column suddenly appeared out of the muck. Instantly flicking the DOGFIGHT switch, I called up my cannon symbology and shoved the nose forward.

But it was too late.

I saw enemy vehicles, several armored personnel carriers, and lots of running figures as I flashed overhead. What I looked like to them I couldn't imagine, but the whole area disappeared behind me in about three seconds.

Jabbing the MARK button on the keyboard beneath my HUD, I banked up hard to the west.

"CHIEFTAIN . . . CHIEFTAIN . . . ROMAN 75 is off west . . . re-attack in ninety seconds . . . from the north."

He didn't answer.

Swearing slowly and fluently, I put the target directly behind me and headed due west. The visibility sucked, but I thought I saw a rounded bit of higher ground and some movement. It must be the Marines.

Hang on, guys . . .

The MARK point was just that. When I hit the button, the F-16's computer wizardry marked the point on the earth I was flying over, like a pin on a map. It generated a latitude and longitude with steering and distance to the exact position I'd overflown. That particular function had been created for just this type of situation. I now knew precisely where the Iraqis were—and how to attack them.

At four miles from the target, I pulled up to 2,000 feet and swept north. I'd fly an arc until I found the road and then attack the rear of the convoy with my cannon. They'd never see me coming out of the dust.

"ROMAN Two . . . One on Victor." I pulled the throttle back and looked at my dwindling fuel readout.

"Go ahead One." My wingman was still up there somewhere, thankfully.

"Call LUGER and have him bring a tanker as far north as possible. You meet the tanker and stay with him." LUGER was the orbiting AWACS. Theoretically, he knew where all the fighters and tankers were operating at any given time. Theoretically.

"Two copies." Good man. No questions or chatter. All he added was, "It's getting a little shitty up here."

"One copies . . . I need to re-attack. Get the tanker. You're cleared off."

I was now truly on my own. But my wingman was carrying anti-radiation missiles, utterly useless in this situation, so he might as well go get gas. I didn't expect the tanker to cross into Iraq, but it was worth a try. Unhooking my sweaty mask so it dangled against my cheek, I glanced outside. *What I wouldn't give for a drink of water.*

"ROMAN . . . ROMAN this is CHIEFTAIN . . ." The radios exploded to life again. " . . . moving . . . vehicles . . . the road. APCs and trucks . . . battalion strength . . ."

He was breathless, and as he broke off, I could hear the clanging of a heavy weapon firing. One of ours, I hoped.

4.2 miles.

The target was now back over my left shoulder and completely obscured by dust. I was also getting bounced around a bit by the turbulent winds on the front edge of the storm. Oh, and the ground had disappeared again.

Fucking terrific.

But I couldn't wait any longer. Racking the fighter up, I pulled a hard, quick five-G turn and came around heading southeast. I knew I'd be angling in over the road, but maybe if the Iraqis saw me, they'd leave the Marines alone for a few minutes.

Rolling out, I called up the gun symbology and rehooked the oxygen mask.

"CHIEFTAIN . . . ROMAN is in from the north . . . thirty seconds."

"ROMAN . . . God's . . . hurr . . ."

And he broke off again. *For God's sake hurry.*

I'm coming buddy . . . hang on.

Anger lanced through me and my fatigue vanished. There were American Marines down there fighting for their lives. Guys like me from towns like mine. Men with mothers and girlfriends and kids of their own.

Fuck it.

I shoved the throttle and the nose forward.

At a thousand feet I still couldn't see the ground, since the weather continued to deteriorate. Nudging the jet slightly left, I dropped down to 500 feet and slowed to 400 knots. Brown crud whipped past the cockpit and sand was caking into any part of the jet that wasn't slick. Like ice. Brown, dry ice. What a weird place.

In 2.7 miles, I nudged the fighter down to 200 feet, praying there were no towers or cables to hit. The gun was up and I . . . *there it was!*

The road.

Holding rock-steady, I craned my neck sideways to see around the HUD and lined up on the road.

"ROMAN . . . ROMAN . . . more trucks . . . from the north . . . we . . . overrun." The Marine sounded like he was right next to me. He sounded scared.

"C'mon . . . c'mon . . ." I muttered, straining to see.

Suddenly a boxy shape appeared at the edge of my vision . . . and another. Trucks! Big military trucks. About twenty of them, lined up on the road and heading south toward the Marines as I dropped out of the dust like an avenging angel.

My left hand touched the MASTER ARM switch as I stared through the HUD. Long-ingrained habits took over, and I lined up on the far end of the string of vehicles. I was less than a mile and a half from the closest truck.

Bunting the nose down, I let the little aiming circle with the dot in it wriggle around at the bottom of my HUD. The idea was to drop toward the earth while the circle, the gun pipper, rose up toward the target. You made surgical adjustments to your airspeed and your aim to put the pipper on the target close enough to kill it. It was good not to kill yourself, either, by hitting the ground at 800 feet per second.

Passing a hundred feet, the pipper was still well short of the truck, so I eased back slightly and physically pulled the nose of the jet—and, hence, the gun—up to point at the truck. The moment the little green pipper touched the big tailgate, I squeezed the trigger with my right forefinger.

"BUURRRPPP . . ."

The jet rocked sideways as the Gatling gun spat out a few hundred 20-mm shells. I instantly pulled up again and then bunted forward, aiming at the middle of the convoy.

"BUURRRPPP."

Rolling and pulling off to the right, I cranked up on one wing and flew sideways down the column. Dark little figures were scattering both ways off the road and jumping behind bushes or into ditches. I was so low I could see small Iraqi flags painted on the doors of the vehicles.

Several things happened next.

Groups of soldiers turned, and I clearly saw them bring weapons to their shoulders. Seconds later, they began shooting at me—I was well within their range.

"BINGO . . . BINGO . . . BINGO . . ." The audible warning system, called Bitching Betty, also started screaming at me over my low-fuel state.

Then two of the trucks at the back of the convoy blew up. Zipping down the road at a bare hundred feet, I booted the rudder, rolled again, and zoomed up to about 300 feet.

"CHIEFTAIN . . . ROMAN 75 is off to the south and west . . . vehicles burning. The column has stopped in place."

"ROMAN . . . hit 'em again . . . hit . . . Rags are . . ." And he faded away again into crackling noise.

I knew I didn't have enough fuel left to go all the way back out and re-attack as I'd just done. So, when the front of the convoy passed off the left wing, I turned and locked my eyes to it, staring so hard that my eyes watered. As it began to disappear in the dark, blowing sand, I slammed the throttle forward, popped straight up, and rolled nearly inverted to the right. Using the 200 feet of altitude I'd gained, I sliced down toward the ground and the leading Iraqi vehicle. It was a Russian-made armored personnel carrier (APC).

And it saw me, too.

Pulling the throttle back, I skidded sideways to line up, and the thing opened fire at me. A double line of green tracers arced off to my left and began correcting as the gunner got a better look at me.

I ignored it and rolled my wings level, letting the pipper come up to the target. I was close enough to see that the gunner wasn't wearing a helmet and he had a mustache. As the pipper reached the front bumper of the APC, I squeezed the trigger again.

"BUURRRPPP." The vehicle disappeared in a sudden fog of chewed-up dirt and sparks. As I pulled up and bunted over again, my eyes flicked to the ROUNDS REMAINING counter and then to the radar altimeter. Fewer than a hundred rounds left, and I was less than 140 feet above the ground.

There wasn't time for finesse, so I just manhandled the pipper to the leading truck and opened fire for the last time.

"BUURRP." And the gun shuddered to a stop as I passed through 50 feet.

Cranking up hard off to the west, I kicked the rudder to spoil anyone's aim, pulled on the stick, and looked over my right shoulder. Just then the truck exploded, shooting off thousands of rounds of ammunition, and I flinched reactively. One cannon shell must've hit the next truck in line, because it blew up, too. As the ground vanished into the brown haze, I saw the remaining trucks and BTRs sliding off the road into the ditch.

Swallowing several times to get some spit back in my throat, I selected the point for the TWITCH refueling track and began a steady climb.

"CHIEFTAIN . . . ROMAN 75 is off to the west . . . Bingo . . . Winchester and RTB."

That was the short way of saying I was leaving the target area, out of gas and weapons, and returning to base. But it didn't matter, because he didn't answer and I had other things to worry about now.

Seventeen hundred pounds of fuel.

I was so far below Bingo that I wasn't sure I could reach the border, much less a forward-divert base in Kuwait. I felt the cold sweat drying on my skin as I safed up my weapons and eyeballed the engine gauges to make sure I hadn't picked up a stray round or two.

Passing through 8,000 feet heading southwest toward the border, I broke into the clear. Not much in my life has looked better to me than that weak blue sky. Dropping my mask again, I wiped my stubbled chin and rubbed my eyes.

"ROMAN Two . . . One on Victor." I keyed the mike and waited.

No answer. I changed frequencies and tried the AWACS. "LUGER . . . this is ROMAN 75."

Again, no answer.

And now I had a decision to make. Maybe my last one. The tanker track was roughly 120 miles off my nose, but there was no guarantee I'd find a tanker there. Or, if I did, he might not have any gas to spare. In which case, I was screwed.

About the same distance off my left wing was Kuwait. There were several bases I could probably coast into and manage to land. But without talking to AWACS, I had no way of knowing which ones were open or in good enough shape for me to land. And then I was still screwed.

What a shitty day.

I'd now been strapped in a fighter cockpit for more than eight hours, and I'd refueled five times. I'd planned on a normal six-hour mission and hadn't brought food or water. My butt hurt and my eyes ached. I turned the heat up because my sweat-soaked flight suit was making me shiver.

I'd flown more than one hundred combat missions by the time *this* war began and was no novice in combat. I had a hatful of campaign ribbons and medals, including a Purple Heart, from earlier conflicts, and by the time I retired, I had been awarded four Distinguished Flying Crosses with Valor—one for the First Gulf War, and three for my service in the second war in Iraq. But that was all either in the past or the future. For right now, not far to the west, one of nature's true nightmares was fast approaching. The khamsin, the sandstorm, was an ominous wave of dirt stretching north and south along the horizon as far as I could see. The sky above the storm was gone.

It was appalling.

The momentary relief I'd been feeling leaked out of me. A storm like that could ground every aircraft on the continent, and I realized maybe that was why I hadn't heard from anyone. *That* was a nasty thought. Swallowing again, I passed 15,000 feet and stared out at the brown carpet stretching out before me. If I managed to get to 25,000 or 30,000 feet, I could glide to the border and at least eject over friendly territory.

Like I said, it had been a shitty day.

And it wasn't over yet.

1

YGBSM

"You've Gotta Be Shittin' Me": that's the battle cry of
the Wild Weasels. Surface-to-Air-Missile (SAM) killers. The first
pilots sent into a warzone. Men who purposefully provoke fire
from enemy missiles and anti-aircraft guns on the ground—then
hunt and kill the SAM nests, making the sky safe for all other aircraft and helicopters to follow. I was proud to be one. True, like
every F-16 fighter pilot, I'd fly many other types of missions in my
career, but I always came back to being a Weasel. Why? It's where
the action is. SAM hunting is the most dangerous mission faced
by today's fighter pilots, a job more hazardous and difficult than
shooting down enemy jets. With 151 combat missions, twenty-one
hard kills on SAM sites, eleven aircraft destroyed (on the ground,
unfortunately), plus many tanks, trucks, artillery, strikes on high-
value targets, and other assorted operations, I've been called the
most lethal F-16CJ Wild Weasel in the U.S. Air Force.

To truly understand what I used to do and how I got there, you
need to understand the mission itself. So, before we go any further,
here's a little history lesson.

SINCE MAN FIRST COMBINED FLIGHT WITH WARFARE, OTHER men have been trying to shoot aviators down. As early as the American Civil War, when manned balloons were used by Union forces to spot enemy troop movements, Confederate sharpshooters immediately started firing at them. Five years later, during the Franco-Prussian War, the Germans mounted a small cannon on a horse cart for the sole purpose of putting holes in French balloons.

With the advance of tactical aviation during World War I came corresponding advances in anti-aircraft capabilities. By December 1914, the British Royal Air Force had become sufficiently concerned about the German bomber threat to London that they developed a 37-mm pom-pom gun. In June 1917, their caution was justified when fourteen plywood-coated German Gotha V bombers lumbered over London at eighty knots and dropped their bombs. Among the 162 dead were 46 children killed when their kindergarten was destroyed. Within a year, twenty-eight of these "heavy" bombers had been shot down, stopping the raids. These missions, though puny by modern standards, marked the first real use of strategic airpower and ushered in the age of air defense.

As aircraft improved, the systems designed to kill them also became more lethal. Weapons that could bring down wooden bombers flying straight and level at eighty knots were hopeless against the much faster and more maneuverable planes of World War II. This meant more accurate aiming systems had to be fielded, which could cope with more aggressive targets. Eventually, the British developed the Kerrison Predictor. Though ineffective against fighters (it was designed to track bombers), it was the first truly automated Fire Control System.

Weapons improved as well. Ironically, two of the best pieces of anti-aircraft artillery (AAA, or Triple-A) came from neutral countries. Bofors, a Swedish company, manufactured a 40-mm piece which proved lightweight, rapid-fire guns were tactically feasible. Bofors also exemplified the concept of "business neutrality" by selling its weapons to both the Axis and the Allies. Incidentally, the man who transformed Bofors from producing raw steel to manufacturing armaments was Alfred Nobel, the inventor of dynamite. He also founded the Nobel Prize—for peace.

Swiss-built Oerlikon 20-mm cannons were used with much success during the war by both the United States Navy and the Royal Navy as short-range anti-aircraft weapons. Interestingly, derivatives of this cannon were standard armament in two of the greatest World War II Axis fighters: the Japanese Mitsubishi Zero and the German Luftwaffe's Messerschmitt 109.

The Germans also developed Fliegerfaust, arguably the first surface-to-air missile system. This was a portable system that looked like a Gatling gun and fired manually aimed 20-mm rocket projectiles.

Wasserfall was a derivative of the large V-2 rockets being fired at British cities and factories. It had a radio-controlled aiming system called Manual Controlled to Line of Sight. This meant the operator had to manually track his target *and* steer the missile to intercept. Designed to counter the strategic threat posed by overwhelming numbers of American bombers, the system proved an abject failure.

The period between the end of the Korean War and the beginning of Vietnam saw tremendous technical advances in both aircraft and weapons. This resulted in the development of new air-combat missions, including close air-support and high-altitude precision bombing. There was also a reconnaissance aircraft, the U-2, that could operate higher than any gun could shoot or any fighter could fly. Such a capability would also put it beyond the range of surface-to-air missiles.

On April 9, 1960, an American pilot named Bob Ericson seemed to confirm this when he crossed the Pamir Mountains into the Soviet Union. MiG fighters, guns, and thousands of Russian curses failed to bring him down as he calmly flew over four of the most sensitive targets the Soviets possessed, including, somewhat ironically, their surface-to-air missile test center at Saryshagan.

But weeks later, on May 1, another U-2 pilot wasn't so fortunate, and Francis Gary Powers suddenly became a household name. To the astonishment of the Air Force and CIA, his plane was brought down by several surface-to-air missiles. The Russians called it the S-75. (NATO, to keep everyone confused, named it the SA-2 Goa. There actually was an SA-1 system, but it was deployed around Moscow to stop American B-52 bombers.)

Thirty-five feet long and more than two feet in diameter, the SA-2 could reach speeds exceeding Mach 3 (three times the speed of sound, or about 2,600 miles per hour) on its way up to 80,000 feet. If this 5,000-pound flying telephone pole hit an aircraft, there wouldn't be much left of it.

Fortunately for Gary Powers, radar-guided systems, though not new, were a long way from being perfected. This was an age of vacuum tubes and slide rules, not microchips and supercomputers, so figuring aiming solutions on jet aircraft seven miles above the earth was not a simple proposition. However, bombers and reconnaissance aircraft like the U-2, unlike fighters, fly nice, predictably straight lines, and this certainly helped three missiles detonate close enough to Powers's U-2 to knock it down—thankfully, without obliterating the aircraft or himself. Powers was captured and humiliated, but he eventually returned home alive.

Another U-2 pilot, Major Rudolph Anderson, wasn't so lucky.

In October 1962, the South Carolina native was killed over Cuba by the same SA-2 system. During the past two years, the missile's tracking had greatly improved, and the Cuban-launched weapon shattered Major Anderson's U-2.

These incidents finally forced the Pentagon to seriously consider electronic countermeasures. These include radar-warning receivers, which tell a pilot that he's being targeted; chaff-and-flare dispensers that would confuse tracking solutions; and offensive jamming pods that could deny or defeat enemy radars. It was a new field and all of this equipment was either primitive or nonexistent. Despite the U-2 losses, there was time, the Pentagon thought, to develop these capabilities.

IN THE EARLY 1960S, VIETNAM WASN'T REALLY ON ANY AMERican's "give a shit" list, and by 1963, President John F. Kennedy had even publicly disengaged the United States from Southeast Asia. Unfortunately, he departed this world before we could extract ourselves from Vietnam, and in August 1964, two American destroyers—the *Maddox* and the *Turner Joy*—were "attacked" in the Gulf of Tonkin. President Lyndon Johnson now had his excuse to go to war, and the subsequent Tonkin Resolution permitted combat operations without a congressional declaration of war. Despite the rather silly notion that two U.S. destroyers had been attacked by the North Vietnamese riverboat navy, the president could now fight whomever he wished.

And that's precisely what he did.

As usual, America's involvement started with air and sea power. Flaming Dart, Rolling Thunder, and Arc Light were air campaigns designed to protect U.S. ground troops and destroy the North Vietnamese capability to fight the war. However, by March 1965, some

3,000 Marines had been deployed into Vietnam, and by December that number reached 200,000.

To counter this, Hanoi began importing huge amounts of Soviet hardware, including the latest surface-to-air missile systems and anti-aircraft artillery. You see, the Vietnamese knew they could win a ground war. They simply had to wear the Americans down and outlast their political willpower, just as they did the French during the 1950s. But the Americans were different. They had air support with advanced capabilities the French had never possessed and stopping them was a serious tactical problem. The Vietnamese needed modern air-defense technology and again turned to the Soviet Union. The Russians, of course, were happy to oblige, since they got to test their equipment *and* kill Americans.

U.S. pilots flying strike missions were suddenly faced with a very dangerous and unanticipated air-defense threat. On a summer day in 1965, an event tragically highlighted the enemy's lethal capacity—and gave birth to the Wild Weasels.

It was to be Captain Ross Fobair's fifty-fifth and final combat mission before going home. Once more across the line for Fobair, an F-4C Phantom pilot from the 45th Tactical Fighter Squadron, it was now almost routine. The twenty-nine-year-old captain had packed up the night before, and he planned on departing Vietnam after landing from his afternoon mission. The Freedom Bird, a transport aircraft back to the States, was leaving that very night. He was going home to California and a well-deserved rest, a reunion with his wife, Anita, his sister, Betty, and his young nephew, Bruce. It was July 24, 1965.

It was Ross Fobair's last day.

With him on the mission was Captain Richard "Pops" Keirn, who was flying in the front seat of the Phantom. (Keirn was a retread on his fifth mission in Vietnam. A former bomber pilot from World War II, he'd been shot down over Germany and spent nine months in Stalag Luft 1, courtesy of the Third Reich.) The mission was fairly straightforward. It was a Combat Air Patrol, called a MiGCAP, to protect a strike force of F-105 Thunderchiefs from stray North Vietnamese fighters. The F-105s—or Thuds, as they were known—were hitting a munitions factory at Kang Chi some forty miles west of Hanoi. MiG sweeps were what fighter pilots lived for—essentially, roaming around and looking for trouble. The idea was to force enemy fighters into engaging the Phantoms and thus leaving the Thuds free to drop their bombs. So, the F-105s would smack their target and the F-4s would get to dogfight.

A perfect day.

But it didn't quite work out that way. Forty miles northeast of Hanoi, over the Vinh Phu Province, a SAM shot up through a soggy cloud deck and hit the Phantom. There hadn't been time to react, and the F-4C didn't carry the threat-detection gear that became standard equipment on later jets. Unfortunately for Keirn and Fobair, the previous shoot-downs involved spy planes, so the CIA and the Air Force hadn't released much useful threat information. Nothing was really known about this new type of threat, and so the pilots hadn't been trained to defeat it. The missile was the same radar-guided SA-2 that had knocked down Gary Powers and killed Major Anderson. It left little margin for error.

The spine-jarring impact immediately put the Phantom out of control. In the front seat, Pops Keirn struggled to assess the flashing lights, aural warnings, and acrid smoke filling the cockpit. He got no response from the back cockpit. Twisting around against the mounting G-forces, he saw Ross Fobair slumped in his seat, blood streaming from his nose. As the F-4 spun into the clouds, Keirn ejected and would spend the next seven and a half years in the infamous Hanoi Hilton, a POW for the second time.

But Ross Fobair disappeared. Thirty-two years later, his

nephew, Bruce Giffin, returned to Vietnam and discovered his uncle's fate. Near a remote village on the slope of a 4,000-foot mountain, Ross Fobair's remains were found and finally returned home for a full military funeral.

Answers to a combat death are rarely clear, and finding a meaning, especially in any modern war, is difficult. But this combat loss has a legacy that endures today: Fobair's death was the final link in the chain that created the Wild Weasels. Many, many lives have been saved over the years because the USAF dedicated men and machines to hunting and killing SAMs. If a meaning can be found in Ross Fobair's fate, then perhaps this is it.

LESS THAN TWO WEEKS AFTER FOBAIR AND KEIRN WENT down, Air Force officials conducted a secret meeting to arrive at a solution for the new threat. Navy and Marine aircraft were also being lost to the SAMs, and the U.S. military, not just the Air Force, needed aircraft that could kill such a threat. To torment, track, and follow prey into its hiding place just like a fierce and relentless wild weasel.

Project Weasel, also called Wild Weasel One, was born.

But there were problems. First, how do you find a SAM site? Especially when it's camouflaged or hidden in a jungle? So, Applied Technologies Corporation built the AN/APR-25 radar homing and warning receiver (RHAW) that could locate an SA-2 by the emissions of its own radar. For this to work, the enemy radar, called a Fan Song, had to be operating. The RHAW receiver could see the enemy emissions and would then provide a rough bearing to the site for the attacking aircraft. In theory, anyway.

It worked like this. As a missile gets closer to its target, much more accurate tracking updates are required for the SAM to hit the aircraft. The APR-26 was supposed to detect this shift in guidance beams and trigger a flashing red warning signal light in the cockpit to warn the pilot that a missile was close. An additional receiver, the IR-133, would permit an Electronic Warfare Officer (EWO) to identify specific threats by analyzing the signal. This became more important as more types of SAMs were created, because different threats were defeated by different methods. If you knew what was after you, then you'd know how to beat it—again, theoretically. None of this equipment was really battle-worthy, and everyone, from the scientists down to the aircrews, was feeling their way. The pressure was on, though, since Americans were dying every day.

Another problem was being aware a SAM was tracking you. Threat reactions had always been done visually, but the loss of Fobair and Keirn changed all that. They'd never seen the missile coming and had no warning they were being targeted. Even if they'd spotted it, no one knew how to defeat such a missile and it was obvious that a more sophisticated solution was needed. This new equipment would have to be placed in an aircraft that could survive against a SAM and also employ weapons to kill the things. The Air Force's answer was to retrofit the AN/APR-26 warning receiver onto a fighter.

But which fighter? You'd need a jet that was very fast and could maneuver well enough to give the pilot or aircrew a chance at survival. Bombers and reconnaissance aircraft could try to rely on jamming and countermeasures, but that wouldn't cut it for a fighter working right on top of the threat. Especially a jet that was *trying* to get shot at so the SAM would give away its position.

Pressed for an answer, the Air Force chose the F-100F Super Sabre to accommodate the two-man crew of a pilot and Electronic Warfare Officer. Made by North American Aviation, the Super Sabre was about ten years old when Project Weasel was conceived. Originally a training aircraft, the Super Sabre was only equipped with two 20-mm cannons. In retrospect, it wasn't an ideal choice, but Project Weasel was making a heroic effort to counter the growing losses in Vietnam, and time was short.

The last problem was, who to fly it? Fighter pilots, as anyone who has ever been involved with them can attest, are a breed apart. The uninitiated or envious often call them arrogant, but that's not really *it*. *It* is an absolute belief in their own invincibility, aggressiveness, and skill. Without this mentality, no sane man would go near a supersonic coffin that flings pieces of high explosive at the ground and other jets.

Fighter pilots regard combat as a challenge, so Project Weasel got to choose from the top aviators already flying the F-100F—but the EWO was another matter. The Air Force had never put EWOs into fighters before, and initially turned to the B-52 bomber community for radar experts. Training started in October 1965, at Eglin Air Force Base, Florida, barely three months following Ross Fobair's shoot-down.

They were trained to fight the SA-2. Everything that was known or suspected was thrown at them, along with best guesses at defensive tactics. Practice missions were flown against simulated SAM sites, and, eventually, one of the EWOs understandably asked what the point of all this was.

They were told that they would lead the strike packages into North Vietnam and would hunt and kill the SAMs. A properly puzzled pilot then asked how *that* was to be done, given the equipment limitations, intelligence uncertainties, and the thickness of the jungle. How do you find a SAM site? There was really no other way to locate a SAM with absolute certainty except to allow the SAM to shoot at its target—then, as long as the Weasel survived, he'd know the location. *As long as the Weasel survived.*

Right.

In the immortal words of EWO Captain Jack Donovan, "You

want me to fly in the back of a tiny little jet with a crazy fighter pilot who thinks he's invincible, home in on a SAM site in North Vietnam, and shoot it before it shoots me? You've gotta be shittin' me!"

You've Gotta Be Shittin' Me. YGBSM. It instantly and irrevocably defined the Wild Weasel mission. It remains so to this day.

In November 1965, the first five Wild Weasel Super Sabre jets arrived at Korat Air Base in Thailand to begin combat operations. Right from the beginning, the Weasels knew that the only way to deal with a SAM was to kill it. You could temporarily suppress a radar by lobbing anti-radiation missiles at it, but that wouldn't solve the problem, and it would still be alive tomorrow. No, you had to kill it with bombs or cannons. So they teamed up with F-105Ds—a supersonic bomber known as the Thunderchief—and went to work.

Called Iron Hand missions, they would hunt the SAM by flying down into its engagement zone, or envelope. This made the Weasel an attractive target, and the SA-2 target acquisition radar would try to lock the Super Sabre. Once the radar was on air and trying to lock the Weasel, then it could be tracked in turn and located. You could locate it by radar homing or, if the SAM launched, you might see the smoke trail. Sabres and the Thunderchiefs would then bomb and strafe the site to finish it off.

Over time, several essential aspects of this process have not changed. First, the SAM has to stay "on air" long enough to track the target and be seen in turn. Second, the Weasel has to live long enough to find it and successfully attack. Lastly, you couldn't miss when you attacked, or the SAM—and all the guns around it— would kill you.

Sounds simple enough, right?

Right.

Three days before Christmas, not quite five months since Ross Fobair's death, Captains Al Lamb and Jack Donovan engaged and killed an SA-2 in North Vietnam. The Weasels had proven their worth and would remain in Vietnam for the duration of the war.

But the F-100F Super Sabres would not.

After nine confirmed SAM kills and a staggering 50 percent Weasel casualty rate, it became apparent that changes had to be made. As far as a new aircraft went, the choice was obvious. The F-105 Thunderchief—called the "Thud," because of the noise it made while landing—had been involved with the Hunter Killer mission from the beginning, playing the role of the Killer. Why not modify the formidable single-seat fighter bomber into a two-seat variant and make it the new Weasel? Weasels could then do their own killing.

The Thud was definitely a man's fighter jet, and it outperformed the Sabre in every respect. Much faster—twice the speed of sound at altitude—it was twenty feet longer and some 20,000 pounds heavier. Even so, the F-105 could travel twice as far into enemy territory as the F-100F. Most important, the Thud had five underwing hard points capable of a 6,000-pound weapons payload with a further 8,000 pounds of bombs carried internally. Lots of choices to make SAMs go away.

The U.S. Air Force had Republic Aviation modify the F-105F to incorporate the lessons learned from Southeast Asia. A tandem cockpit was added for the APR-25 RHAW receiver and the EWO. Radar altimeters, better ejection seats, armor plating, and an updated weapons delivery system were also included.

By June 1966, less than a year after Ross Fobair's shoot-down, the Wild Weasel 3 Program was in combat in Southeast Asia. In all, eighty-six F-105Fs were modified as Weasels, evidence of the seriousness of the Air Force program. The next month, the earlier-generation F-100Fs flew their last combat missions; meanwhile, Operation Rolling Thunder successfully continued turning big trees into toothpicks, and the war dragged on.

It was Secretary of Defense Robert McNamara's notion that slowly increasing the pressure on North Vietnam would make Ho Chi Minh realize the utter futility of opposing the world's greatest military. The idea, dreamed up by the Beltway theorists who were somehow permitted to run the war, was called "graduated escalation."

And it didn't work.

A true politician, McNamara didn't understand the application of military power, nor did he accurately assess his enemy. Rolling Thunder simply committed American forces in a piecemeal fashion, and gave the North Vietnamese time to repair damage, shift resources, and study our equipment and tactics. The amateurs in Washington never fully grasped that time was on Hanoi's side. As the war moved farther north, the Johnson administration gave the enemy every opportunity to learn how to counter American airpower by improving Soviet SAMs.

Five of the first eleven F-105Fs were lost by the end of August 1966, and it was again evident that further improvements to the Weasel were necessary. So along came the F-105G. The G model was a true Weasel, designed and equipped for the sole purpose of hunting and killing SAMs. The APR-25/26 RHAW was replaced with the upgraded APR-35/37 series. Its increased fidelity and sensitivity would allow greater targeting accuracy and, hopefully, better survivability for the crew.

The G model also carried Westinghouse AN/ALQ-105 electronic jamming pods in a pair of blisters under the fuselage. This permitted a much more powerful countermeasure response and freed up two more underwing hard points for additional weapons.

The more capable ALR-31 system necessitated a redesign of the wingtips to give the warning sensors greater coverage of the surrounding sky.

All of these improvements represented lessons learned the hard way and, in many cases, from lives lost. With the APR-35/37 passive detection system to find the SAM radars, the ALR-31 to warn of a missile launch, and the ALQ-105 jammer to confuse enemy radars, the F-105G was ready to fight.

And fight it did.

From the latter half of 1967, Weasels flew from their Royal Thai Air Force bases to hunt and kill the rapidly proliferating SAMs. All told, the F-105s flew more than 20,000 combat sorties. Over 300 Thuds were lost in the fighting, 126 in 1966 alone, though not all were Weasels. Of those, 103 were brought down by SAMs and Triple-A. It was an enormously dangerous and costly mission.

The enemy's Tet Offensive of 1968 had shown that the North Vietnamese were in no way defeated and Robert McNamara's amateurish meddling in tactics had failed completely. His Rolling Thunder plan had cost hundreds of aircraft and the loss of more than a thousand highly talented aviators. McNamara himself had resigned his position in late 1967 and fled to become president of the World Bank. He never lived down his culpability nor justified his God complex. Lyndon Johnson, also personally and politically finished, announced in March 1968 that he would not be seeking reelection. Johnson would die on his ranch in January 1973; McNamara lingered on until 2009. I like to imagine that the ghosts of the 58,178 Americans both men sent to early graves were waiting for them on the other side.

With LBJ and McNamara gone, the air war over North Vietnam slid to a halt. Rolling Thunder was officially and conveniently ended in November just prior to the 1968 presidential elections.

By 1970, the F-105 was no longer in production and still-mounting combat losses necessitated a revised Wild Weasel.

Enter the F-4 Phantom II.

Made by McDonnell Douglas, the Phantom began its military career as a Navy fighter attack jet in 1961. In 1962, a USAF version, the F-4C, was approved and made its first flight in May 1963. It was stubbier and heavier than the Thud but carried an improved fire control system. F-4Ds and Es followed, each with improvements that increased weapon accuracy, maneuverability, and range. Thirty six F-4Cs were re-designated as EF-4Cs and called the Wild Weasel IV. But it was a Band-Aid solution to the worsening situation in Vietnam and a SAM threat that continued to evolve.

In early 1971, the Vietnam lull began to come apart. Air activity over the north increased, and a new enemy offensive kicked off in March 1972. Operation Linebacker was unleashed against Hanoi to drive the enemy back and to win the war. By the middle of April, almost everything in North Vietnam was fair game, and President Nixon, acting on his promise to end the war, turned loose the U.S. Air Force.

The Weasels were once again thrown into the fray, sometimes flying four sorties a day, as rail yards, airfields, and storage facilities were attacked. Infrastructure that had kept the enemy functioning for the past seven years was finally on the target list and being hit hard. The success of this campaign led to the Paris Peace Talks, and on October 23, 1972, air operations above the 20th Parallel were temporarily halted. Linebacker II, the final push, began on December 18, with the Weasels paving the way for massive B-52 strikes that finally brought Hanoi to its knees. But, in true American political fashion, whatever is paid for in blood is usually given away by Washington, and in early 1973, the U.S. began a massive pullout of forces. By January 1975, the North Vietnamese army captured Phuoc Long Province, only eighty miles from Saigon, and on April 30, the Republic of South Vietnam ceased to exist.

So the Weasels came home. Some of them, anyway. Twenty-six Phantoms had been lost and forty-two more officers killed, missing, or captured. Two Weasels, Leo Thorsness and Merlyn Dethlefsen, had been awarded the Medal of Honor.

The advancement of the surface-to-air missile had ushered in a new and revolutionary form of warfare. It would eventually grow and morph into the Integrated Air Defense System, the deadliest technology to ever threaten aircraft. Countertactics had progressed, in turn, from Weasel I through Weasel IV. These techniques would continue to evolve, sometimes forgetting the fundamentals learned in Vietnam and sometimes remembering. Equipment and weapons were proposed, improved, or discarded, but one thing, as we shall see, didn't change. Never again would American airpower attack in force without the Wild Weasel.

2

Cold War and Hot Times

"IF THE TREES ARE GETTING BIG, PULL BACK TILL YOU SEE blue."

Those were the immortal first bits of flying instruction I received from my dad. Followed shortly by "pull up now or we're going to die."

Dad was a businessman and a highly skilled engineer by the time I came along. He'd designed cockpit instruments for NASA spacecraft and helped save the Alaska pipeline by redesigning their flow meters. But he was also a retired Marine fighter/attack pilot. Flying was something I'd always been around as part of a colorful family. Ours is a lineage that includes several generals, one of whom was a Confederate cavalry officer. I also had a great-grandfather who managed to charge up San Juan Hill with Teddy Roosevelt, and another who shipped off to fight in France during World War I to escape a nagging wife.

Despite the family tree, Dad was never the Great Santini. He didn't pressure me to join the military, and, in fact, I went to college to become an architect. No, flying was just something we did. It was fascinating to master a machine well enough to get it off the ground, yank and bank through aerobatics, then bring it back to safely land. Humans were never meant to fly, and most can't learn, so I loved the special freedom of it—and still do. Fighter pilots usually are too busy to appreciate the miracle of flight, but it's always there and I've been under its spell from the beginning.

Later I found it was a great way to entice young ladies into a date. Suppose you're a girl and Bozo Number 1 asks you out to dinner and a movie. You're tempted but along comes Bozo Number 2, who says, "Hey . . . how 'bout going flying with me before I take you to dinner?"

Yep. Guaranteed.

During my second year at college, something clicked inside, drawing me to become a professional pilot. I'd worked for architects the previous two summers, seen the business, and I enjoyed the creativity of designing structures. But I had a decision to make, because if I was going to seek an officer's commission as a military aviator, it had to be started then, since the whole painful process took about eighteen months. So, it was wear a cloth tie and sit in an office for forty years—or cheat death and fly fast jets.

No contest, really.

BY THE SPRING OF 1986, I'D COMPLETED A FIVE-YEAR COLLEGE degree in four years so I could be commissioned on time and keep my "slot" for Undergraduate Pilot Training (UPT). This is Air Force basic flight school and is only open to commissioned officers who've been physically and mentally screened to absurd levels. In the late eighties, there were five air bases devoted to washing out future pilots, and I'd been given a choice: to wait nine months and head off to beautiful, sunny Williams Air Force Base in Arizona or go in five months to Vance Air Force Base, Oklahoma. With the eagerness and ignorance of youth, I chose Vance. You know that "nowhere" place everyone is always in the middle of? That would be Enid, Oklahoma. A small town right out of the movie *Footloose*. No kidding. They legalized dancing there in 1987.

UPT was generally composed of guys like me: newly minted second lieutenants fresh from a university, the Air Force Academy, or Officer's Candidate School. We'd been selected by several different boards, who minutely examined the sum total of our lives up to that point. That included background checks, grade-point averages, sports, letters of recommendation, extracurricular nonsense, and probably how we parted our hair. There were physicals, eye exams, psych evaluations, interviews, and a comprehensive qualifying exam. This was just to get commissioned as an officer. The vast majority of the seventy thousand Air Force officers stop right there and enter one of the mission-support fields, like personnel, maintenance, or supply. There are additional batteries of tests designed to trip up prospective pilots, make you feel stupid, and, yes, specifically test your aptitude to enter the flying world. Only about ten thousand of the seventy thousand officers eventually become pilots, and less than three thousand have what it takes to become active fighter pilots.

So, assuming you pass all that with high enough scores, you get past the gate and up to bat. For your efforts, you're guaranteed nothing except a *shot* at the silver wings of an Air Force pilot. Everything that comes later is up to you. Contrary to popular belief, it doesn't matter where you came from, who your daddy knows, or what university graduated you. Air Force pilot training is an equal-opportunity destroyer of hopes and dreams. I saw all types wash out. Academy guys, 4.0 GPA engineering types, and men who arrived with a thousand civilian flying hours who couldn't fly formation or land a jet.

You've either got it or you don't.

IT WORKED LIKE THIS.

The first two weeks were spent doing everything but flying: registering with personnel, the flight surgeon, security police, etc. For brand-new lieutenants, this usually meant doing it two or three times to get it right. We also began academics immediately. The USAF is big on technical classroom instruction, and any formal training course, whether you want to become a parajumper or a pilot, has a syllabus. The Air Force requires the highest qualifying scores of the four main service branches just for enlistments, let alone for officers. Given the extreme complexity of modern jets, especially fighters, this is understandable. Since we were recent college graduates, the course load was familiar to us, and we were happy to finally be on the "flight line."

On any USAF flying base, the flight line consists of the squadrons, maintenance facilities, and everything in between that makes an aircraft go up and down. Located immediately adjacent to the runways and taxiways, this usually remained a pilot's home until he became a field-grade officer and had to pay homage to gods of paperwork on a staff somewhere. Of course, we weren't pilots yet. We were "Studs"—short for STUDent pilotS. (Naturally, that was not the explanation we gave girls at the Officer's Club.) Think of it as a kind of yearlong, performance-based purgatory between being nothing and *maybe* becoming what you dream.

Then came that first sweet moment when, alone in my BOQ

(Bachelor Officer's Quarters) room, I shrugged into the new, stiff flight suit. It even smelled sweet (that would be the NOMEX material), and with my patches and lieutenant's bars, I was smokin'.

So I thought.

So did we all.

One problem with that: no wings. This painful fact was pointed out to us at least once per minute by the instructors and any girl who wandered into the O'Club. It was like wearing a nice custom suit with no shoes. Obvious, embarrassing, and the first in a long series of humbling sprays from the Reality Hose. So, like everyone who eventually graduated, I made up my mind to have those prized silver wings, no matter what.

The first half of UPT was conducted in little horrible T-37 jet trainers. It was loud, obnoxious, underpowered, and sat low enough to the ground for the crew chief to look *down* at the pilot. The Air Force has since switched to T-6 Texans, and they have to be an improvement over the "Tweet," the T-37. Anyway, the initial phase of pilot training was called "Contact," and it was the first real chance the instructors had to wash out students. Everything dealing with basic flying was covered here—ground operations, take-offs and landings, spins, aerobatics, and, as always, emergency procedures.

The instructors came from several sources. The best were those who'd had operational assignments and were back in the training command against their will. These were former TTB (tanker, transport, bomber) pilots and, thankfully, a few fighter pilots. Without exception, the fighter guys hated flying trainer aircraft. And why wouldn't they? Flying in a front-line fighter squadron was as good as it gets in the Air Force, and now to come back to the shiny-boot, scarf-wearing world of the Training Command was a plunge into the abyss. Fortunately for these guys, they only had to do one three-year tour and then it was back to the real world.

Thank God all the operational guys were there, though, to muzzle the Others.

The Others were First Assignment Instructor Pilots, shortened to FAIPs, and they were universally a pain in the ass. These were pilots who didn't get assignments out of the Air Education and Training Command after they graduated from UPT, and they had to stay on as instructors. Sure, they had to go off to San Antonio, Texas, for a few months, where they supposedly learned how to teach students to fly, but the bottom line was this: the only military-aviation experience they had under their belt was UPT and the Texas course. So, you've got a guy with less than two years of flying training trying to teach and, most important, evaluate a student's ability to be an Air Force pilot. In my opinion, some were actually quite good but most were bitter wannabes. This is precisely why the operational pilots were brought back—to keep their thumbs on the FAIPs and give a reality check to the program. Otherwise we'd have an Air Force of close-order drills, sock checks, and spell-checkers.

My primary instructor pilot was a gruff, irreverent former B-52 pilot with the unlikely call sign of "Daddy Rabbit." There were six of us assigned to him, and we were lucky. Jets are like pets in that the people who fly in them, like pet owners, end up resembling them eventually. The B-52 was known as a Buff (Big Ugly Fat Fucker), and though Daddy Rabbit wasn't fat, he was big and ugly—*and* a superb pilot. His gift was instilling the "Big Picture" in his students, i.e., teaching us to not get mired down in minutiae but be aware of all that was going on around us. DR was also calm, unlike FAIPs.

"Punk," he once said smoothly as I waffled through a spin recovery while Oklahoma filled the windscreen, "ya wanna try and do it right this time so we live to drink at the club tonight." He also hated the training command and passionately loathed most FAIPs. So, Daddy Rabbit, if you're reading this, thanks for everything.

Within a week, guys began washing out for air sickness, failure to master emergency procedures, or just a basic inability to think and fly at the same time. If a student busted a ride, he got a repeat, called an "X" ride. If he busted that, then he flew a "Double X" flight with a more experienced, non-FAIP, squadron officer. If he failed again, he went next to a Proficiency Check with a Flight Examiner, and if he didn't pass it, then he was out. There were students who were fully enrolled and engaged on Monday and gone by Friday.

The Tweet phase progressed through formation flying and basic instrument procedures, and guys continued to drop like proverbial flies. As always, through all of this, there were endless academics. Aerodynamics, aircraft systems, weather, instrument flying procedures—anything that could affect you as a pilot. Emergency training was nonstop. More classroom instruction, simulator flights, and a little ritual each morning called "Stand Up."

This occurred in the big flight-briefing room. Each instructor pilot had a table and usually four to five students (at the beginning). Every morning, before flying and academics, there was a Mass Brief. This covered weather, the schedule, and general announcements. One instructor would then give a thirty-second scenario involving a flight situation and turn it over to a random student. The Stud would then "Stand Up" and take over, in real time, whatever near-death situation had been presented. With an audience of instructor pilots and his peers, he'd have to take this to a logical conclusion and, hopefully, get the plane back on the ground. It was very effective in teaching a young pilot the basics of thinking on his feet and ignoring outside pressures during a crisis.

AFTER SIX MONTHS AND TWO CHECK-RIDES, THOSE OF US WHO were left got to move across the street to T-38s and the advanced flight phase of UPT. About 40 percent of the initial class was gone by this point, and those remaining were seasoned by now. Not cocky, certainly, because we still didn't have wings and also had seen too many buddies wash out. But we'd recovered a bit of the misplaced confidence we'd all walked in with.

The attitude was different on the 38 side. Instructors still washed people out, but they figured we'd proven ourselves over the past six months by simply surviving to this phase. The Air Force also had a chunk of money invested in us by this point and would work a bit harder to keep a potential pilot around.

I loved it. Whereas piloting the Tweet had been brute-force mastery over ugly machine, the T-38 called for finesse. It flew like a fighter (at least a 1970s-vintage fighter); the Air Force had several fighting versions in the form of the AT-38 and the F-5 Tiger II. It sat high above the ground and had the tremendous virtue of tandem seating. This was much better than the Tweet, where the instructor was sitting right next to you.

Jet flying clicked for me during the next six months. I'd come out of Tweets in the middle of the pack, but my hands and brain caught up with each other with the T-38. It had an afterburner, and we now wore G-suits to counter the effects of gravity during maneuvering. Compared to high-performance fighters, the T-38 wasn't a tough nut to crack. But as I saw my reflection in the glass doors, with my G-suit and helmet, I thought I was already there—a fighter pilot on his way to deal death. Maybe it helped. Maybe not. But I liked the look.

About eleven months into the program, all the instructors and commanders went into a huddle over a long weekend. They examined everything about us; each test score, simulator flight, and actual flight had been graded and scored. This mass of sleepless nights and sweaty palms was compiled into an objective score. If there was a tie, then subjective aspects were called into play: attitude, aggressiveness, appearance, "military deportment," etc.

After the instructors emerged from their powwow, the class survivors were now rank-ordered; in my class, from Number One to Number Twenty-two. A line was then drawn at the 20 percent mark, and everyone above the line was Fighter, Attack, Reconnaissance (FAR) qualified, while those below were going to Tankers, Transports, or Bombers (TTB). In my class, there were five of us above the line—the Air Force rounded up or down, depending on their requirements.

Through a combination of Boolean equations, black magic, and an honest attempt to predict operational needs, a small number of each type of aircraft would be apportioned to each graduating class. We were handed three fighters, so the top three names got them. The two poor bastards who were above the FAR line, but not in the top three, got to stay behind and become FAIPs. Every pilot had filled out a "dream sheet" with his top choices of aircraft and location. So the rankings and student preferences were matched up with the types of aircraft the Air Force had dealt out for that assignment cycle. The results were revealed during Drop Night.

This rite of passage took place on a Friday evening at the Officers Club. It was the first order of business for the night—before the effects of an open bar, music, and female groupies could take hold. The new pilot's name was called, and, in conjunction with some properly embellished tales from his training, a picture of his next aircraft was shown on the screen. Sometimes, as a spirit-crushing joke, another plane would be flashed just to see the reaction. I mean, if you're expecting a fighter, you'd slit your own throat if you thought you were getting a lumbering C-130 or a trainer. Remember, this night was the culmination of lifelong dreams, four years of college and a year of UPT. They put up a T-38 for me initially, and as my soul fled my body in shame, I remember actually grabbing the chair so I wouldn't stagger. But amid the guffawing, hoots, and screams, there appeared a picture of a beautiful F-16. In the end, with lots of backslapping, each dazed pilot would walk to the front, shake hands, and receive his official orders. You got what you earned—I had a great night.

I left Vance after that year, considerably skinnier but with silver wings on my chest. As with most military programs, you soon realize that you actually haven't finished anything, because there's always the next course or school to attend. Everything you complete just opens a new door. For an aspiring fighter pilot, there was another full year of various training programs before you got to your first operational squadron.

First came the three-month Lead-In Fighter Training (LIFT) course at Holloman AFB, New Mexico. This was conducted in AT-38 aircraft, and the instructors were all fighter pilots. Actually, the real point of this course, and what made it great, was to teach the young punk *how* to be a fighter pilot. So, besides the obvious flying stuff like dropping bombs, strafing, and dogfighting, they taught other essentials—drinking games at the bar, hymns like "Sammy Small" and "Dear Mom, Your Son Is Dead." We were stripped of all Air Training Command patches and issued Tactical Air Command (TAC) name tags and patches. It was a true mark of distinction to walk into any Officer's Club bar wearing a TAC shield and a squadron patch with the initials TFS—Tactical Fighter Squadron.

We also went through centrifuge training here. Think of the little seat that got spun around the room at 400 miles per hour during *The Right Stuff* or *Spies Like Us,* and you've got the picture. See, we were really part of the first generation of fighter pilots going into high-G aircraft, and no one was certain about the long-term effects. When blood drains from the head during high-G forces, the brain goes to sleep. Obviously, in a jet fighter traveling at 900 feet per second, this is a bad thing, and too many pilots were getting killed. Where planes like the T-38 and older fighters could *instantly* pull, say, seven Gs, the engine and airframe couldn't hold it very long. The Gs would "bleed off" to a very manageable four or five Gs. The danger in the F-16 was that it could *sustain* eight or nine Gs long past the point that the pilot could remain conscious. So the physiology folks, flight surgeons, and paper-pushers all had their panties in a wad over this, and the centrifuge training was supposed to acclimate a pilot to the sensations of high, sustained G forces. That means they strapped you in the seat and spun you till you passed out. Guys like me didn't care. What's one more risk in a profession built on them?

Actually, the biggest threats at LIFT were the "Holloman widows." These gals, usually divorced from enlisted men, had been left there when their ex-husbands moved on. They were determined to do it right the second time around and marry an officer. Think of slightly older women from *An Officer and a Gentleman,* maybe with a kid or two, and you've got it. Since I couldn't spell *matrimony* and had absolutely no desire for a wife and instant family, I avoided them like the plague.

After a year at Vance, Holloman was paradise. Well, Alamogordo, New Mexico, is hardly a metropolis, but, unlike Enid, it did not boast of eighty Baptist churches, nor did it have blue laws, and it *did* have the Sangre de Cristo Mountains. Albuquerque was only a few hours away, and there was moderately good skiing in Ruidoso. It was positively cosmopolitan after Oklahoma.

Following LIFT, I was sent to Advanced Survival training at Fairchild Air Force Base in Washington State. In February. Part of the course included an escape-and-evasion situation, where you are plopped down on a mountaintop with only the survival equipment you'd have after an ejection. This is to say, not much.

After being given a suitable head start—about an hour—you were pursued by armed soldiers whose sole excitement in life was chasing officers through the wilderness. In those days, the Soviet Union and Eastern Bloc countries were the big enemies, so that's who these guys simulated. They only spoke Russian or German. Their uniforms, weapons, and attitudes were authentic. I think they all studied method acting in East Berlin.

I figured that trying to escape and evade in the snow, without snowshoes, while being chased by deranged sadists who intimately knew the terrain, just wasn't going to work. It was, as we say, a nonstarter.

But what else could I do but try, right? So I thrashed my way down to a stream that was moving too quickly to freeze, and then, using a trick picked up from some bad western movie, I walked backward in my own boot prints to a tree. Swinging around to the side, away from my prints, I managed to pull myself up into the branches.

Okay. Maybe not the best of plans but it was all I could come up with at the moment and was certainly better than trying to blindly sprint through four feet of thick snow. And it actually did work.

At least long enough for me to start feeling cocky again.

I watched them pass my tree and stop at the riverbank. I was feeling quite pleased with myself as Hans, Fritz, and Yuri (or whatever they called themselves) looked puzzled for a few moments. They actually poked around in the bramble, looking for my body, before one of them took a closer look at my prints. I think he would've figured it out but the dogs arrived at that moment and beat him to it. No one was amused, except me, and that didn't go over so well.

Once captured, I was thrown into a mock POW camp with all the others. "Mock" in the sense that they couldn't really beat us senseless, electrify our gonads, or kill us. After a strip search and lots of shouting and shoving, I was tossed into a "cell" the size of a wall locker. There was no way to sit down, so the best you could do was to brace yourself against one wall and sort of sag. You could nap for maybe seven or eight seconds like this. It wasn't much fun but was obviously no comparison to the real thing. However, to a young officer who'd spent the last few years getting a college degree, a commission, pilot wings, and a jet fighter assignment, it was a bucket of cold water in the face. I began to develop the small and thoroughly disconcerting notion that I wasn't nearly as important as I thought I was.

The psychological games they played weren't much fun either. Music and noise played over and over. And over. And it was not a light classical medley with some falling-water sounds thrown in for relaxation.

There was the opening line from "You Say It's Your Birthday," along with a witch's laugh and my personal favorite—a baby crying. Over and over. And over. I think that put me off having kids for a good fifteen years.

There were also mind games and other physical abuse, though I think it was called "stressing." But after my four years as a cadet in the Texas A&M Corps, there wasn't anything along those lines that was going to get under my skin. I listened to Pavarotti in my head until they lost interest.

Besides the POW camp experience, there was useful training in all kinds of survival situations, evasion techniques, codes, and assorted other things designed to improve your chances of living through such an ordeal. I figured your luck would already be pretty bad to get into that type of situation, so I paid attention. These were all lessons that some poor guys had learned the hard way in Vietnam.

Unfortunately, as with much of military training, we were fighting the last war. Or, in this case, a war with Russia that had never happened. Still, I reasoned later, if we were trained to fight the Soviets, the Arabs weren't going to cause much of a problem.

Following that cheerful interlude, I went off to the primary F-16 Replacement Training Unit. This was located, thank God, in beautifully sunny Phoenix, Arizona. Oklahoma had left me culturally starved and Washington gave me frostbitten testicles, so Luke Air Force Base was nearly heaven. After packing everything into a blue Stingray (I obviously didn't own much), I showed up at Luke's main gate thawed out and, again, very full of myself. I got over that quickly.

At that time, the F-16 was only nine years old; the newest and hottest fighter in the U.S. inventory. Incidentally, only the uninitiated call it a "Fighting Falcon." Everyone else calls it a "Viper," because (a) it looks snakelike when viewed from the front, or (b) it resembles the fighter from the old *Battlestar Galactica* TV series. Or both—take your pick.

Fielded in 1979 as a lightweight, daytime jet, the Viper quickly showed itself to be much more capable than imagined. This was largely due to a computerized, modular concept that permitted easy expansion as technology and weapons advanced. A lethal dogfighter, the F-16 can only fly by using computers to offset its aerodynamic instability. This designed instability is like starting a fistfight with your first swing nearly complete. The Viper's engine is tremendously powerful and, coupled with the jet's small size, it produces greater thrust than the fighter's weight. Because of this power, the F-16 can sustain nine-G flight, which means it could outmaneuver any threat in the world. The F-16 also uses electronic signals, instead of conventional cables, to move the flight controls. This fly-by-wire system compensates against the instability and helps the pilot physically fly under sustained Gs. As mentioned, this is always potentially deadly to the pilot, as the sheer force of high Gs drains blood from the head, can snap cartilage and tear muscle.

For the next eight months, I learned how to dogfight with another jet at 500 miles per hour. The pain of pulling eight to nine times the force of gravity became a daily event. I learned how to fight as a pair and as two pairs. We slowly qualified in employing each type of weapon the F-16 could carry. General Purpose bombs, air-to-ground missiles, air-to-air missiles, and the cannon.

Every conceivable emergency that could happen in an F-16 was taught, practiced in numerous simulators, and etched forever in the forefront of my mind. All the systems on the aircraft were painstakingly dissected in classroom lectures and presentations until we knew how each component of the jet functioned. A roughly $40M jet fighter traveling at 500 miles per hour with a live human inside was a valuable commodity. We were instrument rated for bad-weather flying anywhere in the world, and we also became qualified to refuel in the air.

We were taught the basics of our various threats. We learned the strengths and weaknesses of enemy jet-fighters, anti-aircraft systems, and surface-to-air missiles. Our own onboard countermeasures and self-protection systems were thoroughly absorbed, as they'd likely save our lives one day. This would be done again, in much greater detail, when we eventually arrived at our combat squadron. It was a process that would be continually revised, updated, and repeated throughout a fighter pilot's career.

At Luke, we experienced the fundamental realization that we, the pilots, were the weapons. The success or failure of fighter operations lay with the pilot. This was one of the many things that made a fighter pilot different from other types of military aviators. The jet was the horse to get us to the fight, but the fighting was up to us.

During the latter phase of RTU, we were given follow-on assignments to our operational fighter wings. This process was loosely based on what we requested, but mostly determined by where we were needed. However, unlike UPT, we'd already proven ourselves and had our wings, so some consideration was given to our wishes. My family came, as always, to my graduation. My grandmother even showed up, and when I took her out to see my jet, she astonished me by asking how long the pitot tube was. It wasn't until years later, after her funeral, that I found a little piece of paper, covered in her tiny, neat writing, with facts about the F-16. This was a woman who had trouble getting a passport because she'd been born in the Indian Territory before it became part of a state.

I began UPT in a class of forty-one student pilots. Twenty-two graduated, and of those, three of us were selected for fighters. My RTU class started with thirteen pilots, and we graduated eleven. About half of these guys were married, and they generally wanted to stay at one of the bases in the United States. This was before the First Gulf War and the sweeping changes that would transform the military; at that time, there were no long-term deployments to nasty places. Squadron life was fairly predictable and consisted mainly of training and social events. I was single and had no ties to anyone in the States except my immediate family. I wanted to go overseas and see the world.

Germany sounded like a nice place, so I listed the three bases there that had F-16s. The first two, Hahn Air Base and Ramstein Air Base, had no vacancies during my assignment cycle, so I ended up with my third choice. I'd never heard of Spangdahlem Air Base, home of the 52nd Tactical Fighter Wing, but it didn't matter. It was in Germany.

With the Cold War still in full swing, Europe was the primary theater of operations. We had bases in the Far East, but I wasn't interested in that part of the world.

Now, the operational (that is, non-training) Air Force was

divided up into several large sections. There were the strategic aircraft—like bombers, transports, and air-refueling tankers. The bombers were there to fly deep into enemy (Soviet) airspace and drop nuclear bombs on Russian cities. Transports and tankers kept everyone supplied and full of fuel.

Then there were the tactical assets, like fighters, forward air controllers, and reconnaissance types. The fighters, in Europe at least, were basically speed bumps. We were to be thrown into the melee to slow down Russian tanks. You see, prevailing wisdom had decided that the big Soviet armored thrust, which would sweep across Europe to the English Channel, would come through the Fulda Gap on the West German border. This was a narrow pass in the Hartz Mountains and was assumed to be the focal point for the opening tank battle of World War III. Naturally, the U.S. Army and NATO were deployed around it, and the airspace above was nicely divided into chessboard sections called Restricted Operating Zones. Maps were drawn and color-coded, procedures exhaustingly created by officers with too much time on their hands, and, over the course of three decades, everything was neatly organized. There was, however, one problem.

It was nuts.

We were outnumbered ten to one by an enemy that had no problem turning Western Europe into a wasteland. They had nukes and would use them in a heartbeat if an all-out hot war broke out. This, of course, meant we would also have to use nukes. So Europe, with its beautiful cities, rivers, art, and good wine would become an immense, glowing parking lot for several generations. This war would make all previous conflicts look like Little League games.

Like I said, it was nuts.

To this day, I'm still not certain how we avoided all that. Mind you, I wasn't too interested in geopolitical considerations at the time. Like most young warriors, I was a fairly simple tool. I had silver bars on my shoulders, wings on my chest, and a cool jet to fly. I didn't care too much about who I was supposed to fight. And if you're one of the guys doing the fighting, you have to believe you're more vicious and lethal than the guy sitting in the opposing cockpit.

And we *were* the best.

The Royal Air Force, and maybe some NATO types, might take issue with this statement, but they used our equipment and had been through our training programs. We also had a generation of fighter pilots who'd seen combat in Southeast Asia within the past twenty years. The ones that survived and stayed in the Air Force were generally first-class aviators. They passed on tactics and techniques that had kept them alive in combat, as well as lots of other lessons you can't learn from books. They also taught me how to think. Well, tactically, anyway.

When I arrived, the 52nd Wing was composed of the 480th, the 81st, and the 23rd Tactical Fighter Squadrons. It was a Wild Weasel flying wing, dedicated to hunting down and killing enemy air defenses, and I ended up flying in the 23rd Tactical Fighter Squadron—the famous Fighting Hawks. This was an unusual squadron, as it contained two types of aircraft. The venerable F-4G, left over from the Vietnam War, and the F-16C, which hadn't seen any war with the U.S. Air Force. I discovered that one big reason I'd been able to get to the 52nd Wing was that very few F-16 pilots wanted to be here. The wing had mixed aircraft because the Air Force had decided to replace the aging F-4G but, of course, hadn't given much thought to what would take its place.

We had a generation gap. Actually, two gaps. One between the pilots and one for the aircraft. Most of the pilots were great guys and had remained with the F-4 because, in the curious fashion of men and machines, they loved it. Others were within a few years of retiring and didn't want to learn new technology or incur the extra years the Air Force would make them serve in return for the training.

So, I found myself in a new world. It was the real thing. We were less than ten minutes flying time from the Fulda Gap and the vodka-swilling Russian Horde; here, no one cared much about shiny boots or trivial rear-echelon bullshit. We'd been told that if the balloon ever went up, our average life expectancy was about ninety seconds—that does a lot to your outlook.

I also came face-to-face with another peculiar form of life, something called an EWO. This was short for Electronic Warfare Officer, and I'd never met one before. I was dumbfounded that the military could find a guy to ride along in the back of a fighter with absolutely no control over his destiny. I'd seen *Top Gun,* watched Goose die, and vaguely understood that certain planes, mostly Navy, had such people. But I'd never met one.

However, in 1988, the military still had aircraft like this. The USAF had its F-4G, F-15E, and F-111, while the Navy had the F-14 and EA-6. Egocentric F-16 pilot that I was, I'd never paid any attention to any of them. This, I later discovered, had been an intentional goal of the F-16 training program. The wave of the future was single-seat, multi-mission aircraft. That is, a jet that can do many things and only use one guy to do it with.

Of course, there'd been lots of single-seat combat jets before the F-16 came along. F-86s, F-104s, F-105s, etc., but the future, according to the Pentagon, was even more advanced technology. Technology that made cockpits and displays so good that one pilot could do what used to take a crew. This philosophy had been shoved into our craniums from the beginning.

Single seat, single engine, baby.

It's a great motto.

In short, rely on yourself, because if you don't do it then it won't get done. This had been preached to us, fed to us, mixed in our drinks, and by now was habit. So I, and every other F-16 lieutenant, was unprepared for non-pilots inhabiting our flying world. To make it worse, many of the EWOs had washed out of pilot training or couldn't get in to begin with. They'd gotten as close to the action as they could by becoming "backseaters." The fact that they wore the same flight suits and patches, although with different wings, didn't seem to make much of a difference. With the arrival of the F-16, they could see that their time was limited, and this definitely didn't improve their attitude or our reception. Neither did the arrival of a flock of young, single-seat fighter pilots who were just starting their careers.

NOW, EACH TIME A PILOT COMES INTO A NEW BASE, HE GETS trained. It doesn't matter who he is or what rank he holds, there will be some sort of training program. It is, of course, tailored to the experience level of the pilot and his previous qualifications. My checkout, like that of all inexperienced new arrivals, was very involved. Despite the past two years of continuous training, I was still a Fucking New Guy (FNG). I wasn't Mission Ready (MR) yet, since this was a qualification quite properly reserved for frontline combat units. A squadron in Germany would never trust the readiness of their pilots to instructors sitting back in the Arizona sunshine. Besides, different bases had unique areas of responsibility. Some were primarily air-to-ground attack units, others did nuclear strike or night attack. The 52nd was officially a Suppression of Enemy Air Defense (SEAD) wing. Wild Weasels.

The first flight in this, or any local training program, was called a Local Area Orientation (LAO). Sort of a wake up, look around, learn the procedures and local landmarks type of ride. It was always done with an instructor pilot (IP), and, like all training sorties, it was graded. As this was a mixed squadron, the lead aircraft was an F-4G, so I got an instructor pilot and an instructor EWO. Again, something I'd never seen before.

Planning for tactical mission starts at least one day in advance, and being a typical Type-A FNG, I wanted to make a good first impression. So, for days prior to the flight, I pored over maps, talked to other pilots, and did all the other FNG things. There are lots of booby traps in any elite unit, and fighter squadrons are certainly no different. Anyone new is treated with wary politeness until he proves himself, which I was intent on doing in a hurry.

Now, older guys who had been in other squadrons have less of a row to hoe than someone like me. Yet still, until the performance matches the paperwork, no one gets a break. And that's the way it should be. There are too many lives and too much insanely expensive equipment at stake. So people were nice enough, but in a distant sort of way, because FNGs could get you hurt.

After planning, briefing, and going through the complicated dance of getting a fighter started up, checked out, and to a runway, I was finally airborne. It was exhilarating to be here, and I was determined to make no mistakes.

Germany was green, and the rolling, continuous hills of the Mosel Valley were dotted with clean little red-roofed towns. We zipped around, practiced flying in formation, flying at low level and getting oriented to the area. I was just a wingman, which meant I would almost always fly with a flight lead. My somewhat limited responsibilities included not losing sight of the leader, not hitting him, and not flying into the ground. Just as with any mission, everything that occurred, from the first radio call to my landing, would be graded, evaluated, and discussed.

After ninety minutes of this, we came back, landed, and met up again in the same room to debrief. I was sweaty, a bit pumped up, and fairly pleased with myself. Most of the mission had taken place at 450 knots, and I'd spent the majority of my time staring at the Phantom and keeping position. This meant I didn't really have a great awareness of where I'd been exactly, but I never lost sight of him or did anything stupid. In the extremely unforgiving world of flying fighters that was good enough for a new guy on his first sortie. At least, I thought so.

So, when the instructor EWO, not the pilot, leaned across the table and began jabbing his finger at me and listing my inevitable transgressions, I didn't quite know what to do. I mean, here was a guy who couldn't fly an airplane giving me instruction on flying. I don't remember how it started, but after a few minutes this is how it ended.

He said, "Your tactical formation was a little wide . . . and you were too far behind the wing line. You've got to stay completely line abreast."

"Why?"

"Why?" He looked surprised and I noticed a vein in his forehead began throbbing. "Because that's where I expect to see you, and if you're not there, then I've got to find you. That takes up valuable time and pisses me off."

"Why does it matter if you see me at all?"

"Excuse me?" His eyes went kind of pointy and his mouth tightened. Out of the corner of my eye, I saw the F-4 instructor stop writing on the grade sheet and look up.

"Well . . . you're not a pilot so why does it matter if you see me or not?" The EWO's lips disappeared and I clearly remember that his face turned a deep, dusky red color. Like every blood vessel he had just exploded beneath his skin. "I mean, aren't you busy doing something in the backseat?" Like winding the clock? I didn't say that but I was thinking it.

It really was an innocent question; not contentious, because you had to earn the right to argue. I was just confused. However, the

EWO made a little choking sound as he struggled to comprehend the enormity of what I just said. I saw his mouth open and close like a guppy, and he sat there with a stupid, stunned expression on his face. Lots of F-4 guys, this one included, had a cheesy mustache left over from the 1970s, and his was pointed straight out with rage and indignation. From his point of view, I was a peon. A Fucking New Guy. And in his world, he was a minor deity who dispensed knowledge to peanuts like me. If he'd been a pilot, I would've listened without question or comment. But he wasn't a pilot, and in my world that meant you didn't tell me how to do my job.

When the F-4 instructor pilot blinked a couple of times and managed to clear his throat, I was all ears, but it was too late to salvage the situation. As he pulled me out of the briefing room, I swear I saw the soles of the EWO's boots sticking out from the ceiling, the rest of him having just shot up through the roof.

So it was a rocky start.

F-4 guys would also end every flight brief by adding, "Remember your crew coordination items," and then the pilot and EWOs would talk among themselves. A few days after the exploding EWO incident, I was sitting in a four-ship briefing when the flight lead closed with that statement. The other F-16 pilot, also a lieutenant, with fantastic comedic flair but very bad timing, started talking to his fingers. I mean, they were his crew, right? The F-4 guys were not amused *at all*, but it got me off the hook. See, I wasn't the only one.

Some of these EWOs were bitter wash-outs hanging on by their teeth to a doomed profession. A few of them just lived to belittle young fighter pilots, because we were a constant reminder of something they could never be. However, many EWOs were truly gifted, and I came to appreciate that fairly fast. They could listen to a few seconds of the audio signal from our Threat Warning Receiver (RWR) and instantly tell what type of enemy radar was trying to bite you. The good ones knew everything about the enemy systems we thought we'd face one day. A few could even identify individual radars by their unique sounds, and they were happy to share the secrets of their art. It was truly amazing to a young officer like me, and I soaked it in because, until technology caught up, the EWO was the heart of the Wild Weasel mission.

THE ORIGINAL SA-2, AND ITS FANSONG RADAR, HAD BEEN built to kill bombers and reconnaissance aircraft. Jammers, countermeasures, and threat-warning equipment had leveled the playing field somewhat, but the most expedient countertactic was low-altitude flying.

You see, radars all have a gap, a blind spot in coverage, called a "notch." FANSONG's blind spot was its inability to separate the radar return of the target from the much larger return generated by Earth. If you flew low enough, you could hide in the ground "clutter," and the radar would never see you—like wearing a black T-shirt to hide in the dark. If the radar can't see you, then it can't track and kill you. And if it had already launched and exposed its position, you could defeat the system by dropping down and flying very low. This kind of flight is impractical for most big aircraft, but it's ideal for fighters.

Newton, ever the father of tactics, correctly stated that every action has an opposite reaction. Everyone started going low after Vietnam, so, to counter the low-altitude threat, Soviet and American engineers developed systems that had no real clutter notch, because they tracked an aircraft's velocity. These missiles could also be launched visually using TV cameras, since a fighter at low altitude was easier to see than one at 20,000 feet.

The new radars were designed to be faster and more accurate, because they had to acquire, track, and launch in seconds rather than minutes. They were also mobile. Big, fixed SAM sites like the SA-2 were easy to see and therefore simple to avoid unless they were deployed around high-value targets we needed to destroy. The Soviets were aware of this, so they'd developed a particularly nasty family of mobile SAMs and greatly improved anti-aircraft guns. These systems filled in the gaps in distance and altitude coverage and were deployed around the larger strategic sites for overlapping coverage. They were highly mobile and attached to ground forces for air defense. This meant there were lots of them, and they could be anywhere.

The next-generation model, called SA-6, was fielded in the late 1960s. A mobile SAM on a tracked vehicle, it used a STRAIGHT FLUSH radar and each battery contained about twenty-four missiles. NATO called it a "GAINFUL," though it was known to the Soviets as a "KUB," meaning "cube," as there were three missiles per launcher. It was guided by the launching radar, so the steering commands for most of the intercept came directly from the STRAIGHT FLUSH. However, during the terminal phase of flight, the missile "sees" the reflected signal from the target and provides its own steering. This is called Semi Active Radar Homing (SARH) and is much deadlier than command guidance, as the reaction times are far faster.

Soviet SA-6s were sold to Egypt, among others, and were responsible for most of the Israeli Air Force F-4 Phantom and A-4 Skyhawk losses during the 1973 Yom Kippur War. They were also used, though not very successfully, by the Syrians in the Bekaa Valley. The SA-6 brought down at least one American F-16 during the First Gulf War and another in Kosovo.

Then there is the SA-8 GECKO. Though it looks like a six-wheeled Winnebago, the system isn't funny at all. Extremely mobile, the SA-8's LANDROLL target-tracking radar could switch on, find you, pass the information to the missile, and shoot in a matter of seconds. It was also a short-ranged system, so there wasn't much time to react anyway. In fact, if you got an SA-8 spike, then you reacted instantly or you wouldn't survive to fight back.

There were others. One of the most dangerous systems was the ROLAND, which the French were good enough to sell to anybody with cash. The French have been lousy warriors since Napoleon died, but they did make good equipment. Man-portable systems, called MANPADs, were also further refined and manufactured in huge numbers. These were particularly dangerous to low-altitude fighters, because as infrared (IR) trackers, they tracked heat sources and gave no warning at all unless you happened to see them launched. If you did see one, it could usually be thrown off by a series of flares. But there were always more than one, and spotting it is next to impossible. IR SAMs are simple, cheap, and ideal for the Third World.

The American military had long been enamored with radar-guided SAMs. They were more accurate, longer-ranged, and much harder to defeat, but the problem with that was we assumed everyone else had gone high-tech as well. U.S. fighters weren't then equipped with any kind of IR warning device. The only warning you had, if any, was when the nasty things zipped past your canopy or your engine blew up.

LEARNING THE STRENGTHS AND WEAKNESSES OF THE ENEMY and his equipment took up a great deal of a new pilot's time. He also had to study the local flying procedures, remain instrument-qualified, and perfect his fighting skills. And there were always tests. Written exams, check-rides, spot evaluations, and formal training programs called upgrades. It was endless and all-consuming.

And I loved every minute of it.

After the initial two years required just to get into a fighter squadron, a pilot is only a wingman. In order to be listed as Mission Ready, he then goes through additional three or four months of checkout in the various missions for which his squadron is responsible. He's still a wingman, so he always goes up with a "flight lead."

There are "two-ship" and "four-ship" flight leads. That is, a pilot who can command the essential fighting element of two aircraft, or one who can lead two pairs. The two-ship, also called an "element," is the basic fighting pair. These are usually combined into four-ships, six-ships, or even bigger packages, depending on the mission.

Progressing upward through the various tiers of fighter aviation is called "upgrading." Every wingman aspires to become a flight lead, and his acceptance into that first big upgrade is strictly a matter of performance and individual ability. Lives are at stake, in the air and on the ground. Tens of millions of dollars are at risk every time a flight takes off, so this is not entered into lightly. After a year or two of being a wingman, a young pilot has his name put forward at a weekly meeting of the squadron Instructor Pilots, and his record is discussed. This includes all of his check-rides, test scores, and previous performance in his Mission Qual checkout. His attitude and, most of all, his maturity. On this note, we're talking about professional maturity and decision-making related to flying. If we were judged by O'Club maturity, everyone would still be a wingman.

This first upgrade is important, because for the previous three to four years you've been following others, learning, and generally trying to stay alive. Though there's considerable autonomy in a single-seat fighter, there's still always a more experienced pilot nearby to plan, direct, and make most of the decisions. To lead. This mentality change is the first big step.

The actual program is straightforward. Like all upgrade and training programs, it is well organized. There is a syllabus outlining minimum requirements for every aspect of each training flight and the proficiency level needed to pass. It's all graded.

One of the most significant hurdles for a prospective flight lead is learning the art of the briefing. Briefings are supposed to last no longer than an hour and a half. This sounds like a lot of time, but I can tell you it really isn't. Now, except in rare cases, the pilots taking part in the mission all helped plan it the day prior. Peacetime briefing rooms are in the part of a fighter squadron called "The Vault." This is behind a huge metal door, like a bank vault, and contains all the classified information necessary for the squadron's various missions. No one gets in but pilots and intelligence types. The rooms are about ten by fifteen and set up to accommodate a four-ship briefing. The pilots sit around a central table and the flight lead stands up front and talks. There are white boards for drawing details and tactical scenarios. Sliding panels along the front wall contain things that are usually "standard" for most missions. Rules of engagement for employing weapons, divert field data, ground operations, etc.

The flight lead is responsible for the organization and "flow" of the brief. It starts with a time hack—a synchronization of watches. The "Overview," which is the intended mission sequence, is discussed. This is called the "Motherhood," and is all the non-tactical aspects of getting jets off the ground, to and from the base, and back on the ground. Types of takeoffs (afterburner or not), rejoin formations, routes, communications, and the expected return-to-base procedures are all briefed. These events vary considerably with the experience level of the pilots, training requirements, and weather. Contingency plans are a big part of each phase of a brief. How does a four-ship operate as a three-ship if a jet breaks? Who leads the flight if the flight lead doesn't make it? Air-refueling, night procedures, and a host of other "what if"s? The permutations are endless. Emergencies are also reviewed quickly and concisely, just as they'd be dealt with at 400 knots. There's always an EP (Emergency Procedure) of the day, where the causes, indications, and solutions are discussed.

A typical briefing will spend about twenty minutes discussing and reviewing this before getting into the point of the mission. Called the "Meat," this occupies the remaining time. Say it's a Wild Weasel mission to find and destroy an SA-6 battery protecting a target that is to be hit by strike aircraft. The first step of the Meat is laying out the "Big Picture." This would include composition of the strike package, their routes into the target area, call signs, radio frequencies, and timing. The latest intelligence is also reviewed— location of the main target, locations of SAMs and Triple-A, and the expected reaction from whomever you're trying to kill. The "Ingress" to the target area is outlined, including the type of tactical formations, reactions to enemy fighters and SAMs, and communications. A good flight lead will blend in extra information, like countermeasure usage, countertactics, or combat search-and-rescue in the event a jet goes down.

The type of attack is painstakingly detailed. This is, after all, what it's all about. Weapons with their plethora of settings and variations are discussed. As always, contingencies and how to deal with them at 500 knots, when people are shooting at you, are a major point of discussion. *Everything* bad that could happen can't be addressed, of course, but the main idea is to have plans that will adapt and work when the shit hits the fan. For instance, suppose a SAM targets you during your attack, or a MiG appears. How is it dealt with? And how do you then re-attack the target? What if the weather over the target area is too bad for your primary chosen attack? Again, lots of variables.

WHILE THE COLD WAR WAS ENDING, WE ONLY DEPLOYED from our home bases for training. These were never very long, and usually to nice places. In Europe, we had Sardinia for air-to-air training, and England or Spain were our primary deployments for air-to-ground training. Requirements—called "currencies"—are endless in the flying world. You had to drop so many bombs, shoot missiles, land so many times at night, etc. . . . so many per month, every month, or you became non-current. We had to drop a required amount of bombs, within various accuracy parameters, to maintain our Mission Qualified status. When the weather in Germany was bad (about six months out of the year), then we went elsewhere.

A fighter pilot's first trip to Spain's Zaragoza Air Base was a chance to participate in a small squadron deployment, which was good practice, and also to go fly in the sun for thirty days with your buddies. Much better than winter in Germany. Zaragoza—or Zab, as we called it—began several thousand years ago as a Roman settlement for army veterans. Goths, Arabs, the Inquisition, and Napoleon had all harassed this place long before we got there. It's a beautiful city, where bright flowers soften the beige medieval fortifications and Moorish architecture still reigns supreme.

We would usually fly at least once a day; a beautiful, low level along the Spanish coast or through the mountains to the Bardenas bombing range. Wingmen became better wingmen, flight leaders better leaders, and upgrade training was conducted for those who deserved it. Evenings were spent at the Officer's Club, drinking the local sweet sangria, singing songs, and cooking out on huge open grills. The smells of honeysuckle, charcoal smoke, and fresh fruit are forever etched in my memory. Spain.

It was superb . . .

Every few nights, when the flying schedule permitted, we'd take little taxicabs downtown to eat or see the sights. One of the initiation rights for an unworldly American pilot on his first trip to Zab was the fabled Green Bean Tour. It worked like this. The new guy was assigned an "instructor" to take him through the narrow, dark streets behind the big cathedral in downtown Zaragoza. These little streets were called the Tubes and were lined with carts, street vendors, and hole-in-the-wall snack shops. I use the word *snack* only because you *could* physically eat the stuff.

Actually, that was the game. The new guy had to eat whatever the instructor told him to eat. Between courses, he also had to drink the local red wine, called Tinto, from a leather bouda bag. The rest of the squadron came along to assist in this.

The idea was to survive this haute cuisine gauntlet, and the Tinto, without puking. To my knowledge, no one ever did. At the end of the Tubes was a small stone plaza, where the squadron commander and the higher-ranking officers waited. Having seen this just a few times over the years, they usually opted for a quiet drink together while we promoted goodwill for America among the locals. Well, not really, but they did love our money.

I did fine for most of it. I mean, to the point where I thought I was going to make it to the end. I'd used the Tinto to wash down and disinfect the candied snake, locust poppers, and half a dozen other Spanish treats that had been shoved in my face. But near the end my guide refilled the bouda bag and handed me something on a stick.

"You gotta try this."

There was some snickering from the crowd.

"Whaddacallit?" I burped back.

"Kinda like a Spanish . . . corndog. Yeah . . . a corndog."

More snickers.

Well, it was dark and I'd figured out pretty quick not to look closely at the things I was eating. Besides, this was the last stop and I thought I'd made it. Feeling cocky, I swallowed some Tinto to numb my one remaining taste bud, closed my eyes, and took a bite of something crunchy.

I remember briefly feeling quite proud. Whatever I was eating wasn't too bad and then I'd be finished. The two other lieutenants were already on their hands and knees, getting a better view of the thousand-year-old gutter. Everyone else was chuckling, since they'd been in the same situation at some point in their careers.

"Howizzit?" someone asked.

I nodded, now an expert on all Spanish snack food, and replied with total confidence, "Good. How 'bout another?"

More chortling.

Just then I felt something wedged between my teeth and stopped chewing long enough to pull it out. I burped again and then made the mistake of holding it up against the faint light.

For a long, nasty moment I stared at the thing as my Tinto-soaked brain processed.

"Whatchagot?" someone asked innocently.

It was a foot.

Actually, it was a curved bird's claw, complete with little talons. So the alley spun and the stars blurred. I felt the awful burning rush of all that Tinto, and the candied hummingbird I'd just eaten, come shooting up through my nose, mouth, and out of my ears. I joined the other lieutenants on the ground and everyone roared with satisfaction.

No one beats the Tubes.

Now, this particular ritual ends in a ceremony simply known as the "Naming." This is where fighter pilots get awarded those cool-sounding nicknames, or call signs, you hear about in the movies. I mean, who wouldn't want to be "Maverick" or "Iceman" or "Thor." Right?

Right.

The reality is a bit different. There are some manly, warlike call signs, of course. I've known Slash, Magic, Crusher, Bruiser, and Storm'n. Even Ghost, Spook, and Zing aren't too bad. Usually call signs are given for something noteworthy, and not necessarily good, that a pilot has done. Or maybe the guy is just an asshole— "JRay," "Barney," and "Moses" are prime examples of that.

"Slider" is usually given for landing gear-up; "Scratch," you guessed it, for scratching the belly of the aircraft on a low level or dinging the speed brakes on the runway; "Boomer" for inadvertently breaking the sound barrier and every window within a five-mile radius. The possibilities are endless.

"Toto"—for accidentally shutting the engine down (throttle on, throttle off—get it?). I even knew a "Bubbles," who'd ejected over the Atlantic Ocean. Anything, including personal traits or physical appearance, is fair game. So we have "Opies" and "Wookies" and even a "DDong" (short for "Donkey Dong"). I'm sure his mother would be proud.

There are a few rules with this. First, and most important, if you've carried a call sign into combat, then you can never be renamed—it's yours for life. Second, if you've managed to keep the same call sign while flying in three different theaters (like Europe, the Far East, etc.) then it's yours to keep. Third, and most common, if you really hate a call sign then it's probably also yours for life.

I was named Two Dogs in loose reference to an old joke about how American Indians name their children. ("Why do you ask, Two Dogs Fucking in the Night?") You see, I suntan to a deep reddish brown and my nose is beaked, so it kind of made sense in the Tinto haze on that sultry Spanish night in the gutter. Hey, there are definitely worse things to be called. Like Homer, Kraken, or Moto ("Master of the Obvious"). Anyway, it stuck. Honestly, at that stage of the night, I wouldn't have cared if they'd named me Cindy, as long as it got me back to the Officer's Quarters and my toilet any sooner.

At least once during the trip, there would be a mass exodus to the Spanish Riviera—Costa Brava. Americans with wild, long shorts and Europeans wearing extra-small Speedos would mix on topless beaches, burn in the sun, and watch girls. I'd like to say the beaches were filled with young Penthouse Pet types, but it just wasn't true. There's really nothing like a saggy, half-naked, middle-aged German housewife to kill the picture. Still, nothing's perfect.

We'd also have to spend at least two days up at Bardenas Range in the north of Spain. A qualified fighter pilot had to act as the Range Control Officer (RCO), a duty that inevitably fell to the lieutenants and younger captains. The RCO was there as the approval authority for aircraft to drop bombs and to strafe with their cannons. He was also on hand to deal with aircraft emergencies and to officially score the bombs that each pilot dropped. This was a big deal, since Mission Qualification was the life blood of a fighter squadron. That and Jeremiah Weed whiskey.

The Air Force had a detachment permanently assigned at the range to maintain targets, scoring equipment, and facilities. They all seemed to be Hispanic and loved being up there where they could speak the mother tongue. The senior sergeant was a guy named Vic. I never knew his last name, but we always said "stick with Vic." Vic would shuttle us around, take us out to dinner and to see the sights. He also helped perform one of the more harebrained stunts in my short career. Running with the bulls in Pamplona.

Five hundred years ago, the merchants of Navarre sold their cattle at a market in Pamplona. They would move the beasts through the narrow streets to holding pens and await the sale. To speed things up, they'd "run" the animals through the streets. Eventually, some young, brainless Alpha-male types, undoubtedly fortified by Tinto, decided to see if they could outrun the bulls. Over time this became a rite of passage and a tradition. So, during the Feast of San Fermin, a weeklong festival emerged and the bulls were run every morning. Any excuse for a party, right?

Technically, we were prohibited from doing this, because several hundred people were hurt each year and a few were even killed. But there's no quicker way to provoke a fighter pilot than to tell him something is prohibited. I remember the fireworks and the thousands of red bandannas and flags flying everywhere. Some of the locals were barefoot and wore baggy peasant outfits, all white, no doubt to see the blood better. I also recall sprinting with the crowd (all men and all young enough to be that stupid) through the narrow, uneven streets. This wasn't so bad, I thought, then something bobbed past my head at eye level and I realized it was a horn. So I zigged over to the nearest wall and managed to scramble up most of the way. A few hands appeared to help me into the beautiful, and extremely thorny, rosebushes on the other side.

So why risk your eyes and balls, not to mention your career and life, to dash around in front of enraged bulls? Because it was there, of course. Besides, in college I'd read *The Sun Also Rises,* and if Ernest Hemingway had done it then I had to do it as well. So much for the positive effects of literature in higher education.

All in all, it was a terrific time. Fast jets, European travel, and the constant challenge of staying alive. Other life-altering events, like marriage, children, and war, were still in the future. I had my hands full but I also had the advantages of first-rate instructors and a young squadron commander who took an interest in my career. I upgraded to four-ship flight lead as a lieutenant and was approved to begin instructor-pilot training in the fall of 1990.

That all changed rather quickly in August, when a dictator I'd never heard of, named Saddam Hussein, invaded Kuwait. As I tried to locate Iraq on a map, vacations were canceled and all upgrades were halted. A few of us who spoke French were sent to France to talk with pilots who'd actually trained the Iraqis. We came back smelling like cheese but feeling relieved. I mean, Arabs taught by Frenchmen? Come on. Tactical analyses appeared from Nellis AFB, CIA country studies showed up from someplace in the Virginia countryside, and we all got busy as the future rapidly became the present.

The Wild Weasels were going back to war.

The Elephant

January 19, 1991
Mosul, Northern Iraq

"TORCH . . . FENCE in."

My hands darted around the cockpit, performing the FENCE, or pre-combat check of my weapons and equipment. I eyeballed the chaff and flare settings, turned up the volume on the radar-warning receiver, tightened my seat straps, and ran through all my loaded weapons. Staring at the big master-arm switch for a long second, I put my thumb on it. Glancing around to make sure it all was where it should be, I gently moved it to the ARM position—my various weapons switches were now "hot." Mortally afraid of screwing up, I carefully avoided the pickle button that would release my bombs and kept my finger off the trigger.

Sighing a little, I stared out at the big F-4G a mile and a half to my left. Beyond him by another mile was another Phantom/F-16 pair. We were spread out in what was called a fluid-four formation. An ideal combat formation, this kept lots of space between aircraft for maneuvering and was extremely difficult for an enemy to see all of us. It was a beautiful, absolutely clear morning covered by a powder-blue sky with hundreds of miles of visibility. Behind us, the big KC-135 tankers were wheeling back in dignified left-hand turns over the snow-covered mountains of eastern Turkey. We were on our own.

Ahead lay the jagged peaks of the Zagros mountain range and, just beyond, through the Zahko Pass, was Indian Country—Iraq. A nation most of us hadn't cared about or devoted the least thought to until the previous August. Saddam Hussein, in a monumental error in judgment, had invaded Kuwait and threatened the Ghawar oil fields in Saudi Arabia. I really couldn't have cared less. I was going to war and, with the ignorance of the inexperienced, all I could see was a grand adventure.

And it *was* exciting. After four years of college and nearly three more of advanced flying training, I was finally on the cutting edge. Here, on the front end of the first combat strike package into Iraq from the northern front, exactly in the right place, at the right time, and with the right jet. Despite my cockiness, my breathing matched my heart rate as the mountains slid away under my wings and the great plain of northern Iraq opened up before me. Contrails appeared overhead as the escort F-15s zoomed up above 30,000 feet and headed south to deal with any MiGs.

"CHAINSAW, this is RAZOR One. Pushing . . . picture."

RAZOR One was the Mission Commander. He was asking the orbiting AWACS what the situation, or picture, was south of us in Iraq. I'd heard communications like this all the time in training. It was familiar and comforting. What happened next was not.

"RAZOR . . . picture . . . three groups, Bull's-eye One-Five-Zero for forty-five, angels medium . . . northbound. Bandits."

Every tactical area had a common reference point on the ground called a Bull's-eye. It could be geographically significant, like a mountaintop, or tactically significant, like an airfield. In any event, the idea was that all aircraft could give their compass bearing and distance *from* the point and everyone listening would have a decent idea of their position. Today the Bull's-eye was the city of Mosul.

Obviously, the bad guys didn't know this. We also generally used special radios, called HAVE QUICK radios, that the enemy couldn't listen to. The HAVE QUICK frequencies changed every day and, once loaded properly, would jump around in an unbreakable coded sequence. Anyone listening would hear only broken bits of words, if anything. I froze for an instant as my brain processed that there were three distinct groups of unknown enemy fighters, called Bandits, southeast of Mosul and heading north.

Toward us.

The Mission Commander, an F-16 squadron commander from Torrejon Air Base, calmly replied. I heard the F-15 Eagle flight lead acknowledge and the contrails got longer as they lit their afterburners and raced south to fight the MiGs.

"Lucky bastards . . ." I muttered. But we were certain we'd have enough fighting of our own in a few minutes, when we got within range of the surface-to-air missiles around Mosul.

Everything got quiet for roughly thirty seconds. The Eagles were working out among themselves who would kill which group of Iraqis, and everyone else was listening. Then it all came apart as the strikers broke through the SAM engagement zones.

"CONAN One . . . spiked south." The F-15 flight lead radioed that an enemy fighter had locked onto him.

"RAZOR Three . . . Mud . . . SA-2 . . . southwest!" One of the F-16s up front was locked by an SA-2 somewhere south of him.

"TRON . . . Music on!" Somewhere an EF-111 had activated his jamming systems.

"CONAN Four! Missile in the air . . . Mosul."

I didn't know if he meant a SAM or had picked up the inbound contrail of an enemy air-to-air missile.

"SAM off the ground . . . missile in the air from . . . Mosul . . . I . . ." Whoever it was had picked up a missile from the SA-2 batteries around Mosul.

"TORCH One . . . Magnum SA-2!"

That was us! Snapping my head left, I saw fire shoot out from beneath my flight lead's wing. The big HARM missile nosed over for a second then leveled off and accelerated. I watched, fascinated, as it abruptly zoomed up, trailing thick, white smoke. I'd never witnessed one actually launched. Managing to look out ahead of me, I was amazed to see three or four long, gray trails reaching up from the ground like disembodied fingers.

SAMs!

Four of them that I could count. Even as I watched, they began to arc around in our direction. I glanced at my warning display and saw several big "3" symbols overlapping each other in the middle of the scope. A sharp, cold spear shot up from my belly, through my chest, and I tried to swallow but couldn't. I had just caught my first glimpse of the Elephant.

Seeing the Elephant, a symbol of combat since Hannibal crossed the Alps, is looking Death in the face. Your first real glimpse of your own mortality.

It hadn't really sunk in until that moment that all of this was very real. The distant black smears against the pale sky had been aircraft with men inside, a few moments ago. Those smoke trails coming up at me were live SAMs. High-explosive warheads traveling at three times the speed of sound and coming directly at my butt . . .

My skin felt prickly and, as time slowed down, my awareness increased. I noticed that the cockpit smelled like a wet dog—we had sheepskin covers over the ejection seats, and this one had gotten wet and mildewed. The big engine vibrated through the floor and I felt it throbbing against my heels. There was a fly crawling across the HUD. I had just seen the Elephant. No amount of training can prepare a man for that first realization that other men are actively trying to kill him. Hopefully, you don't freeze; ideally, you just react.

I did.

"TORCH Two . . . SA-3 . . . south . . ."

Clouds of white-feathered brown dust rolled across the ground as the missiles lifted off.

My flight lead was a big, gruff pilot called Orca. He calmly zippered the mike and pulled sideways to put the missiles off his left wing. This should've given the missile's tracking radars trouble but they kept coming. Chaff blossomed behind the F-4, and I groped for my own dispense switch. The big Phantom flipped over, pulled down toward Iraq, and I followed. Being shot at while inverted at 20,000 feet over enemy territory was definitely a new experience. As the earth spun around beneath me, the Phantom lumbered upright, and I snap-rolled the F-16 to follow.

Looking south, I could only see one contrail left. My RWR was still cluttered with "3" symbols, and the audio warning was screeching in my helmet. But Orca pulled straight up in a classic last-ditch maneuver. White vapor trails streamed off his wingtips as we came up through the horizon and pointed at the sun. Almost simultaneously, we both rolled in the direction the missiles had to be coming from. More chaff spit out behind him as we zoomed up and continued to roll until we were upside-down again.

He came through the horizon inverted, then sluggishly leveled off. I found myself between the Phantom and the SAMs, so I instantly barrel-rolled over his tail to about a mile behind him. My face was sweaty and I was breathing hard, but it occurred to me that the maneuvers and chaff had worked. At least three SAMs had been shot at us, and we'd survived. And those were three SAMs that hadn't been shot at the strikers.

"Two Dogs . . . Slapshot SA-2 bearing two-zero-five . . ."

My personal call sign penetrated the noise, confusion, and fog of combat, and that was precisely why we used them. A "Slapshot" was a quick-reaction HARM fired along the given bearing. It was supposed to force the SAM radar off the air or, if he stayed up, it would theoretically go right down its throat.

Almost of their own accord, my hands moved, and I pulled the F-16 to a heading of 205 degrees and stared at the HUD. The big pointing cross symbolizing the HARM's nose hovered over my heading display. My eyes flickered to the bottom of the HUD and I confirmed, again, that my weapons were armed. Swallowing once, hard, I mashed down on the red pickle button and held it. For a long half-second, nothing happened. But as I looked out at my left wing, the jet shook violently and the HARM snaked off the rail.

"Sonofabitch . . ." *It actually worked.*

"TORCH Two, Magnum SA-2!"

I immediately pulled up and away from the launch. We did this at low altitude, because the HARM left quite a trail and the enemy was quite capable of doing to us what we did to him. That is, following the smoke back to the aircraft and shooting it out of the sky.

Then the radios went batshit. The F-15s were talking about splashing MiGs, more SAMs were off the ground, and several strikers in front of us jettisoned their bombs as they reacted to an air threat behind them.

Behind them?!

My head swiveled like it was on rollers. I tried to calmly scan the sky in sections, as I'd been taught, but my eyeballs just bounced around. If there were MiGs behind the lead group of our jets, then they'd be . . . here.

Suddenly, I knew what had happened. Some Eagle driver had seen our HARM launches and thought they were air-to-air missiles! I chuckled, but it was understandable. We'd never fired those things off in peacetime, and it must've looked suspicious.

I quit looking at my air-to-air radar.

"RAZOR One . . . rolling in from the north . . . RAZOR Three, arc southeast for the roll-in."

The Mission Commander's calm voice came over very clear—a true professional. His flight acknowledged, and I glanced forward long enough to see a whole flock of F-16s flip over on their backs and dive toward the ground.

A surface attack like they were doing was fairly straightforward. There would be a route and separate altitudes, usually in 4,000-foot blocks, into the target area. These would keep you clear of other flights attacking the same target. Theoretically. The Initial Point (IP) was like the doorway. Systems would be checked one more time, air-to-air radars would sweep for enemy fighters, and countermeasures activated. Past the IP, a pilot would fly a specified heading and distance to his "action," or "roll-in" point. Here, he'd put the jet into whatever weapons delivery parameters were needed to release, fuse, and detonate his ordnance. It was all planned in advance and relatively predictable.

Wild Weasel attacks weren't like that for the very good reason that air defense sites were unpredictable, and mobile SAMs were just that—mobile. You can't plan specific attacks without fixed targets. So we needed something that could work "on the fly" against most any threat.

"TORCH Three . . . defending SA-3 from the south!"

That was the other F-4G in our four-ship. I couldn't see him but I did see two more SAMs lift off. I was much closer now and could plainly see Mosul. The Euphrates River was almost turquoise in the early-morning light, and I could see there were cars moving across the four bridges. The city center was green with a big park of some kind. Gray suburbs stretched out in all directions except to the southwest. In that direction, on the west bank of the river, was the airfield. A tan bar of concrete paralleling the Euphrates, it was a huge military complex protected by MiGs, Triple-A, and SAMs. It was our target, and if we destroyed the hangars and runway today, then there'd be no air threat from Mosul as we fought south, toward Baghdad. The Weasel's mission was to suppress or kill the SAM sites so the strikers could drop their bombs on the airfield.

Orca didn't answer, but I saw his F-4 crank up and over to point at the airfield and the SAMs. This time, his HARM came off and dove straight at the winding trails of smoke.

He'd turned into my flight path to shoot, so I yanked the nose up and barrel-rolled over him to the other side. There were jets everywhere. Far below me, like swirling gray gnats, the striker F-16s were coming off the target, twin vapor trails streaming from their wingtips. Snapping the jet upright, I leaned forward and stared down at the base. Huge cones of dust and smoke sprouted as dozens of 2,000-pound Mark 84 bombs exploded, completely obscuring the airfield.

Suddenly, flashes caught my eye and I flinched. Ahead were countless gray and black puffy spots blossoming against the pale blue sky. *Anti-aircraft fire*. Triple-A. I groped for the mike switch.

"Triple-A, ten o'clock . . . a little high." I managed to get it in and, fortunately, my flight lead recognized my voice. That type of call did no one much good, since I'd forgotten to give a position or my own call sign.

The F-4 ramped over and I followed. By simply changing altitude, we'd confuse the gunners. At least for the next salvo.

"LASER Three is re-attacking . . . thirty seconds," I heard as

I finally remembered to check my fuel. One of the strikers hadn't dropped and was going in again.

"TORCH copies," Orca immediately responded. "We'll cover from the east."

I glanced up and was amazed at the number of contrails criss-crossing the sky. Thin pairs that had to come from fighters, and the much thicker ones that could only be missiles.

"LASER Three is in!"

"Two Dogs . . . Slapshot SA-3 . . . Mosul," Orca barked.

This time, much more deliberately, I turned in, refined my aim, and hosed off my remaining HARM. Pulling up and rolling toward the F-4, I was surprised to see that he continued pointing at Mosul only six miles away.

"TORCH . . . Magnum . . . Magnum . . ."

I frowned under the mask. What the hell was he doing? Neither of us had weapons remaining and he kept jabbing at the SAM batteries.

"Magnum . . . Magnum SA-3 . . . Mosul."

But then I learned another combat lesson. The Iraqis didn't know we were out of missiles, and we knew they listened to our radio traffic. Maybe his bogus radio calls would force a SAM down. Orca was covering the last two-ship of strikers as they re-attacked the airfield. He was making them look and shoot at us instead of the strikers—he was Weaseling. I floated a bit high and aft so I could keep him in sight and watch the ground. Five thousand feet below me, I saw the vapor from an F-16 wingtip as it pulled off-target.

"LASER's off-target . . . north for the egress."

"TORCH has you in sight. Come off zero-three-zero."

As I watched Orca, he pulled the Phantom's nose up and did a big barrel-roll over the airfield. Several little orange balls zipped past and exploded just like corn popping. But after the last ten minutes, it didn't seem like much to worry about.

As we headed north in a slow climb, I realized that we were probably the last fighters heading for the border. The Weasels have another motto—First In, Last Out. And that's exactly what we were doing. I turned and looked back as the funnel-shaped clouds spread out over the airfield. Wispy, gray SAM contrails still hung in the air.

On the common strike frequency, I heard a pair of F-15s up above us, thumping their chests over splashing some Iraqi fighters, and I wished I'd gotten to shoot a MiG. We zoomed up above 20,000 feet and headed north toward Turkey. It was an amazing sight. The mist had burned off, and the dark green peaks along the border jutted upward against the blue sky. To the west, the light brown of the Syrian plain stretched as far as I could see. To my right, past the Zagros Range, was the blue-green smudge of Iran. Way off toward the north loomed the enormous, white-crowned peak of Mount Ararat, beyond which lay the Soviet Union.

I was exhilarated. Dropping my mask, I wiped off my face and wished I'd remembered to bring a bottle of water. And food. Tomorrow, I told myself, and jotted that down on my lineup card that had become quickly cluttered with lessons. NEVER FLY IN A STRAIGHT LINE. CHANGE ALTITUDES RANDOMLY. ATTACK WITH THE SUN BEHIND YOU IF POSSIBLE.

These things hadn't changed since World War I. I'd been taught all of them but nothing sears in life-preserving habit patterns like combat.

Suddenly a thin, pole-shaped object shot up exactly between the F-4 and myself. For a second, I was too surprised to react. But Orca instantly weaved away to the west and I saw a string of glowing flares drop away from his tail section.

"Shit . . ." Weaving the other way, I also thumbed out some

flares. Rolling up on my left wing, I stared down and realized what had happened. The Iraqis had lugged some shoulder-launched missiles, MANPADS, onto the 12,000-foot peaks, and they were shooting at our contrails.

Orca knew it, too, because he shoved the nose over and descended below the layer of air that caused contrails. And then we were past the peaks and into Turkey. More lessons. Don't ever fly in the contrail layer unless you want to be seen, and never relax in enemy territory.

Exhaling, I shook my head as we headed for the air-refueling tanker track over Lake Van. What a morning. But we were back in Turkey, relatively safe and—

"CONAN One . . . pop-up threat . . . Bogey . . . nose fifteen . . . low."

CONAN was the flight of F-15s above us.

What the fuck?

"TORCH flight . . . bracket . . . bracket!" Orca snapped and instantly rolled hard away to the west. Reflexively, I cranked away from him to the east, and we were set in a classic pincer maneuver that was supposed to force an enemy fighter to pick a side. This would expose him to the jet he didn't attack—and then he'd die.

"CONAN . . . this is CHAINSAW . . . say again?" The AWACS controller sounded incredulous.

But we were in Turkey. How in the hell did a MiG slip past and get behind us? The tankers, I realized, as I fumbled with my mask and tried to pull my head out of my ass. The MiG must be attacking the tankers! There was no time for a radar search, so I pushed in with my left thumb and instantly brought up the "Slewable Air Combat Maneuvering" mode. This was a quick-reaction mode, utilized to point the radar at threats less than ten miles away: it would automatically lock on whatever it found.

I glanced up, saw the Eagles making contrails and eyeballed

where the threat must be. Slewing the pointing cross left and down in the HUD, I let go and waited as the two F-15s began their attack. They'd called it a "Bogey" instead of a "Bandit" which meant they couldn't positively identify it as hostile. Identification could be done with a variety of electronic systems on both the F-16 and F-15, but there hadn't been time. So the aircraft would remain "unknown" until it could be visually identified or committed a hostile act. Like shooting at one of us.

"LOCK . . . LOCK . . ."

To my astonishment, the radar actually grabbed a contact. I stared, wide-eyed, at a dark speck coming straight down the "snot locker"—between us—at over 500 knots. It was eight miles away and charging up at us from below.

I snapped the master arm back to ARM and strained forward against my straps to see over the F-16's nose. The Target Designator (TD) box was there, sliding over the mountaintops as the strange jet raced toward us.

"CONAN One is visual . . . bogey . . . ten o'clock low!"

"CONAN . . . CHAINSAW . . . say again?"

AWACS was doing its normal bang-up job. Out of the corner of my eye, I caught a flash of sunlight on something shiny and saw the Eagles, about four miles in front of me, sweeping down from the north. The F-4 and I were split apart by about five miles but now beginning to turn in. This unknown fighter was sandwiched in three dimensions. It was the perfect intercept.

He was screwed, whoever he was. It was just a matter of who would kill him first.

I grinned and uncaged my AIM-9 Sidewinder. This let the missile's infrared seeker to try to track whatever target I was locked to. It just growled at me though, unable to tell jet from earth, so I'd have to get closer. That wasn't a problem at these speeds, since we'd close the eight miles to shooting range in about fifteen seconds.

There! In the TD box, I could see an aircraft. It was tiny and its exhaust left a smoke trail. With the exception of the Phantom, no U.S. aircraft smoked. And this was no Phantom. I kept trying to lock the Sidewinder but it wouldn't.

Shit.

If an Eagle killed this MiG in front of me, I'd never forgive myself. Probably spend all my money in therapy.

I'd descended a few thousand feet when we broke apart so I wouldn't give this asshole a nice, look-up shot at me. I'd also been able to pull my power back as I'd glided down, and this cooled my engine off so any infrared missile shot against me would have a tough time. I didn't put out any preemptive flares, because if he hadn't seen me yet, flares would certainly give away my position. It was risky though, because if he shot, I'd have only a second or two to pop the flares. I didn't like thinking defensively.

Fuck it. Shoving the throttle up to mil power, I pulled back and up toward the oncoming jet.

He was about four miles in front of me and slightly high, so I uncaged the Sidewinder and the clear, steady tone said it finally liked what it saw. With a good firing solution and a visual on the bogey, this was almost perfect. Squinting against the sun and the Gs, I still couldn't tell what it was except that it was painted brown. I grunted and moved my right thumb just over the pickle button. That about clinched it. We didn't have any brown aircraft.

For a long count of two, I waited. Waited for a smoke trail coming off his jet. Waited for the Eagles to identify it.

"CONAN One . . . ID Friendly! Repeat . . . ID Friendly." The Eagle pilot sounded disappointed.

What in the hell . . .

My thumb came away from the pickle like it was hot. But I continued pulling into the other jet, carefully avoiding the two F-15s that had settled in behind the thing. As they all flashed past me, barely a mile away, I caught sight of a brown cylinder with incredibly stubby wings.

MiG-21! my brain screamed.

"It's a fucking MiG-21," I yelled into my mask, and my thumb came back down above the pickle. My first shocked thought was that the Eagles had made a colossal blunder. The Iraqi Air Force had MiG 21s, and this was exactly where you'd expect to find one. Close to its home base and hiding in the mountains.

Then I saw the red flag with the white crescent and star on the tail, and my thumb again came quickly away from the pickle button.

Unbelievable. Un. Fucking. Believable.

Türk Hava Kuvvetleri. Turkish Air Force. My brain clicked on again and I remembered why the jet was familiar. It was an American-made F-104 Starfighter, and I'd seen one in a museum once. Shaking my head as the thing zipped by, I very carefully moved the master arm to SAFE. What kind of idiot would be out trolling the border *today* in front of a hundred armed fighter pilots? I shrugged my shoulders against the seat straps and took a deep breath. A Turkish idiot, that's who. As we continued north, the F-15s stayed with the F-104 and were voicing the same sentiments to the still bewildered AWACS.

Air-refueling was always satisfying. Every time was different and yet each instance required absolute precision to bring it off. In peacetime, in normal airspace, air-to-air refueling was tedious and very rigid. But combat refueling was more straightforward. Each track usually had a cell of three KC-10 or KC-135 tankers flying in trail of each other. They were about three miles apart and stacked at different altitudes, so we creatively named them the High, Medium, and Low tankers. The Low tanker was usually leading the cell. This was done for several reasons. The other tankers, which had no air-to-air radars, could fly off him visually during the day or night if the weather was clear. If it wasn't, then they were de-conflicted by altitude and wouldn't hit each other. Lastly, with the Low tanker in the lead, his jet wash, which could be considerable, didn't affect the aircraft behind him. Flying through invisible turbulence while you're impaled on a boom twenty feet from a jet filled with jet fuel isn't much fun.

You had to find the tanker on your air-to-air radar and talk to him. You had to run a three-dimensional intercept to wherever he was, watching out for the remaining tankers and dozens of other fighters. It doesn't matter how many times you've done it; slowly sliding up behind the big plane and watching the boom come down was always a thrill. Unless it was nighttime, or the weather was bad, and you were running out of gas—then it was a sweaty nightmare, like a monkey fucking a skunk.

But not this morning. This was a bright, clear day over an exotic corner of the world that seemed even more beautiful because I'd survived my first combat mission. After getting our gas, we slid back and pulled away low to the southwest. Our home base was about 200 miles away on the Gulf of Iskenderun.

A half-hour later, we were overhead Incirlik Air Base. Normally, there were well-established procedures for getting into and out of an air base, like overhead patterns and instrument approaches for bad weather. There were also "minimum risk" procedures, designed to get as many jets as possible off the ground or down to land without exposing them to ground fire. In retrospect, it was fairly silly to worry about shoulder-launched SAMs and small-arms fire. This being the first day of the war, no one knew what to expect and, until sanity prevailed, we could do whatever we wanted. Besides, it was fun to fly up the runway at 500 knots or do the "Stack."

The Stack was basically a long glide in idle power down from

20,000 feet to the overhead landing pattern. You could see every-thing below, and it kept your engine cool to thwart an infrared threat. Besides, as I said, it was fun. Orca and I were almost the last aircraft at the top of the stack. The two F-15s that had followed us out of Iraq were somewhere behind us, and two KC-135 tankers were orbiting at 25,000 feet until all the fighters landed.

"TORCH One . . . High Stack."

He made the call and went into a sharp, descending turn. I was supposed to wait until he called "mid-stack," and then I'd start down. Dropping the mask again, I loosened my seat straps, wiped my face, and actually relaxed a bit. And why not? What else could happen?

Under normal circumstances, that's a risky thought to have. Under these circumstances, it was downright cocky. And stupid.

As I watched the jets spiral down and cross the runway thresh-old, a wholly unbelievable plume of white smoke lifted off from the north side of the base. My mouth dropped open. Really.

SAM.

Holy shit . . . I was trying to think of what to say and fumbling for the mike button.

SAM!

But an extremely excited voice beat me to it.

"Mi . . . Missile . . . Missile launch! Launch at . . . EXXON 21!"

EXXON was one of the orbiting tankers, and the pilot sounded like he was getting an enema.

Suddenly, the amazingly fast missile detonated in the middle of the stack with fighters swirling all around it. For a long, long moment, there was dead silence and then the tower frequency ex-ploded.

"Tower . . ."

"LIK Tower . . . TARZAN Three . . . there was a missile launch from the base."

"What the hell was . . ."

" . . . North of the base . . . exploded at . . ."

" . . . About 7,000 feet."

"Two . . . are you all right . . ."

We found out later that the Patriot base defense missile battery was in auto-mode. Among other things, this meant that if it detected jamming, then it would lock onto the jamming source and fire. No one had foreseen the effect that a hundred jets, all with jamming pods, radios, and electronic equipment would have on the Patriot. It saw all that and interpreted everything as hostile, locked the biggest thing it could see, and fired. The poor tanker pilot had probably wet his pants, and who could blame him?

Everyone finally calmed down and normal calls continued. I landed uneventfully and found Orca waiting for me at the end of runway (EOR), getting "de-armed." This meant that the explosive charges that released our bombs, missiles, or countermeasures were deactivated and pinned to keep them from coming off on the ground. I looked over at him, barely thirty feet away, and gave him a few enthusiastic fist pumps. He nodded, and I saw him smile. The EWO had his arms up on the canopy rail and his head back like he was asleep. But then I saw the visor turn toward me, and he gave me a thumbs-up.

One hour later, we'd shut down, visited maintenance debrief to explain any problems with the jets, gone by life support and gotten out of our gear, turned in our paperwork, and were back in the squadron. This was a long, low building that had been built during the Cold War and smelled like it hadn't been used since the Cuban missile crisis. It was "hardened," or reinforced, with six-feet-thick walls to withstand the nuclear attack that never came. Pilots coming back from missions would drop off their paperwork at the duty desk and then wander into the intelligence vault for yet another debrief. This was a sealed room with no windows. There were lots of secret computers, and all the classified information pertaining to our aircraft, weapons, and missions was kept here. Maps covered the walls with the latest and greatest updates on MiGs and SAMs. We'd pass on our enemy encounters and then discuss the target area.

Finally, after all this, we'd find an empty briefing room and discuss the flight in detail. We'd talk through each phase of the mission, tear apart the good and bad aspects, and arrive, hopefully, at ways to make it better. We'd dissect our videotapes and analyze each weapon that was dropped, shot, or fired. From this, and any intelligence reports, we'd arrive at a preliminary Battle Damage Assessment. This would get passed up to the Mission Planning Cell, which would use all the gathered information to plan the next round of missions.

I'd followed this process throughout my tactical career in training, so it was nothing new. This time, however, we concentrated almost exclusively on the combat engagements and our weapons effectiveness. The non-tactical stuff was limited to ensuring a smoother flow of a hundred aircraft back and forth into enemy territory. Like not having the Turkish Air Force run practice intercepts on us, or making certain that the Patriot batteries were not firing on auto tomorrow. Little things like that.

Three hours after we'd landed, we'd beaten today's mission to death and were planning tomorrow's. It was to be a similar strike package against the well-defended city of Kirkuk. SA-2s and SA-3s, of course, with a possible SA-6 and lots of Triple-A. The F-15s had claimed a dozen Iraqi fighters with no losses, but they were anticipating more of a fight tomorrow.

All the results from today were put together against the desired results for tomorrow. This was all dumped on a small group of fighter pilots attached to the Combined Wing Staff. Usually majors and lieutenant colonels, these guys were thoroughly frustrated, because they were planning the war and not fighting. Nevertheless, they took all this information, plus whatever general guidance was provided by the Coalition Headquarters, the Pentagon, the White House, the God of War, etc., and put together The Plan. This was published in a thick sheaf of papers called an Air-Tasking Order (ATO), or "Frag," and it delineated targets, backup targets, weapons, and timing.

The Time Over Target (TOT) was a hard number that had to be met within thirty seconds. With hundreds of aircraft dropping all kinds of bombs, this was critical to minimize confusion and prevent fratricide. The border-crossing, air-refueling, and takeoff times worked backward from the TOT. The appointed Mission Commander, always a senior, field-grade pilot and, if possible, a Weapons Officer, would plan the tactics for his mission. How would the air escorts deal with the MiGs? Which SAMs were priorities for the Weasels? The target area was divided up between striker four-ships, and he'd decide who would attack what and when it would happen. Endless contingencies were taken into account—bad weather, backup attacks, and rejoin plans, to name a very few. Everything tactical had to be simple and easily executed when The Plan fell apart—which it always did, to some degree.

The Mission Commander would determine the taxi times and ground flow plan based on the takeoff order. He would then arrive at a Mass Brief time, when everyone involved in the mission would sit together, hear the latest intelligence, and go over things that affected everyone. These included radio frequencies, formations, and border-crossing points. The Combat Search and Rescue (CSAR) plan for the day was also briefed in the event of a shoot-down.

Once the Mission Commander posted the Mass Brief time, each squadron would build its own flying schedule, deciding who would fly in which positions and when their flight briefings would occur. It was a long, tedious process but one we'd all done before, so it went surprisingly smoothly.

As the excitement and adrenaline wore off, I realized I was glassy-eyed from hunger, with a throat that felt like sandpaper, and thrilled to be alive. It was that pins-and-needles, heightened-awareness feeling you get when you've come through a particularly dangerous event and discovered all your pieces and parts still work. I wanted a scotch.

Now, unlike our brother fighter pilots flying out of Saudi Arabia, we had an Officer's Club and, more important, a bar. As the four of us strolled into the main lounge, it seemed like we were back in the States. The place was packed with guys drinking and talking with their hands. In fact, the only way to keep a fighter pilot from talking with his hands was to put either a drink or a woman in them.

Most of the pilots were wearing survival vests, festooned with various weapons, over their green flight-suits. There was a long, highly polished mahogany bar along the far wall complete with mirrors and glass shelves full of liquor. Men slouched against the bar rail or perched on bar stools trying to get the harassed bartender's attention. Ceiling fans slowly circulated the cigar smoke and the lights were dim. All fighter bars were about the same. They smelled of sweaty Nomex from the flight suits, stale beer, sweet brandy, and burned popcorn. Somewhere a jukebox was cranked up, playing "Fat-bottomed Girls," and in the corner another squadron was singing a touching hymn called "Sammy Small."

I was home.

None of the fighter pilots were wearing their normal squadron patches, because we didn't fly with them in combat. Most had a name tag with embroidered wings and a call sign on their chest or left arm. These differed in color by squadron, and there were at least six different types that I could see. F-16s from Tor-rejón and Spangdahlem; F-15s from Bitburg and Soesterberg; F-111s from Upper Heyford. Officers from the AWACS crews were also there, and, astonishingly, two very drunk KC-135 pi-lots. Turns out, they'd been flying the tanker that the Patriot used for target practice—they'd gotten a glimpse of our lives. They weren't getting much sympathy from the fighter guys, but we bought them drinks anyway. After all, we got paid to get shot at—they didn't.

"Hey, Two Dogs!" someone shouted, and I looked at the undu-lating wave of green at the bar.

"Over here. Orca, Shadow . . . get your asses over here!"

Orca punched me on the shoulder and waved toward the mob. As the smoke parted, I saw most of our guys, including our com-mander, holding up the far end of the bar. Lieutenant Colonel Dave Moody, known as MooMan, had just arrived that morning. He'd led our deployment out of Germany only to have his jet break down over the Mediterranean; he'd spent two days getting it fixed and had missed leading our first combat mission. Somehow he'd made it out to the end of the runway for our launch this morning. He'd also managed to "borrow" a huge American flag from the deserted elementary school and stood by the taxiway, saluting all his guys as we'd rolled past. Unforgettable. MooMan was one of my heroes.

"Dogs, you little punk." He thumped my chest and shoved a glass of something in my hand. "How'd ya do today? Hit any-thing?"

"I—"

"He couldn't hit his ass with both hands," someone helpfully chimed in.

"Lost in space," another shouted.

"I—"

"Box of rocks."

"You weren't there to hold his peepee, so how could he hit anything?"

"I—"

"C'mon boy . . . spit it out!"

A large, hairy paw appeared on my shoulder and I turned to see Orca standing next to me. "Y'all leave him alone . . . he did just fine. Hosed down a coupla SAMs near Mosul and didn't lose sighta me once."

Catcalls and booing followed that pronouncement, but Orca just smiled. "And he didn't shit his pants when the Patriot tried to kill him. In fact"—he winked at me—"the kid armed up and tried to roll in and strafe the damn thing!"

Slight stretch of the facts there, but we lived by the 10 Percent Rule (only 10 percent of any story had to be true) and, in fact, I hadn't shit all over myself like the two tanker pilots.

More catcalls but everyone laughed and cheered. Arms grabbed my shoulders and propelled me up to the bar. MooMan grinned at me and raised his glass. "To the Elephant!" We clinked and I drank. Then gagged. He chuckled.

"What . . . is this . . . stuff?" I wheezed as my eyes glazed over.

"Applecorn . . . with some Jeremiah Weed for flavor."

Apfelkorn was a thick, sweet liqueur beloved by American fighter squadrons in Germany. Jeremiah Weed was a pet drink of fighter pilots everywhere, along with Jack Daniel's and Drambuie. Individually they were bearable, but mixed together they were nearly lethal.

There was lots of action all around, and I sat and watched, happy to be one of the boys. To be part of any elite group is something you can carry with you for the rest of your life. At first it's all about ego and "making it." But that gets beaten out of you one way or another, as others quit, wash out, or die. In the end, if you make it, you're left with the greatest prizes of all: the quiet respect of your peers and the knowledge that you have nothing left to prove to anyone but yourself. I took another cautious sip of the horrible stuff and thought how lucky we were to be part of this. Bases back in the States were full of fighter pilots who were home with their wives tonight and wishing they were us.

I was proud. As I saw it then, America's interests had been threatened and we'd been brought in to solve the problem. Iraq had the fourth largest military in the world, hundreds of jet fighters, thousands of SAMs, and we'd just kicked open the front door. They'd actually shaken their hairy fist at the most powerful country on Earth—basically, gave the United States the big middle finger—and today we'd snapped it off at the knuckle. Tomorrow we'd go and cut off their balls.

And here I was, to do it.

Off to my right, beyond some tables, a huge group was playing Crud. This is a combination of pool and rugby played on a billiard table. To the left, against the far wall, was a stage, although there was no band. A rainbow-colored jukebox the size of a Dumpster was cranked up, and about a dozen flight-suits were jumping around to "Viva Las Vegas." Looking closely, I saw a few female officers from the AWACS surrounded by swarms of men. The girls weren't good-looking, and the flight suits definitely didn't help, but they were the only women in the place, and they were having a good time. The male officers from AWACS were nowhere to be seen. Go figure.

Squinting at the shadows, I saw one table of four very serious, dark-skinned pilots with perfect hair, clean flight suits, and all their patches. They'd given up trying to figure out the Crud game and were watching the women and the dancing.

Turks.

I thought they were drinking water, until one of them poured another round of something clear from an unmarked bottle.

"What's that?" I yelled in MooMan's ear and pointed at the Turks.

"I'll show you. Raki!" he screamed at the bartender, who returned with two shot glasses and a bottle of the clear stuff.

He winked again and gave the standard German toast: *"Prost."*

My eyes watered and the room wobbled. Raki. Turkish hooch. It tasted like tobacco spit mixed with licorice. I tried not to throw up, and very carefully cradled the toxic shot glass in my hand. MooMan laughed and wandered off. I found my young captain buddies, and we leaned against the bar to watch the Crud game.

It's actually a pretty simple game, which only uses two balls—the colored "object" ball and the white "shooter" ball. It's played with two teams of almost any size, and the goal is to kill off your opponents by sinking the object ball into any pocket. Naturally, this is resisted by the other team. Everyone takes turns shooting, and if you sink the ball, then whoever shot before you loses a life. When you lose three lives, you're gone. There are really only two rules. You can't hit the referee (at all) and you have to shoot from the ends of the table. Beyond that, the rules vary depending on who's playing, who's watching (women), and how much everyone's had to drink.

Tonight was the full menu of testosterone, adrenaline, and alcohol. After a day of combat missions, with some women watching, it was a wild game. Any force, short of lethal force, was allowed to block shots, keep shooters from the table, and otherwise screw up the other side. A few of the players were limping, and several had been sidelined with gashed faces and broken noses.

Now, Officer's Clubs are open to all officers. But on fighter bases, it's a rare or clueless non-fighter type (male, that is) who wanders into such a place. Bad things can happen to them. I had just noticed two such officers standing back against the wall, watching the game. They were obviously disapproving of the noise, drinking, and general savagery. Both wore battle dress uniforms, a fancy way of saying "fatigues," and they were very clean. They had shiny boots and were also wearing gas-mask satchels over their shoulders. Gas masks—utterly ridiculous, so, of course, it was mandatory equipment. So, of course, we ignored it. I had no idea who they were or why they thought being here was a good move.

Suddenly the TV screens began flashing red.

"What the . . ." The guy next to me pointed. Then the Giant Voice, the base public-address system, penetrated the walls.

"INCOMING . . . INCOMING . . . ALARM RED . . . ALARM RED . . ."

This meant *something* had been shot at the base and everyone was supposed to take cover immediately. The Crud players laughed and kept playing, and the drinkers didn't even look up. The civilian staff did dive under the tables, but the only ones in flight suits who vanished were the AWACS crews. Go figure. The fighter pilots took the opportunity to go to the bar, and when the Turkish bartender refused to come up from under the ice machine, everyone helped themselves.

I noticed the two staff officers, also known as Shoe Clerks, were huddled together under a table, clutching the center pedestal. One of them had opened his satchel and was pulling out the gas mask.

"Why the fuck do they think a half-inch of plywood is gonna save them from anything?" I slapped one of the Phantom pilots next to me on the arm.

"Dunno." He shrugged and poured a big scotch. "I'd rather die drinking."

"C'mon," said Cujo, another Phantom pilot, and jerked his head toward the tables. "Let's sit." We pulled up chairs and settled down at the table the staff guys were using as a bomb shelter. There was some shuffling and muttered curses from under the table as our boots violated their personal space.

So, for about ten minutes, as the TV continued to flash, we drank and played Crud, and the weenies hid under the tables. When the all-clear sounded, they wriggled out and stood up.

"Hey . . . glad you could join us." Cujo wasn't very subtle. "It was pretty hairy up here."

He hiccupped loudly and lurched off to the bar, leaving me alone.

"I suppose you think you're funny," one of the staff guys said. I thought he was talking to his buddy, so I just watched the Crud game. Turned out he was talking to me and didn't like being ignored, because he walked around to stand between me and the game.

"Did you hear me?"

I glanced up at him. He was in his thirties, with beady eyes and that slightly pudgy, well-fed look that most staff officers get. Too much food, coffee, and no stress. He was also wearing major's oak leaves and no wings. Of course.

"Trying not to," I answered. "You're in my way." Cujo had returned and chuckled loudly. The major put his chubby little square hands on his wide hips.

"Get up."

"Fuck off."

The skin around his eyes tightened a bit at that. "I'm Major Carlson and you can't talk to me that way . . . captain or lieutenant or whatever you are."

Our ranks and patches were attached with Velcro and we took them off to fly combat. I'd forgotten to put anything back on.

"Maybe I'm a major, too. Ever think of that?"

He kind of smirked and said, "No chance. You'd have to grow up first."

"Your wife thinks I'm grown up."

He turned red at that and began to inflate. Normally I'd never speak to a major that way, but this guy didn't have wings, so in my book he just didn't count. Besides, he was an asshole. And a dumb asshole, because he didn't let it go.

"Why are you wearing a weapon in a bar?"

And a jackass.

I mean, what type of ass-clown would say something like that on the first day of a war? If I'd spent the first day of the war staring at a computer, like he did, I'd be in my room, crying and measuring my dick.

"Fuck *off.*"

I felt movement behind me and then saw several of my buddies standing there. Apparently, they'd smelled confrontation through the burned popcorn and Drambuie.

"I want your name, rank, and unit. You will also give me your weapon." This guy was a real work of art.

"Why? Are you taking me prisoner?"

"Name," he snapped.

"I lost it somewhere over Iraq today while you were eating doughnuts."

His entire face tightened at that. Like someone just shoved something up his butt.

"You arrogant bastard. I'm a *major* . . . you can't talk to me that way!"

"Well," a new voice drawled unpleasantly. "Maybe he can't but ah can." The pilot who spoke up was called "Lips" and always reminded me of David Lee Roth. Same hooked nose and intense eyes. He was also a superb pilot and a totally irreverent, excellent man. Moving around beside me, he looked at this Shoe Clerk like he was a cockroach. "Ah'm a major, too. So I'll say it fur us both. Fuuuck off."

To help him on his way and make sure there were no hurt feelings, my squadron buddies immediately started to sing the "Wild Weasel Song"—a gentle, rather touching hymn.

"*We are dirty bastards . . . scum of the earth . . .*"

The staff guy's face suddenly lost its color as he realized that he was more or less surrounded by large, armed men who'd had too much to drink.

"*Filth of creation . . . motherfucking sons-a-bitches and forni-cators . . .*

Known in every whorehouse . . . smoke, drink, and screw . . ."

His buddy realized it, too, and I saw him tug the first guy's arm. Carlson took a step back and jabbed a stubby finger in my direction. "I'll be back."

"*We are the Wild Weasels . . . so . . . FUCK . . . YOU!*"

Everyone laughed as he angrily waddled away.

About thirty minutes later, I'd had enough and was trying to muster enough energy to leave when the doors swung open. A big, lean man about fifty years old strode in and stopped just inside the doors. He had iron-gray hair, cut very short on the sides, high cheekbones, and a faded flight suit. He was also wearing on his shoulders the eagles of a full colonel.

I was wondering if he was one of the wing commanders, as they're all full colonels, when Major Carlson's puffy face peered around this guy's shoulders.

"Uh-oh." Cujo and Lips saw him, too.

The major was pantomiming something about what a first-class prick I was, and pointing in my direction. The colonel looked at me and nodded. You can always tell a truly tough man by his eyes, and this pilot had a hard, steady look. As he approached, I got to my feet, which is what you did when a colonel showed up. He looked me up and down slowly, then stared at my face.

"And you are . . . ?"

I cleared my throat. "They call me Two Dogs."

"Sir."

"They call me Two Dogs, sir."

He had a dry chuckle with absolutely no humor whatsoever. Like he was clearing a hairball.

"Rank."

"I'm a captain, sir."

"When? Yesterday?"

"No sir. The day before." This was actually true, but he obviously thought I was being a wiseass. My buddies helped me out by chortling loudly, and this did not amuse the colonel.

He leaned forward and said, very softly, "Get your feet together when you speak to me." It was much more menacing than a shouted command, and I sort of shuffled my heels toward each other.

The colonel looked around at his audience, and I noticed that he was wearing the star and wreath of a command pilot on his chest. He was also wearing a U.S. Air Forces in Europe shield and, most significant, a gray-and-black Fighter Weapons School patch on his left shoulder. I swallowed and, for the first time, felt uneasy. Whoever this man was, he was no rear-echelon staff puke.

Looking back at me like a cat about to eat a canary, he calmly asked, "Didn't somebody once teach you that captains can't tell majors to take a hike?"

"That's not what I said, sir."

He raised an eyebrow and cocked his head. "No?"

"I told him to fuck off."

"Sir."

"I told him to fuck off, sir."

"So did I, Colonel," Lips chimed in helpfully, and the older man glanced at him.

"Major, you'll know when I want your opinion, 'cause I'll kick you in the balls."

"Be hard to miss those . . . sir."

The colonel's eyes went sort of flinty and shifted long enough to make Lips melt back into the crowd. It occurred to me that I might actually be in some trouble here. Nevertheless, I felt a little thrill of anger shoot through me.

"And why did you tell him that?"

Because he's a pussy and a toady and he was hiding under a table. Because he sat here in his creased uniform 900 miles behind the lines while I got shot at today. Because he's got a smug smirk on his fat face, and I'd enjoy tearing his throat out. These were all good answers but what I really said was, "He wanted my weapon, sir."

"Is that so?"

Apparently, that was news to him, and he shot the major a brief look that wasn't good. He stared at the Crud game and the dancers like he'd seen it a thousand times before. Actually, I thought he was listening to the music. It was "Viva Las Vegas" again, by the way.

"Well, he happens to be correct. A bar is no place for weapons. Even during a war." No one moved. He stared at me and held out his hand.

He was probably right about that. However, we hadn't set up our armory yet and there was no place to store our guns. Besides, we were all on twenty-four-hour ops now and had to be constantly armed.

"I can't do that, sir."

Tilting his head back slightly, the colonel looked at me like I was a bug. After a long few seconds, he flipped his thumb at the door. "Come with me, Captain."

What could I do but follow? The major smirked again and my hands began itching. I really, really wanted to smash this Shoe Clerk's teeth in.

I thought the colonel was being remarkably calm until we got to the front door, which he proceeded to open with a tremendous kick. My second miscalculation of the evening. This man was really, really pissed off.

"Out!"

I swallowed again and stepped out. "Stay," he barked at the major, who promptly dropped his smirk on the tile floor.

I breathed in the cool night air, straightened my shoulders, turned around, and got a face full of finger. This made an immediate impression on me, because somewhere along the way he'd lost the fingertip. Like maybe it had been shot off.

"Listen to me you little shit," he snarled. I backed up a step, but the finger followed. "I flew 127 combat missions over North Vietnam. I've killed gooks and saved lives and been through more crap than a snot-nosed puppy like you could understand at this point in your so-called career. Your one combat mission doesn't impress me . . . one . . . fucking . . . bit." The finger, now about ten feet long, jabbed in time with his words, and I tried not to back up any farther.

"Get it?" He didn't wait for a reply but stabbed at my nose again. "I was shot down twice, rescued once, and I've *fucked* the Elephant. Now—" and I swear his eyes actually narrowed—"give me . . . the . . . fucking . . . gun."

For an incredibly long moment, we stared at each other. My slight buzz had long since evaporated, and I was fully aware that this was one extremely agitated senior officer. But I was still a man, and he was wrong—at least from my point of view. Besides, how the hell would I get my weapon back for the morning mission?

"I can't do that, sir."

He looked genuinely shocked. And before he shot me, I added, as respectfully as I could, "I have another mission in ten hours, and I'll need the gun, Colonel."

He stared at me again, but as I met his gaze I saw some of the anger slowly leak from his eyes. They were brown, by the way, except the parts that were red. Finally, he sort of puffed out his cheeks and exhaled. Looking down at his boots, he slowly shook his head then gazed out past the street at the lights of the flight line. The night mission was getting cranked up and the unmistakable whine of jet engines floated over the trees.

For a second, I saw a younger version of the same man. Just like me, only flying his combat missions over the jungles of North Vietnam instead of the Iraqi plains. With rare insight, I thought of how hard it must be to sit and watch this when you've done it for real. Maybe that was the reason this guy was so angry. He was completely frustrated.

The colonel looked up. "Captain. You are without a doubt the cockiest prick in an O'Club full of cocky pricks." He stared out over the trees again for a few seconds, sniffed the jet fuel, and then looked back at me and sighed. "So here's what's gonna happen. You're gonna call it a night. You keep your weapon, and you go back to your foul little hooch and get some sleep."

I blinked. He wasn't going to kill me.

"And don't show up in the bar again with a gun."

I had an out. Brainless fighter jock that I was, even I could see that. So I got my heels together all on my own, straightened my slouch, and saluted like a cadet.

"Yessir."

He gave me a direct, steady look and then slowly returned the salute. He started to turn away and then did something I didn't expect and would never forget. He slowly held out his hand. Somewhat cautiously, I took it, and he nodded, shook once, and let go.

"You're still a pain in the ass. Now get the hell outta here before I stab you in the eye."

MY HOOCH WAS A TEN-BY-TEN WOODEN SHACK WITH A COR-
rugated tin roof and several pairs of feral cats that mated continuously in the tiny attic. The noise was interesting and the smell was
repulsive. This hooch, and the others like it, would normally house
two enlisted men who worked on jets. As it was, we had eight officers in each one. This spectacular feat of spatial geometry was
only possible because we "hot-bunked." That is, I shared a cot with
another pilot, who flew night missions, and vice versa. Incidentally,
he was an Italian who always left a fine layer of dark hair on the
blanket. This stuck to my face, so I usually looked like a young
werewolf with mange.

In any event, there was a critical billeting shortage, and, naturally, the really nice quarters had to go to the transport pilots, who
flew in once a month with more toilet paper. The staff guys also
needed rest, so they could keep the coffeepots full. But it was war,
and we were all too tired to care at the time.

As I lay down on my cot that night, I stared up at the ceiling and
thought about all that had happened during this long and dangerous day. I was glad to be alive, and I'd heard there were many others
who hadn't survived. I'd never doubted myself or my abilities, but it
was good to have my youthful overconfidence confirmed. Still, I was
smart enough to realize that this alone might not save me. We'd lost
planes and good pilots elsewhere in Iraq, and I knew I'd face a worse
threat tomorrow now that the enemy was awake and ready.

I'd always been proud—it goes with the occupation. But right
then my heart was pressed against my chest. I'd passed the test. I'd
fought and survived.

I'd seen the Elephant. In fact—I smiled, as I finally drifted off to
sleep—I'd kicked him right in the nuts.

4

FLY LIKE AN EGYPTIAN

THIRTY MINUTES PAST SUNRISE, THE FIGHTER'S WHEELS RE-
tracted and the F-16 was airborne over central Egypt. It was
0601:45 on a Wednesday in January 1992.

I glanced rapidly between the outside world and the HUD's
green digital airspeed reading. A ruined Soviet-era bomber, a fence
line, and even a small crumbling pyramid all flashed past as the
dirty runway unrolled beneath the speeding jet.

This was one of the beautiful moments of being a fighter pilot.
Thundering down a piece of concrete in the calm, cool, early-
morning air. Strapped into an intimately familiar cockpit filled
with warmly glowing displays. The metal around me throbbed
with the power of forty thousand angry, charging horses, and I held
the jet perfectly steady at twenty feet off the ground. The runway
was 12,000 feet long, a bit over two miles, and I'd covered most
of it with twenty seconds of full afterburner. As the little green
number reached 510 knots, I took one more glance at the engine
instruments, stared straight ahead, and smoothly pulled back on
the stick at 0602:03.

Bursting free, the fighter surged upward, gulping thinner air, mixing it with jet fuel, and shooting the exploding mix out the back. Egypt fell away beneath me, and, within seconds, all my eyes could pick up was the distant horizon. Bunting forward slightly, I held the climb angle at sixty degrees and rocketed into the brilliant morning. The F-16 ejection seat is tilted back to counteract the tremendous G forces of dogfighting, so, combined with my climb angle, I was sitting perpendicular to the earth. The air-conditioning vent between my legs coughed and spit out a stream of misty, smelly air; dust from the Egyptian morning, hot plastic canopy baked in the sun, jet fuel, and a faint whiff of burned oil.

I frowned. Hot oil wasn't normal, but this aircraft had just come out of maintenance after having the engine changed. It was also an Egyptian F-16. Anything was possible, which was precisely why I was flying it this morning on a functional test flight. This was a combination of specific maneuvers, called a profile, designed to thoroughly and brutally punish the aircraft before it was returned to normal flying with squadron pilots. The Egyptians always refused to take the chance of a test flight, so it fell to the Americans. I didn't mind—it was extra flying time with no brief or debriefing. A few seconds after pulling vertical, I passed 5,000 feet, smiling under the oxygen mask and dark visor. Everything was working perfectly.

Briefly.

It was 0602:11.

"WARNING—WARNING . . . WARNING—WARNING . . ."

Shit.

My eyes snapped to the engine instruments, then to the row of RBLs ("really bad lights"). These were just under the glare shield at eye level maybe two feet in front of me.

Shit.

ENG FIRE . . . HYD OIL . . . all the serious ones were suddenly glowing red. The jet was dying. Just like that. In less than a second.

0602:16.

Reacting instantly, I yanked the throttle back to IDLE and continued pulling over the top. Without the awesome thrust of its engine, the fighter slowed rapidly. Four hundred fifty knots and falling. If you were watching from a nearby cloud, the F-16's flight path would have looked like the profile of an egg. At four hundred knots, the jet reached the top of the egg and was gracefully curving back, falling toward the horizon. Inverted now, I pushed the stick forward slightly into "negative" Gs and felt my butt float off the seat. This more or less kept me at the same altitude for a few moments while I hung upside down and decided what to do.

From the beginning of their career, pilots are taught how to troubleshoot complex and potentially fatal in-flight emergencies. The ability to diagnose, evaluate, and choose the correct action while still managing to fly an aircraft is fundamental. It's another skill that separates a single-seat fighter pilot from the others. We don't have a crew to read checklists or help evaluate the situation.

Doing all of this in a complicated F-16 loaded up with weapons and traveling at the speed of a rifle bullet is a big challenge. There are two types of emergencies—the kinds that won't kill you and the ones that will. As this was definitely the latter, there was no time to do anything but react.

The huge, dry runway beneath me helped. European and American runways I'd used were much, much shorter and often wet or icy. On the other hand, the Russians had built this one for bombers, and it was enormous. Also, unlike American runways, which were aligned with the prevailing wind, this one seemed purposely built so there would always be a direct crosswind to complicate landings.

None of that mattered at the moment. I had no engine, and I was going nowhere but down. Eyeballing the gauges, I saw that the engine temperature, called Fan Turbine Inlet Temperature (FTIT), was spiked in the red range. Not good. But the hydraulics and electrics were okay, meaning the flight controls worked and I could still physically fly the jet.

0602:22.

I could smell burning oil; in a plane loaded up with 7,000 pounds of jet fuel and carrying missiles, this was definitely bad. The oil gauge in this $40M fighter was the size of a quarter, and I had to squint to see it. It was low. Not at zero, but well below normal. If I was truly on fire, I would have to either shut the engine down or eject.

Neither option appealed to me.

Or I could pull the throttle back to IDLE, glide to the runway, and hope I didn't explode. Swiveling my head around to look past the tail, I saw there wasn't any smoke from a burning engine, so I had that going for me. Hanging there, upside down, with cockpit dust floating in my face and a mile above an air base in the middle of Egypt, I had a brief thought that this wasn't so bad. I mean, a wing hadn't fallen off, and I hadn't taken a missile up the tailpipe over hostile territory, right?

Right.

Without looking down, I reached to the left console by my knee, lifted the protective guard around the switch, and turned on the Emergency Power Unit (EPU). Immediately, a steady "WHRRRRR" vibrated up from behind my seat, as the system fired up. The EPU would provide essential power for hydraulics, flight controls, and the radios in the event the engine failed or I shut it down. There was also a Jet Fuel Starter (JFS) system. This was a small turbine shaft that ran through a gearbox and connected to the main engine. Using a mixture of compressed air and an extremely toxic gas called hydrazine, the main turbine would spin up to begin the ignition sequence. This allowed a startup independent of the old cumbersome "start" carts you see beside older jets.

0602:26.

Just then a violent shudder ran up from under the ejection seat, through the cushion and into my spine. Flipping the fighter upright, I blinked as the dust settled back to the floor. Rolling up on my left wing, because fighter pilots prefer to look left, I stared down at the field. I was too high and too close. Dumping the nose slightly, I angled away to the right, so I could look left at the runway. Glancing sideways into the cockpit, I squinted against the morning sun at the engine gauges. The EPU was providing minimal hydraulic pressure and enough electricity to keep the flight controls working. Everything else looked bad.

At 4,900 feet above the runway, at 0602:30, I keyed the mike.

"Beni Suef Tower . . . Beni Tower . . . MAKO Four One . . ."

I was now about a mile southwest of the field in a wide, shallow descending turn. Flying was all by the seat of my pants at this point. Distance and altitude . . . distance and altitude. I could see where I needed to be, and my hands worked to make it happen. Flameout landings were a huge part of F-16 non-tactical training. We practiced this technique repeatedly, day or night, in all weather and from random positions. But in the back of your head, in training, you know that if you completely ass it up, your engine still works and you won't crash or eject.

Not this time. Although the engine was still running, the smell was worse, and I knew I'd never be able to go around and attempt it again. I was trying not to think about the Egyptian Air Force's incompetent maintenance. There were thousands of spinning turbine blades, millions of micro-combustions, and miles of tubing, conduit, and wiring running beneath my feet. All repaired by Arabs, who generally didn't read their own language, much less six-inch-thick manuals written in technical English. This was another reason I didn't want to try the ejection seat.

"What the fuck am I doing here . . ." I muttered as I rolled and adjusted my flight path. I was holding about 250 knots and steadily dropping. Jets don't glide well. The oil gauge now read zero pressure and the cockpit smelled like the inside of an oil can. But no smoke yet.

At 0602:34, I put the gear handle down and felt two belated "thumps." Eyeballing the landing-gear lights, I saw only two lights. No nose gear. Perfect. Then the tower decided to wake up.

"Mahhko . . . Mahhko . . . theese Bani Toweler . . . you call?" The Egyptian sounded sleepy.

I swallowed and took a deep breath.

"MAKO Four One . . . Base Key . . . Emergency," I answered calmly. I mean, you have to sound good, even in Egypt.

I was now about two miles southwest of the runway, passing 3,000 feet, and still no nose gear. I pumped the stick a few times to help it down but still had no light. It didn't matter. Dumping the nose to keep my speed up, I steepened the turn and came around to point at the runway, just as the tower controller went bat-shit.

"Mahhko . . . WHAT?" he screamed. Arabs generally aren't known for their ability to stay calm, cool, and collected.

"Say ageeen . . . you have . . . *mish'killah*?" He reverted to Arabic in his panic, although what he had to be excited about was beyond me. I was the one riding the pine, as we say. To help him out, I replied in Arabic.

"*Aiwa habibi* . . . MAKO *jenoob harb* . . . *itneen kilo*." You bet . . . MAKO is southwest, two miles.

As the tower operator erupted into a flood of high-speed Arabic and English, I just turned the volume down. He couldn't do anything for me anyway, and I had other problems. Landing on two wheels wouldn't kill me unless I was a complete jackass, and with a couple miles of concrete before me, it wasn't too critical. I focused entirely on where I wanted to touch down—called an aim point—and my airspeed. If I was too slow, I'd stall and die. If I was too fast, I'd run out of runway and crash in the dirt. In this situation, the only way to get slower or faster was by trading altitude, and without an engine, I had all the height I was going to get.

Base Key was an established position in the standard F-16 flameout landing pattern. It meant I was somewhere between one and three miles at about 2,000 feet and lining up with the runway to land. I was in a decent position. Sufficient distance and airspeed to make it and enough runway to stop on. I exhaled, and for the second time I felt I might reasonably survive this.

Then I saw the smoke.

Little gray wisps of it floated out from my air-conditioning ducts. My eyes flickered back and forth between the ground and the smoke. Getting fixated on the wrong thing right now would be fatal. Besides . . . sometimes the vapor from the environmental control system *looked* like smoke. But vapor doesn't burn, and this stuff stank.

Reacting instantly, I pulled the throttle back over the stop into CUTOFF and heard the engine immediately wind down. The cockpit got ominously quiet except for Bitching Betty's annoying monotone and the sound of air rushing over the canopy.

"WARNING, WARNING . . . WARNING, WARNING . . ."

Yeah . . . I know.

It was 0602:40.

I passed through a thousand feet at 1.5 miles from the end of the runway, slowing to 230 knots. My throat was dry and my hands were clammy as I stared through the HUD. Far off toward the middle of the airfield, I saw the morning sun glinting from the control tower's mirrored-glass windows. Several vehicles with flashing lights were racing down the taxiway, raising twin brown plumes of dust. That surprised me. I hadn't known there were any emergency response trucks here.

Lining up the little green Flight Path Marker on the white centerline stripes, I noticed that the smoke had disappeared, which was good, but that my nose gear was still up, which was bad. Pulling a little on the stick, I let the jet rise slightly and slowly to 190 knots. Sometimes the nose gear wouldn't extend if the airspeed was too high. But nothing happened, and as the controls got sluggish, I pushed the nose back over for more airspeed.

Holding 200 knots, I kept the little FPM nailed to the runway and glided over the threshold. With the ground rushing up, I made a gentle, blended pull, called a "flare," and held the jet off the concrete. As I did this, I heard another thump as the nose gear finally came down. Not risking a look into the cockpit, I eyeballed the last few feet against the rapidly dropping airspeed. Rocking slightly between both wheels, the fighter touched down in wobbly F-16 fashion. I kept the nose off the ground as the runway zipped past.

At 100 knots, I let the nose drop and, despite the green gear light, I winced when the wheel smacked down. Without an engine to continuously power the brakes, stopping would be problematic on most runways, but this one was so long I wasn't worried. Nevertheless, I let the F-16 roll out by itself for a few seconds, then smoothly pressed down on the brakes to completely stop the jet.

The fighter came to a halt 7,000 feet down the runway at 0603:07. I sat there for a few moments, staring straight ahead, my boots pressed hard against the rudder pedals and my hands still gripping the stick and throttle. One minute and thirty seconds had elapsed since I'd released the brakes for takeoff. Fifty-six seconds since the engine decided to come apart.

Reaching over, I toggled on the parking brake and then unhooked the left side of my oxygen mask. Leaning my head back against the seat, I gazed up through the canopy at the blue sky and the beautiful dawn that had nearly been my last. Off to the left, the emergency vehicles were careening in my direction; I exhaled slowly.

Switching off the EPU, I raised the canopy, pulled my helmet from my head, and put it on the HUD as a wave of warm Egyptian air hit me. Rich earth, dust, and a faint whiff of burning trash. I smiled a bit as I wiped my face.

It doesn't get any weirder than this.

AGAIN, I SHOULD'VE KNOWN BETTER THAN TO HAVE THIS thought. I glanced up over the canopy rail to the right and saw an ancient-looking peasant not thirty yards away. He was standing in the dirt beside the runway and had obviously walked through the holes in the perimeter fence. If we were on a U.S. air base, he'd never get through the fence. Or, if he did, he'd be dead right now. The man had a face like a raisin and dark, deep-set eyes. He was wearing ragged sandals and a dirty white *gallibiyah,* an ankle-length robe. Beside him was a donkey even skinnier than he was, and they were both looking at me.

Later I'd come to think that this scene summed up Egypt. They could build 12,000-foot runways but couldn't keep old farmers from wandering onto them. They could buy $40M jet fighters but couldn't keep them working. However, right then I was literally dazed. I'd just landed an F-16 without power, saved it and myself, and was staring at a donkey's face.

So, as I sat there, my sweat cooling and the emergency sirens growing louder, the peasant calmly shuffled in front of my jet, leading the mangy animal. As they passed before me, the donkey raised his tail and shat on the runway. The old man looked back at me and very deliberately shook his head.

I think the donkey did, too.

THE CAREER OF A TACTICAL OFFICER IS NOMADIC. TRUE MILI-tary logic assumes that picking someone up every two to three years and having him start over somewhere else is a smart thing. It *does* offer a great deal of experience in widely varied environments, which, I suppose, is the point. You also get very good at moving and selling houses.

My operational career had been overseas, and I wanted to stay there. No other commitments—why not see the world? Germany had been terrific, but it was time to go. The Air Force figured that a young, combat-experienced, frontline instructor pilot would be ideal for . . . flying training jets in Texas.

I disagreed.

With feeling.

Scrambling around for any alternative, I discovered there were some wild and exotic exchange tours available to fighter pilots. These programs provided American instructors to assist allied air forces that had purchased F-16s. I had friends who went to Greece, Portugal, and Turkey. One lucky bastard ended up on the island of Bali with the Indonesian Air Force and women in grass skirts. He used to send me postcards just to rub it in.

I got Egypt.

Still, I was excited. Land of the pharaohs and the Valley of the Kings. I'd studied it all as an architectural student in college, and now I got to see it firsthand. Pyramids and scuba diving. And it wasn't teaching student-pilot aerobatics for the anal-retentive Training Command in Texas.

Egypt in 1992 had none of the turmoil it is working its way through today. Hosni Mubarak was very definitely in power and the military controlled everything. There were about half a million soldiers on active duty and half a million more in reserve. The Egyptian Air Force was the fourth-largest user of F-16s in the world. Military officers, especially fighter pilots, were treated like royalty. The United States was giving Egypt more than a billion dollars per year in aid, which made American officers doubly welcome.

The Egyptian leadership had watched the Gulf War especially closely. They'd had a long debate over which superpower had superior arms, training, and personnel. The Iraqi military had been largely trained and equipped by the Soviets, yet the Americans had crushed it in less than ninety days. Saddam's armed forces had been widely feared in the Middle East, at least by the Arabs, and, as our allies, the Egyptians were thrilled to get young combat veterans like me to train their pilots.

I was part of a PEACE VECTOR (PV) program, through which American tactical personnel were "loaned" to friendly foreign governments to provide technical assistance and training. As the United States was, and is, the world's largest arms exporter, this is big business, to the tune of $18–20B annually. I was essentially a government-sponsored mercenary.

AFTER SEVERAL COUNTERTERRORISM COURSES AND LANGUAGE training, I was attached to the Office of Military Cooperation in Egypt. The U.S. embassy maintained a beautiful apartment for us in the upscale Mahdi section of Cairo. Marble and earth tones, of course, but very nice and available anytime we wanted to come into the city.

I was sent down to PEACE VECTOR Three at Beni Suef. This former MiG and bomber base was about a hundred kilometers south of Cairo, in the Faiyum Oasis. In the days of ancient Egypt, it had been known as Crocodilopolis, but unfortunately, by the time I got there, all the crocs were long gone. Cairo, Alexandria, and Jiyanklis (on the Suez Canal) also had PV detachments. These usually consisted of two pilots, a maintenance officer, and a handful of senior sergeants who were specialists in their respective fields. Each location hosted an Egyptian fighter wing that was composed of at least two full squadrons. We would be embedded with the resident Egyptian Air Force units and assist them with all aspects of military training.

Beni Suef appalled me at first, but that was only because I was used to Germany. With the notable exception of the Gulf War, I hadn't seen the shitty parts of the Middle East yet. In retrospect, it was a great place. General Dynamics had built a compound within the confines of the air base for its original support folks. It was like a little village. There were nearly a hundred houses, euphemistically called "villas" while in reality they were 1960s-style ranch homes. Other good things included a baseball diamond, volleyball and tennis courts, a splendid pool, and, of course, a bar with hot tub.

Much like McCarthy-era America, which feared the Soviet Union, Egypt suffered from acute national paranoia toward Israel. This meant each fighter wing maintained a different six-day schedule to prevent the Israelis from sneak-attacking. Theoretically. The Israeli Air Force couldn't have cared less about Egypt's alert status. In fact, I met a veteran Israeli pilot who told me that before attacking Beni Suef in 1973, he flew down the runway, in fingertip formation, to give the Egyptians a chance to make it to their bomb shelters. In any event, Egypt had fighters actively flying, seven days a week, all year long. (Apparently, the fact that Egypt and Israel were both American allies didn't bother anyone in the PV program.)

The Egyptian pilots were all brought in from their homes in Cairo or Alexandria via C-130 transport on day one. Days two through five were workdays. This usually meant four scheduled flights, called lines, in the late morning, followed by four more late in the afternoon. So, eight lines a day for four days. By comparison, a typical American fighter squadron would fly ten to twelve lines in the morning, followed by eight to ten lines in the afternoon or night. American pilots also plan meticulously and debrief each mission exhaustingly, sometimes for five or six hours. Egyptian flight briefings were more of a Zen thing. It was hardly a taxing schedule. On day six, they were on a C-130 back home for a four-day weekend. Then the whole ten-day rotation would begin again.

Between the military detachment and the civilian contractors, there were maybe thirty people living on a compound built for a hundred and fifty. There were no children and only two wives. We played lots of volleyball, swam, and cooked out a great deal. Almost every late afternoon we'd sit up on the roofs and watch the sun go down. Sunsets were truly spectacular. Bands of yellow, orange, and gold lay like glowing sword blades along the horizon. It would become thinner and thinner until, at the very end, the orange fire slid abruptly into the darkness. The final desperate rays would shoot upward, splattering the pink bellies of clouds until they, too, were extinguished. This ritual was usually enhanced by drinking Fuzzy Navels and playing very loud classical music. The Egyptians working on the compound thought we were crazy. They'd stand in small groups, talking softly, pointing at us, and shaking their heads. I thought it was great.

Anyway, about six months into this, I was dozing by the pool early one afternoon when my handheld radio started squawking in highly excited pigeon English.

"Captain Dan! Captain Dan . . . many planes come!"

Many planes?

I opened an eye and squinted at the radio, debating whether or not to answer it. It was the second day of the typical four-day weekend and absolutely nothing was happening. Normally we'd drive out to the Red Sea coast and dive, or we'd go up to Cairo, stay in the U.S. embassy apartment and get a real meal. But the other pilot was on vacation in Greece, and the maintenance officer was in the States, so I was just hanging around working on a really fine tan.

Deciding to ignore the noise, I then heard an unmistakable dull roar in the distance. That unique manly whine that only comes from high-performance fighter engines. I opened both eyes and stared straight up. The runway was about a mile east of where I lay, and, as the noise got loud enough to drown out the panicked tower controller, I saw them.

Four F-16s in fingertip formation, each about three feet apart and holding position perfectly. I know my mouth dropped open, but I didn't care. They flew down the runway and pitched out in the classic "break" turn. Only fighters do this, because you pull about six Gs and roll out heading back the way you came. The leader got abeam the approach end of the runway and I saw his landing gear come down. One by one, the other three followed as he dropped and turned to line up on the runway. Egyptians didn't fly that way.

"Captain Dan! Many plane . . . you come . . . *please* . . ." The poor guy was practically in tears. Like he was going to be personally blamed for the unannounced arrivals. Actually, he probably was, given the Egyptian military mentality.

"Easy, *habibi*," I answered. "I'll come now."

I sighed once at the quiet pool. As I jogged to the villa, two other flights of four came screaming overhead and pitched out. Throwing on my flight suit and boots, I paused long enough to grab two six-packs of beer from the fridge. I was excited now. Lots of countries flew F-16s, and the new arrivals were not Egyptians. Now that the Gulf War was over and the danger was past, many of our NATO allies were finally sending contingents of fighters to the "war" zone. These, I thought, were likely Dutch or Belgians on their way into Saudi Arabia.

In any event, this was something different—and novelty was good.

I careened past the startled gate guards and hightailed it up the perimeter road to the entrance to the Egyptian side of the base. Several more guards, in khaki pants and ragged tennis shoes, stood in the road. Recognizing me and my truck, they waved and opened the gate. That is, they lifted the wooden pole from two badly dented oil drums and stood aside so I could pass.

With the truck's windows down, hot air mixed with the flies and dust as I sped down the road. On the right, toward the runway, the very last jet was coming around on final, gear extended and landing light glowing. With a tiny thrill, I realized they were American F-16s. All fighters carry identifying markings that are plain to pilots but look like ancient Hittite to anyone else. I was still too far away to read them but the placement of these markings on the tail told me they were U.S. fighters.

Excited now, I mashed the pedal down and drove faster. For some strange reason, the roadside curbs were painted with alternating two-foot sections of black and white. This made driving after a few Fuzzy Navels a surreal experience. I often wondered how many conscripts it took, and for how long, to paint miles and miles of concrete with these stripes.

Coming to a big, L-shaped main intersection, I turned right and headed toward the runway. There were several big dormitories, now empty, for the pilots to stay when they were here. Behind them were a collection of hovels for the enlisted men and conscripts. Incidentally, conscripts weren't allowed to leave the base on week-ends, and about fifty of them were huddled by the road, looking toward the runway with empty faces.

I raced past the headquarters complex, recognizable because of the date palms planted in the forecourt and the monthly fresh coat of brownish-pink paint on the walls. Think of vomit sprayed on cinder blocks and you've got the picture.

The road led directly onto the flight line. Western military complexes, and particularly American air bases, are harder to get into than a nun's panties. Just to pass onto the main base you need a piece of plastic containing a computer chip with your life history, medical history, and security clearance. Flight line access means going through layers of fences, camera surveillance, more guys with guns, and additional identification. Without the right ID, you'll end up facedown on the ground with a pistol in your ear.

But here I just drove on.

The runway and taxiways opened up before me like the parking lot at Wally World. Or the state of Oklahoma. The Soviet-built TU-16 bombers that had originally inhabited this place needed lots of space. Called Badgers, they were three stories tall and had a wingspan of 108 feet. They'd needed *acreage* just to turn around. In fact, there was a wrecked one that had been pushed off the taxiway and lay rusting in the sun. Next to it was a MiG-21 fighter that was missing a wing. Just beyond these modern heaps, outside the perimeter fence, was the small but authentic Lahun pyramid. Built 3,800 years ago, it was in marginally better shape than the two Russian jets.

As I turned onto the taxiway, I saw them. Twelve F-16s huddled together just off the north end of the runway. They were beautiful—decked out in fresh dark-gray combat paint with a lighter sea-gray splash around the cockpit. The distinctive gold canopy glinted in the sun and brilliant white strobe lights flashed from their tails. Heat-seeking Sidewinder air-to-air missiles jutted from each wingtip, and the white tips of deadly long-range AM-RAAM missiles were visible beneath the wings. Each fighter had a pair of 370-gallon wing tanks and a rectangular electronic counter-measure pod slung beneath the belly. They were clean, with new, black tires and the exposed metal parts gleamed like they'd all been polished. This was typical of American fighter jets, but I hadn't seen one in six months and the Egyptian Air Force didn't spend much time on such things.

As I got closer, I saw the big "HL" on each tail flash and rec-ognized the 388th Fighter Wing, Hill Air Force Base, Utah. I'd never been stationed there but the fighter community was small, so odds were I knew some of these pilots. It didn't matter. They were Americans, and these guys had just become my best friends—even if they didn't know it yet.

I raced up in my four-by-four pickup and skidded to a stop ten yards in front of them. As I got out, twelve helmeted, dark-visored heads turned to stare. I walked over to the leader's jet and stood just beyond the lethal range of the jet intake. The engine was pow-erful enough to pull a grown man through thousands of spinning turbine blades and turn him into shredded wheat. This has hap-pened occasionally, by the way.

Looking up, I saw him raise his oxygen mask to his face and knew they were all talking about me. *Who is this guy? Should we shoot him now? Where the hell are we? Let's shoot him now.*

So I waved.

Nobody moved.

The high-pitched whine penetrated my earplugs, and I didn't want to stay there any longer than necessary, so I made a cutting motion across my throat. This was the international signal to shut down the engines.

He shook his head slowly and they talked some more. I couldn't really blame them. After all, they were on a foreign air base in the middle of a country none of them had likely ever visited. They could take off again if they had to, and this was, no doubt, part of what they were discussing. I had a thought then and trotted back to my truck, with twelve heads swiveling to watch. As I rummaged about in the bed, I could almost feel their fingers tightening on the triggers.

But I turned around, flashed a charming smile, and triumphantly held up both six-packs. I couldn't see faces behind the visors but I absolutely had their attention now. Assuming they'd flown in from the United States, they'd been sitting in those cockpits for at least ten hours and a cold beer was a glimpse of heaven. Within thirty seconds, I heard the dying whine of a jet engine, then another and another. All down the line the big canopies yawned opened as the fighters shut down.

Booze wins again.

I dropped one of the beers in the ankle pocket of my flight suit, pulled a boarding ladder out of the truck and walked back to the lead jet. Carefully hooking the prongs on the left side of the cockpit, I seated the foam supports just forward of the gun and slowly climbed up the ladder.

Clearing the canopy railing, I leaned over and looked into the cockpit. The ejection seat took up most of it. On either side of the pilot were consoles about a foot wide, and every inch was taken. Most of the switches and knobs were things a pilot would set one time prior to takeoff and then leave alone. Radios, jamming pod, and the countermeasure controls were all here. The right side had cockpit lighting controls, environmental controls (air-conditioning and heat), and the sensor power panel for the various pods the F-16 carried. There was also the Data Transfer Cartridge (DTC) port. This was a VHS-tape-size cartridge that could be programmed by a special computer prior to the flight. Thousands of navigation points, threat data, weapons, and other useful stuff could be saved on this and then loaded into the fighter's systems with the touch of a button.

During long combat missions or transoceanic flights, these consoles were cluttered with map cases, food, and water. This guy's cockpit was no exception. Ever wonder how a fighter pilot wearing a G-suit, harness, exposure suit, and survival vest relieves himself while strapped into a tiny cockpit?

Piddle packs. Little tough plastic bags partially filled with absorbent sand. They had a sealable "neck" and were good for one toilet break of the liquid kind. Describing the mechanics of the *other* relief process in an F-16 cockpit would take an entire chapter. Anyway, this guy also had a few used piddle packs tucked against the bulkhead.

Speaking of the pilot, he was leaning as far back away from me as he could get. I noticed he was unstrapped from the ejection seat, and his G-suit hose was disconnected. But he couldn't get out, because I was there.

"Hey dude!" I smiled and slapped the canopy rail. "Good to see ya!"

The pilot looked typical. About thirty years old, very fit, with sweaty black hair cut close on the sides. He was wearing oversize aviator sunglasses that looped behind his ears. His left hand was on the console just beneath the HUD so he could twist and face me. I then noticed his right hand was on the black 9-mm pistol in his vest. That made me blink. Suspicious was one thing but deadly force was another. I tried a different tack.

"How 'bouta beer?"

Dragging the perspiring can from my pocket, I carefully set it on the top of the ladder, and he slowly took his hand off the weapon. We stared at each other for a long moment, then he said, "Where are we?"

Actually, he shouted it at me like Americans do when they think volume overcomes language barriers. I leaned back, somewhat surprised.

"Wha . . ."

"WHERE . . . ARE . . . WE?"

I frowned a little but at least he was talking. I popped the beer and shoved it at him.

"Cut it out man . . . you're in Beni Suef."

He took the beer and nodded, pleased to have his suspicions confirmed. Taking a long swallow, he wiped his mouth with a gloved hand and said something I'll never forget.

"YOU . . . SPEAK . . . GOOD . . . ENGLISH!" he shouted again.

"Wha . . ."

"YOU SPEAK ENGLISH VERY WELL!"

For the second time in an hour, my mouth dropped open. Then, as he stared at me, I saw my reflection in his big sunglasses.

Oh.

And then it all made sense. He thought I was an Egyptian. Seeing myself through his eyes, so to speak, I thought it was an understandable mistake. I was wearing an Egyptian uniform with Egyptian pilot wings and squadron patches. I also had a very bad mustache and was tanned like a piece of unshaven mahogany. Picture Pancho Villa in a flight suit and you've got it.

"Cut it out man . . . I'm an American."

"YOUR . . . ACCENT . . . IS . . . VERY . . . GOOD!"

Anyway, we sorted it out.

Once they figured out that I wasn't a terrorist who spoke East Coast Yankee English, everything was okay. They'd been on their way in country to Dhahran Air Base, Saudi Arabia, for a 120-day Southern Watch deployment. This was done through relays of air-refueling tankers, which started out in the United States. The fighters would then be "handed off" over the North Atlantic to tankers from bases in Europe. Sometimes they'd spend the night in Germany or Spain, but often, depending on the situation, they'd fly all the way in to Saudi or Kuwait. Fourteen hours in a cockpit the size of a desk was about as much fun as it sounded. In either case, the fighters would meet up over the eastern Mediterranean with U.S. tankers temporarily based in Saudi, called the Kingdom, that would take them the rest of the way in.

Apparently, there'd been a big dust storm, a khamsin, that kept these last tankers on the ground. Unable to make it to Dhahran and unable to return to Europe, the fighters had diverted into Beni Suef. Now, every such deployment was planned out to an amazing level of detail. Every leg of the trip, fuel numbers, divert bases, and radio frequencies are painstakingly arranged so when something like this happens, everyone knows what to do. These guys weren't lost—no one gets lost in an F-16 crammed with electronic wizardry—they knew exactly where they were geographically, they just didn't know *where* they were, if you follow. They were simply appalled by their surroundings. You don't see burned-out aircraft, cratered runways, and donkeys on a U.S. air base.

I got the extremely nervous Egyptian maintenance officer and a crew of his minions to bed down the jets. This was done amid much supervision by the still-suspicious Americans. The Egyptians were shocked when each pilot pulled out everything needed for his aircraft from a big travel pod slung beneath one wing. Chocks for the wheels, intake and canopy covers, oil-sample kits etc. . . . The Arabs were even more surprised when our guys did all of this themselves. Egyptian pilots more or less shut their planes down, hopped out, and went to drink tea.

My new friends were less shocked when I led them over to the Oasis (as we called the General Dynamics compound) and into a few of the villas. They got positively enthusiastic when they saw the pool and the bar. I was so happy to have buddies again that, I confess, I didn't work too hard on their logistical issues for a few days. Don't get me wrong—Beni Suef wasn't a bad place, and the two other officers with me were good guys, but I missed the camaraderie. Thirty other men who've survived the same screening, years of training, and the constant attrition are generally priceless to be around. Personal likes and dislikes aside, you know that you will count on them with your life. They'd die for you. There is no real equivalent to that in life beyond a fighter squadron. It's like a fanatically loyal family with brains—and weapons.

I kept these guys around a few days while we worked out their flight plan and clearances to leave one Arab country and go into another. This would normally take about twenty-four hours, but I managed to cram it into three days. Hey, I had to be thorough, right? Right. They weren't in any hurry, because no one—and I mean no one—liked Saudi Arabia. I called it the Great Hijacking.

THE VIPER BROKE LEFT OVER THE RUNWAY NUMBERS AND pulled into a hard, six-G turn. Grunting against gravity, I closed my eyes and grabbed the "towel rack" that ran along the canopy in the back of the two-seat F-16D.

Every squadron had a few of these jets, and they were used for various types of "dual" training. That is, missions or events that had to be done with an instructor pilot physically in the same jet. Americans avoided them whenever possible, but the Egyptians used them a good deal—a relic of their Soviet training. I was always being thrown in the back for some sort of near-death experience that called for instruction.

I hated flying in the damn thing.

"WHUMP . . . WHUMP . . . WHUMP."

What the . . . my eyes popped open as the landing gear thunked down and the Egyptian rolled wings level. For a moment, I was speechless and the jet slowed as the guy up front prepared to turn to final.

"Hamad . . . wha . . . why did you put the gear down?"

"Sir?"

"Why is the gear down?"

"For to land, sir."

I rubbed my face and took a deep breath. You never rolled into a six-G break turn and put the wheels down—it was a wonderful way to rip hydraulic lines and gear doors off the aircraft. Because of this, there was a strict airspeed limit of 300 knots.

So Hamad waffled through the final turn, scaring us both.

"Go around," I directed, and he obediently raised the gear, added power, and off we went. Rather than stay in the pattern, we took the long way back to a ten-mile final, so we could talk a bit. Turned out, Hamad had flown MiG-21s and they always put the gear down in the break turn. This was okay, because a MiG-21 couldn't pull six Gs, and it took about a minute for the crappy Russian hydraulics to get the wheels down anyway. In a patois of French, Arabic, and English, we decided that we were in an F-16 today and we'd do it my way.

He swore he understood.

But, just to make sure, I actually squirmed around enough in the back to wedge my boot under the gear handle. There was no way the sucker was coming down.

As the Gs hit during the break and my knee connected with my chin, I felt the handle bump against my boot.

"Heh, heh, heh," I managed to gurgle from my pretzel-like position, feeling pretty proud of myself.

Then it happened.

"WHUMP . . . WHUMP . . . WHUMP."

Sonofabitch. As we rolled out again, I saw that he'd *blown* the gear down with the Alternate Gear Handle. This was an emergency system only to be used when the wheels wouldn't lower any other way. Doing it now could cause all sorts of problems. In fact, as I took the jet to land, my main hydraulic system failed.

Language was always an issue. Another day, in another D-model two-seater, I was trying to teach a kid how to land. The Egyptians conducted all their RTU-type training in their line squadrons, something we would never do. This was another Russian idea that didn't work but they insisted on it anyway.

This particular pilot, named Moshen, had also come from MiG-21s and was doing his best to kill us both every time we came around to land. There's a position in the overhead pattern, called the "Perch." This occurs when you're abeam the end of the runway about a half-mile away, and you begin to turn to final. In a fighter, this means dropping the nose and flying the jet around in a descending arc, so you roll out on a one-mile final. Every time is different, and you simply play the stick, throttle, and your eyes to make it happen. It's a Zen thing.

This kid didn't have it. He'd dive for the end of the runway with no concept of speed, distance, or death. Our conversation went like this.

"Moshen . . . pull your nose up."

"Sir?"

"Pull the nose up . . . see the men on the ground running away? That's bad."

"Sir?"

"I got the jet."

And I'd recover control, go around, and we'd have our three-language discussion. He'd swear he understood and I'd give him control back.

"Pull the nose up."

"Sir?"

"Pull your nose up . . . we're too steep and we're going to die."

"Sir?"

"Look at the fucking ground, Moshen!" I exploded in Arabic.

"Can't see the ground, sir!"

"What?"

"Can't see ground. My nose is up!"

And my mouth dropped open. Looking around the ejection seat, I saw him sitting with his head all the way back, staring up through the top of the canopy. I saved us again and discovered that every time I'd told him to pull his nose up, he did exactly that. He just hadn't understood I was talking about the *aircraft* nose . . . not *his* nose.

Some days it didn't pay to get out of bed.

LIVING IN EGYPT AND TRAVELING THROUGH THE REGION GAVE me insights into how some Arabs think and act. The sweeping generalizations made against them were as inaccurate as those about Americans. Finding any member of the U.S. military who knew much about Arabs was a rarity in 1992. Sure, we'd won the Gulf War, but after careers spent training for World War III, most military folks, myself included, sat back afterward and said, "What the Hell was that all about?" Iraq hadn't directly threatened the U.S., after all.

I'd fought some Arabs, trained a few, made personal friends and at least one personal enemy among them. There is much to admire about the Arabs and their culture. For instance, my Egyptian friends were always watching American television to improve their English (fat chance) and learn about us. One day, one of them asked me about a show he'd seen, regarding nursing homes. He remarked, "How sad that these old people have no family to care for them." I told him that many did have families but that they lived in homes to receive proper care. This shocked him and he just couldn't grasp the notion that families wouldn't care for their own.

On the other hand, I watched a platoon of Egyptian tanks (American-made M-1 Abrams) level a village that had supposedly sheltered insurgents. They pulled up, gave the villagers thirty minutes to leave, and smoked a few cigarettes. At the end of the half-hour, they simply rolled over the mud-brick houses and flattened them.

Understanding them a little, living within their world, and flying with them was a tremendous advantage. However, this would cause me some problems later in my career. There were lots of guys, especially among the general officers and the up-and-coming batch of lieutenant colonels, who'd all missed the Gulf War. They'd been off on staffs or in one of the Professional Military Education (a true oxymoron) courses, and hadn't fought anybody. These officers were still fighting the Soviet Union in their minds, and were slow to change with the times. But an officer who could quote Sun Tzu and knew about OODA loops was, well, vital. Right?

Right.

That's how a guy who wrote speeches for a general ended up commanding a fighter squadron. It's also how a C-130 transport pilot wound up in charge of the entire U.S. Air Force.

Another obstacle was simply entrenched military doctrine. Decades had been spent creating, packaging, and making careers out of fighting the Soviet Union and its puppets. No one had been thinking of Iraqis or Afghans as a threat, because no one cared. Fundamentalist extremists like al-Qaeda and the Taliban weren't on anyone's radar yet. They weren't a threat to the big military and so they weren't considered—though they should've been. As the Arab proverb says, "A fly in a man's mouth won't kill him but it will make him vomit." I'd seen the entrenched hatred of America even in our Egyptian allies, and if some of them felt that way then trouble from Iraq, Iran, and others couldn't be far behind.

Several months after the Great Hijacking, I was thrilled to get orders back to the United States. I'd been away for more than four years and was ready to come home. The exotic life of an expatriate is great, but I wanted a Sonic double hamburger. I wanted to listen to people talk and not translate it in my head. I wanted to see brainless American television and go to the Home Depot on Saturday morning to buy flowers I'd never plant. I wanted to walk into a Safeway at three A.M. because it was open and I could.

I wanted to come home.

5

PATCHWEARER

FIGHTER SQUADRONS, LIKE ALL ELITE GROUPS, EACH HAVE
their own personality. Same profession, same jets, same types of
people; and yet every one is unique. Some of our active units, like
the 27th and 94th Fighter Squadrons, have lengthy pedigrees going
back to the dawn of air combat during World War I. Many others
were created amidst the huge expansion of military aviation during World War II. In 1941, there were barely a hundred up-to-date
fighters in the U.S. inventory. By mid-1944, the Army Air Corps
(the predecessor of the modern Air Force) owned eighty thousand
combat aircraft.

The structure, from the top down, works like this. The modern
Air Force contains nine Major Commands (MAJCOMs), grouped
by location and mission. Three of these are fighter commands and
the others are for bombers, transports, training, and logistics. I
don't count the Space Command—sorry. Incidentally, this ongoing
money pit has a bigger slice of the 2012 Air Force budget than Air
Superiority and Special Operations combined. Air Combat Command (ACC) is for fighter wings based in the continental United

States; Pacific Air Forces (PACAF) for units in Asia or the Pacific; and U.S. Air Forces in Europe (USAFE) is for Africa and Europe. Pilots can and do rotate between all of these. It's a great way to see the world, learn languages, and live life.

MAJCOMs are composed of Numbered Air Forces (NAF) responsible for a geographic region. Ninth Air Force, for example, is made up of five fighter wings based in Virginia, both Carolinas, Georgia, and Florida. A wing is commanded by a very senior full colonel or a brigadier general and functions like a small town. There are married and bachelor housing areas of different quality, depending upon one's rank. Fire and police stations, a commissary for food, and a military-style Walmart called a base exchange. Fitness centers, pools, a church, and, of course, officer and enlisted clubs.

Each fighter wing is made up of several "groups" that share the wing's number. For instance, the 20th Fighter Wing (FW) at Shaw AFB consists of a Maintenance Group, Medical Group and a few other support organizations like Security Police and Personnel. The 20th Operations Group contains the 55th, 77th, 78th, and 79th Fighter Squadrons. Every active flying pilot on the base is assigned to a squadron. A recently assigned pilot, whether a transfer or a true rookie out of the training pipeline, is called a Fucking New Guy (FNG)—unless he's a lieutenant colonel or above. FNGs are assigned to a "flight," an administrative unit within a squadron made up of about five pilots plus an Assistant Flight Commander and a Flight Commander. These last two guys are senior captains; the Flight Commander should be an Instructor Pilot (IP) but often is only a flight leader.

He takes care of his guys. The Flight Commander knows what upgrades and training each pilot needs, and builds the weekly flying schedule accordingly. He reviews the grade sheets written on each man and helps maintain the all-important grade book. This is a permanent record of the formal training courses and upgrades the pilot has completed.

Besides a flight assignment, a pilot will also have at least one additional duty. He'll be put into one of the squadron functional areas, called a Shop, under the Shop Chief who is a senior captain. These shops allow the squadron to run smoothly: Scheduling, Training, Mobility, Life Support, Standardization and Evaluation, Intelligence, and the Weapons and Tactics.

The Training Shop is exactly that. The Chief and his minions keep track of each pilot's various requirements and currencies. Currencies cover not only tactical issues, like weapons qualifications, but a myriad of other headaches. How many takeoffs and landings per month, how many night landings, instrument approaches, required briefings, etc. . . . The list is nearly endless. Scheduling is the backbone of a flying operation. Every six months, the Scheduling Shop builds a Long Range Schedule outlining known deployments, exercises, and then creates the Flying Window, which are blocks of time available to the entire wing for its flying. Every pilot needs to maintain weapons currency by dropping so many bombs, strafing, and firing a certain number of missiles within preset accuracy parameters. There's much, much more to this, but it's sufficient to say that scheduling is a basic nightmare and an excellent place to stick a new guy.

Mobility is responsible for all the equipment, paperwork, and special requirements necessary for a squadron of three hundred people and two dozen aircraft to deploy at a moment's notice. The life-support shop, with the assistance of specially trained enlisted folks, maintains the helmets, G-suits, harnesses, and survival gear, as well as overseeing periodic refresher training for first aid, water survival, land survival, and personal weapons qualifications.

Standardization and Evaluation (Stan Eval) Shop is like the flying police. Everything related to military and applicable civilian flying regulations is maintained and enforced by Stan Eval. Each pilot, in addition to required training, currencies, and upgrades, must also take at least two check-rides per year. As explained earlier, check-flights are comprehensive oral, written, and flying exams. Normal pilots must take an instrument check that verifies his instrument rating and professional qualifications to fly a military fighter. This involves a session in a flight simulator, where all critical emergencies must be analyzed, solved, and taken to a logical, satisfactory conclusion. Another day is taken up with written tests covering aircraft systems, flying regulations, and the annual Instrument Refresher academic course. The actual flight takes another day.

The check pilot, called a Standardization and Evaluation Flight Examiner (SEFE), evaluates every aspect of the mission. Instrument Qual checks focus on maintaining your instrument rating and advanced aircraft handling through aerobatics and a few dogfighting setups. Several instrument approaches are flown, followed by Simulated Flameout Approaches, since being able to land without an engine is obviously crucial to a single-seat fighter pilot. Once back on the ground, after an extensive debrief, the SEFE gives an oral examination of anything else he feels is required.

Mission Qual checks follow the same format but the focus is on a pilot's fighting skills. The actual flight will be from a scenario provided by the SEFE, which encompasses the specific missions a squadron would be responsible for in combat. Strike squadrons may focus on laser-guided bombing, whereas a Wild Weasel squadron would concentrate on Maverick missiles or cluster bomb attacks against SAM sites. The oral debrief is just as thorough and equally unpleasant *but* absolutely necessary. It's all taken very, very seriously. The examinee is tested up to whatever qualification level he holds and must demonstrate his proficiency at all the inclusive skills. Every pilot, regardless of rank or qualification, is also subject to no-notice check-rides. This occurs when a SEFE shows up at the squadron one morning, points at a scheduled flight, and makes it a check-ride. The idea is to see how ready and lethal a pilot can be with no time to prepare. Kind of like combat.

Evaluators are usually field-grade officers and always instructor pilots. Some of the best SEFEs are Weapons Officers who've been off to staffs and schools, are now majors, and are back in flying units. Evaluating others from your own jet and knowing what's happening in the other cockpit takes a great deal of experience—judgment of critical, dynamic situations with lives and tens of millions of dollars at stake doesn't come naturally to everyone. In a fighter squadron, the commander and the director of operations (DO) should always be SEFEs. This is a credibility issue as well, since guys who lead *should* be the best, and credibility is essential in fighter units. The Weapons Officer is also usually a SEFE, and at least one of the Assistant Director of Operations (ADO).

ADOs are majors or sometimes very junior lieutenant colonels. They usually return to flying after completing the obligatory staff tour or one of the singularly useless professional military education courses. Fully re-qualified to fly, they're put in charge of the functional shops run by captains. As field-grade officers, they're another level of supervision and they work directly for the Director of Operations (DO).

The Director of Operations is the second-in-command of the squadron. He takes care of all the operational and training aspects just discussed. The squadron commander sets the tone and focus, and the DO deals with implementation. Always an IP and a SEFE, this officer rules the flying operations. He's a lieutenant colonel who has served as an ADO or on the wing staff and should know all there is to know about running a squadron. If he doesn't retire or screw up, he'll likely command a squadron of his own.

The squadron commander makes or breaks the outfit. Life is superb with the right commander and miserable with the wrong one—I've had both kinds. When I showed up in Germany, my squadron was just shutting down for two weeks of skiing. The commander had made it an annual tradition to take everyone to the Alps for a big winter party. So, a month after finishing F-16 training in Phoenix, Arizona, I'm sitting on a snowbank on top of an Austrian mountain and drinking Apfelkorn. Surreal.

We also routinely rented boats during the grape harvest season and would take wine-tasting cruises up and down the Mosel River. There were also weekend "cross-country" flights. These contributed to instrument training and familiarity with foreign air bases, but it was also great fun to take a few fighters and tear up a French Officer's Club. Or fly up to Copenhagen to see the Little Mermaid statue or over to England for a weekend in London. You get the idea.

Another great squadron had a weekly ceremony and award called the "HUA." This stands for "Head Up [his] Ass" award and was given—after much serious and sober consideration, of course—to the poor bastard who'd done the dumbest thing that week. This didn't necessarily have to do with flying if you'd been stupid enough to have witnesses for something else.

Like the punk lieutenant who rolled in on a slightly older but stunning woman at the Officer's Club bar only to later discover that she was his new commander's wife. A commander who observed the whole sorry attempt from a few bar stools down. She thought it was funny but the colonel didn't laugh much. Neither did the lieutenant.

Where the commander is the personality of a squadron, the Vault is the heart.

The Vault is a secure, special-access area of the squadron that's only entered through a coded, double steel door. Inside are the briefing rooms, library, mission-planning areas, map rooms, and computers. The Vault is the focal point for tactical operations and is the province of the squadron Weapons Officer.

Also known as a Patchwearer or Target Arm, the Weapons Officer is the squadron expert on combat operations and the training required to survive and win wars. A graduate of the elite Fighter Weapons Instructor Course (FWIC) taught at Nellis AFB in the Nevada desert, he's been through the nastiest, toughest tactical-air-combat course in the world. Think of it as a fighter pilot's version of a Special Forces or SEAL Team—absolutely the best of the best in tactical aviation. Easy to spot by the black-and-gray patch (earned on completion of Fighter Weapons School) worn on his left shoulder, the Weapons Officer is the yardstick by which the other squadron pilots are measured. He instructs the instructors. He takes the squadron to war.

THE PATHWAY TO THE FIGHTER WEAPONS SCHOOL WORKS like this.

Weapons Officers are constantly evaluating the instructor pilots in their squadrons. Target Arms select and train senior flight leads as instructors, so they're aware of likely candidates for several years. Each of these guys will already have phenomenal credentials as a pilot and instructor, so what makes or breaks the application are the recommendations from the few active Patchwearers in the wing. Just being an extremely gifted pilot isn't enough. The guy has to be able to *teach* as well as lead, and this isn't always the same thing.

The Air Force's idea is to train very few individuals to a level surpassing all others and then have them teach the rest. Aside from eye-watering flying abilities, this is why being able to instruct is so vital. To paraphrase one Fighter Weapons Instructor, being the best pilot in the Air Force doesn't matter if no one can learn from you.

Twice per year, each wing will submit a primary candidate and an alternate from its top pilots for the Weapons School selection board to consider. So, out of the hundreds of fighter instructor pilots in the USAF, about thirty get selected to attend each course. For the F-16 world, that amounts to three or four from bases within the United States, one from Germany, and two from the Far Eastern bases.

Once you're selected, but before leaving for Nellis, you get what's called a "spin-up." In essence, the Patchwearers at your base take turns beating the shit out of you. You go out and dogfight every day against your wing's Target Arms for two weeks to hone your skills. Your briefing and debriefing skills are exhaustingly picked apart. Remember, you're already an IP *and* the top pick from your base, so this is humbling.

Fighter Weapons School lasts six months—and the details are almost all classified. Incidentally, all Air Force fighter pilots today have Top Secret/Special Compartmentalized Information (TS/SCI) clearance. The course generally follows the same structure that a pilot will have experienced in every training program he's completed—but the course is on steroids. Remember, besides extremely lethal fighting skills, the goal is to really, *really* teach a pilot how to instruct others.

As you travel to Nellis AFB (located outside Las Vegas, Nevada) and spend your first week there in a classroom, the Weapons School instructors are fighting each other twice a day, every day.

By the time you face off with them, you haven't flown in two weeks, while they've been sharpening their claws and licking their fangs. Not that it would make a difference. They're superb, and no spin-up in the world would save a student from the shredding he's about to receive. It's a necessary attention-getter: until you get thoroughly trounced, somewhere in the back of your mind is the belief that you're still God's gift to the fighter world. You get over it quick.

Basic Fighter Maneuvers (BFM) is the first phase of the course. It's anything but basic and much too complex to describe on paper, but I'll attempt an overview. BFM is aerial hand-to-hand combat at 400 knots. Its purpose is to teach the pilot to truly fly and fight the aircraft. Nothing reveals the physical limits of yourself and the jet like BFM. It is fast, violent, and death is literally a few seconds away. There are midair collisions, out-of-control situations, and blackouts from G-locks. This is the blood-draining agony of sustained, multidimensional maneuvering at seven to nine times the force of gravity.

It will kill you.

There are four types of BFM. Offensive, which puts you at a starting point behind your adversary. He reacts, and you have to kill him before he can reverse positions and kill you. Defensive, where you're the meat and the enemy is behind you. You've got to defeat his initial shots and then stay alive long enough to take away his advantage and kill him. In neutral BFM, the fight begins as both aircraft pass nose-to-nose at about a thousand knots. Each guy then claws through various options at 800 feet per second and tries to arrive at a position to employ his weapons. In this case, barring a mistake, it all comes down to experience and who can outperform the other soonest. Dissimilar BFM is when any of the above are fought against another type of aircraft. This, especially if it's from a neutral setup, is the most realistic dogfighting training there is. In the real world, you rarely know exactly who all the bad guys are, and you're much more likely to meet one head-on rather than sneak up behind him.

BFM is only the beginning.

Air Combat Maneuvering (ACM) is next, and it's BFM on steroids. Here you fight as a *pair* against one enemy fighter. Again, there's Offensive, Defensive, Neutral, and Dissimilar. Communicating with your wingman is vital, and together you must locate the threat, identify it, react, and then kill it. Remember, you're doing all this while zipping around at rifle-bullet speeds.

Air Combat Tactics (ACT) is fighting as a pair against an unknown number of adversaries—because in combat you never really know how many bad guys are out there. Again, this approximates real-world confusion and tests a pilot's ability to be able to think, fight, and win against any number or type of threat.

There are two main categories of air-to-air tactics. Within Visual Range (WVR) is where you're fighting an opponent you can see with your eyes. This usually means short-range weapons, like heat-seeking Sidewinder missiles and the 20-mm cannon. Beyond Visual Range (BVR) is meant to take advantage of the American technical superiority that permits long-range missile employment. If you can kill a guy before he gets close enough to shoot at you, it's always better. Think about a man coming at you with a knife, but you've got a loaded gun in your hand. Would you pull your own knife or just shoot him in the head?

The best part of ACT was the dissimilar combat. We usually fought against American F-15s or F/A-18s, both of which are very tough fights. There were even some Navy F-14 Tomcats (you know, Maverick and Goose) still creaking around, but they were more for trophy-hunting rather than fighting. Sparing no expense, the Air Force also brought over foreign aircraft and their pilots when available. French Mirages, Israeli KIFRs, and German Tornados were all on the menu.

These international guys always had a good time flying across the world to Sin City to dogfight in the sun. One night in downtown Vegas, I watched a British fighter squadron get thrown out of a casino and arrested en masse. The Brits were confused, because it's simply Royal Air Force tradition to get plastered, sing songs, and perform the Prang Concerto—that is, burn a piano. Unfortunately, this particular piano was in the lobby of a very large and prominent downtown casino. If we'd done that, we'd be in jail for a while, but these guys got a headline in the *Daily Mirror* and a hero's welcome back in England. We thought it was great. Do you want fighter pilots or overgrown Boy Scouts?

ACT was also important, because it was more or less the halfway point of the program, and I finally felt I might make it. Maybe. Again, it was a real shock for someone who'd aced everything to date to consider failing a formal course. Shocking and scary. But fear is a very useful motivator.

Throughout the program, we also attended classes every day. More than three hundred hours of academic instruction covering all the aircraft systems at engineering-level detail. All the weapons we could use were dissected and rebuilt. Tactics, countertactics, and every threat we could face in the world was analyzed in detail. We also had to research and write a graduate school–level paper on a related classified subject, and then present it before a panel of FWIC instructors. All of this was commingled with nonstop flying, briefing, and debriefing. I used to fall asleep standing up in the shower at the end of the day. It sucked. I loved it.

The last few flights in the air-to-air phase were called four v. fours—meaning four of us against four of something else. In our case, we traveled to Florida and flew against the F-15s from the 33rd Fighter Wing (Eglin AFB) and the 325th Fighter Wing (Tyndall AFB). Air-to-air fighting in all its variations is what Eagles do.

It's all they do. And the advantage to flying only one type of mission is that you have the luxury of becoming extremely good at it.

However, we were all F-16 instructors *and* we'd been FWIC students for three months. We'd recovered some confidence and were ready to finish ACT and move on. Besides, it was Florida, and everyone, the FWIC instructors included, was looking forward to a little wind-down before we started the most complex sections of the course. Killing Eagles at the beach was fun. I smiled for the first time in three months.

With the air-to-air phase complete, the FWIC course switched into high gear. Viper pilots regard dogfighting as something we might have to do on our way to killing things on the ground. No one ever won a war solely through air superiority. Don't get me wrong—you have to own the air in order to win on the ground, but rarely can you be victorious with airplanes alone. Every American war fought since 1917 is proof of that.

Bomb-dropping in support of ground operations, generally referred to as "Surface Attack," is the bread and butter of the F-16 world. There are low- and medium-altitude attacks with different bombs, strafing with the 20-mm cannon, precision-guided munitions like the Maverick missile, laser and TV bombs, cluster bombs . . . the list goes on.

The point is, as a Target Arm, you've got to be the best at this. From your own jet, you have to be able to watch pilots executing these attacks and be instantly able to gauge their effectiveness. Or prevent fatalities. Several thousand pounds of high explosives delivered in the wrong place can kill you. Or blow up the wrong people on the ground. Missing a target also means someone else will have to fight his way in and risk his life to fix your fuckup. It could also lead to ground troops getting overrun and never coming home again. So we take it seriously—and so did the FWIC instructors.

Basic Surface Attack leads into Surface Attack Tactics (SAT). A student is given "objectives"—the desired results—and a few other specifics, like the Time Over Target (TOT) and the *known* threats. He then designs, plans, briefs, and leads the attacks against the entire catalog of possible threats.

Now, the Nellis threat array is infamous for its lethality, in a training sense. In any given year, more than five hundred aircraft from all over the world fly twenty thousand training sorties against these threats. All U.S. tactical flying units cycle through every few years, including USAF fighter squadrons based in Europe and the Far East. All the NATO air forces attend if they can afford it, and occasionally you can see Israelis and some of the friendlier Arab nations, like Egypt or Morocco. Even the French show up occasionally, when they can find it.

After SAT comes the Mission Employment (ME) phase. Every aspect of the course is rolled into four separate missions. You're given tactical problems with targets, threats, and timing windows. How you solve the problems is up to you. I've seen perfect plans that are poorly executed and bad plans that are overcome by superb execution. You just never know how it's going to play out, and a student's adaptability is a key issue with surviving this phase—or not.

The FWIC student, now only several flights away from hopefully graduating, is the Mission Commander. He has to decide, based on the threats and the target, how to plan and orchestrate the attack. He chooses the weapons, routes, tactics, and designs the attacks. He also runs the entire mass briefing and debriefing.

Each aircraft that flies on the Nellis range carries an Air Combat Maneuvering Instrumentation (ACMI) pod. All the flight parameters and even the pilot's HUD view is fed back to a huge building containing the mission debriefing system. RFMDS, the Red Flag Mission Debriefing System, is the heart of all tactical training at

Nellis. Every mission and every flight can be picked apart thanks to the ACMI pods. It's a tremendous advantage, to be able to sit with a cup of coffee at zero miles per hour and totally reconstruct a mission. All maneuvers, tactics, and every weapon that is dropped or shot is analyzed. This is how we learn, improve, evaluate, and this is another reason for American air supremacy.

For a FWIC student, the ME phase is a rite of passage. However, I knew two pilots who washed out in this final part of the course. If you do survive, your immediate reaction is disbelief. At least it was in my case. That, and the weak-limbed numbness that comes from profound relief. I'd been through every other formal course and training possible for a fighter pilot—*and* had seen action in the Gulf War. Fighter Weapons School was by far the most difficult.

After my final flight, I drove back to the Visiting Officer's Quarters and sat outside on the Wailing Bench. Normally, you only sat on this thing when you busted (failed) a flight. You'd carve your call sign and the mission number into the bench and wait for your buddies to pass you a shot of scotch by way of solace. Needless to say, there were hundreds of names and dates, because everyone busts rides. So I sat there, let the sweat dry, and the realization sink in that I was almost a Patchwearer. There was one final, very closely held initiation that would take place during Patch Night. After this, graduates received the gray-and-black patch they'd proudly wear for the rest of their careers. The idea was now to go back to a fighter squadron with the latest techniques and tactics and pass it along to everyone else.

I'd known for months that my combat experiences in the Gulf were at odds with some of the tactics being taught at Nellis. But remember the environment. FWIC instructors fight other elite American pilots, so their tactics tend to reflect that level of threat—and not necessarily those posed by poorly trained Russian, Chinese, or Middle Eastern aviators. Besides, if you can defeat the Nellis "threat," you can beat anything in the world. One curious result I've noticed is that we often falsely equate the threat's capability with our own standards. We give them too much credit and occasionally derive some flawed tactics from this outlook. I was determined not to do this. I wanted to combine all my previous experience with the magic I'd just been taught—a perfect marriage of real-world lessons with the most lethal fighter training in the world. In retrospect, it was a nice thought.

Fighter Weapons School was a tremendous, life-altering experience and you truly do emerge as someone else. Anyone who has survived to be part of an elite group knows this feeling. No matter what unmanned space-based crap they're gluing to the Nellis main gate these days, that place will always be "The Home of Fighter Pilot" to me and those like me. I'm sure that'll piss off the politically correct ground-pounders, but really, who cares?

6

INTERMISSION

SINCE I WAS ONE OF THE FEW VIPER PILOTS WHO'D STARTED AS a Wild Weasel, I was especially eager to apply what I'd learned from the Fighter Weapons School and Operation Desert Storm to the newly fielded F-16CJ. The F-16CJ, called a CeeJay, was a quantum leap forward in technology. Tremendously versatile, with an amazing capacity for adaptation, the F-16 is a natural Weasel. Due to its composite-material construction, it was difficult to see on radar and nearly impossible to see with the naked eye. The engines didn't smoke and it was the most maneuverable fighter in the world. This meant it was as deadly to enemy fighters as it was to SAMs and, unlike the F-4G, it didn't require escort. Its only shortcoming, due to the relatively small size, was a smaller weapons payload. To compensate, the CeeJay carried precision-guided munitions, like laser-guided bombs and air-to-ground missiles, the rationale being that if you could put a bomb within three feet of its target, then you didn't need to carry many of them.

It was during these years that the pace of deployments to Southwest Asia moved into high gear. George Bush's rush to claim a victory in 1991 had left us with another war to fight, and anyone with a working brain knew this was inevitable. You see, Iraq was basically quarantined between the wars. This meant they owned the ground but we controlled the air, so we really controlled most of the country. No-fly zones were established above the 34th Parallel north to Turkey, and from the 32nd Parallel south to the Kuwaiti/Saudi border. These were patrolled by fighter squadrons that continuously rotated in theater for over ten years. Not just fighters, but the aerial tankers, transports, AWACS, and everything else needed to support them.

It was a colossal drain on our resources, immensely expensive, and an overall pain in the ass. Aircraft service life was shortened by at least 50 percent, due to the added hours flown, and we missed a lot of Christmas holidays, kids' birthdays, and wedding anniversaries. Divorce rates skyrocketed and the fabric of the Air Force was permanently altered as general officers and policy-makers strove mightily to create a replacement threat for the Soviet Union. A military—and most nations—need at least one enemy to grease industry and keep everyone on their toes.

The Air Force and Army particularly needed the Iraqi threat to justify their budgets. The Navy has aircraft carriers and can go virtually anywhere, but they can't remain at sea indefinitely. A carrier battle group also requires significant resupply to remain effective. As for the Army, well, one look at a Forward Operating Base (FOB) is enough. They're not intended to be permanent and it shows.

Only the Air Force has the global logistical capability to sustain long-term, heavy operations. No-fly zone (NFZ) enforcement in the south could be done in a limited way from carriers in the Gulf or from shore-based fighters. But, with the exception of Bahrain, any shore-basing of naval air was done from a USAF air base in Saudi Arabia or Kuwait. NFZ operations from the north could only be done from Incirlik Air Base in Turkey.

However, we now had several footholds in the region from big bases that had been built with all the engineering and logistical expertise of the U.S. military. It is a truly impressive display of American power to see empty desert transformed into self-contained, fortified cities within weeks.

Now, the Air Force has always had the idea that if you take care of your people then they'll take care of whatever needs to be done. Also, the Air Force usually *remains* deployed, so air bases today are what naval bases were in the past: stepping-stones across the world and vital links for force-projection. So bases are built to last, with at least some thought given to those who will serve there. In any event, air bases are built around flying operations. The runways, ammunition dumps, operations and maintenance facilities are the best in the world. I mean, there's no point to having an air base if the aircraft can't fly the missions.

The living facilities are also pretty good, relatively speaking. I've seen little condominiums, prefabricated apartments, and containerized housing. Only in rare cases does the Air Force use tents, and then never for very long. A huge part of any air base is the Morale, Welfare and Recreation (MWR) area. This includes dining facilities, fitness centers, and, if at all practical, a swimming pool—no kidding. Of course, since most of the Middle East is sand, beach-volleyball courts are always a necessity. Depending on the intensity of operations and the longevity of the base, there is also a food court of some kind. I've seen Chinese, Turkish, and Indian restaurants, usually a burger joint, and always some type of pizza parlor.

But no alcohol. General Order No. 1 from Operation Desert Shield reads:

> *Operation Desert Shield places United States Armed*
> *Forces into USCENTCOM AOR countries where Is-*
> *lamic law and Arabic customs prohibit or restrict certain*
> *activities which are generally permissible in Western so-*
> *cieties. Restrictions upon these activities are essential to*
> *preserving U.S. host nation relations and the combined*
> *operations of U.S. and friendly forces.*

Just to be clear—we weren't on holiday as guests in another country, so the "host nation" statement was always bullshit. We weren't there to promote democracy, save souls, or make friends. Oil, economics, and politics aside, we were in the Middle East because Saudi Arabia and Kuwait couldn't protect themselves. They were frightened enough of the Iraqi threat to beg our help and, for many reasons, we gave it. Do you really think any of them would protest the personal conduct of the soldiers who were saving their wealth and way of life?

I don't either.

Most of the Saudi officers I knew drank more than we did, and, during the war, Cairo was full of Kuwaitis who were content to party while the Americans protected their country. The British and French military also had a large presence in the region, and they didn't inflict similar restrictions on their people. In fact, the Brits loved Jell-O parties. They'd put the stuff in ice trays, mixed with vodka or gin, and slurp it down. During twelve rotations to Southwest Asia, I never heard of one alcohol-related incident.

By the way, the civilians working for oil companies, like Aramco, drank like fishes. So did the U.S.-government types assigned to Saudi Arabia. Drinking isn't that important to me personally and it was certainly no hardship to do without. In the Army's case, it's not a bad idea to keep booze away from minimally educated kids with guns. However, regardless of the pros and cons, our government's rush to placate people who weren't in a position to object rubbed us the wrong way. I mean, if you have the biggest stick and you're waving it in everyone's face, then why be afraid to use it? Appeasement nearly always has far-reaching security ramifications and this was no exception, as we shall see.

Aside from being away from home and civilization as we knew it, these weren't really tough deployments. We lived in decent conditions, had lots of time to work out, and very few distractions. Some guys took classes for the master's degree required by the Air Force for promotion beyond the rank of captain. Others indulged in hobbies. I know one guy who made stained-glass windows from bits of broken glass he found around the compound, and another who trained for Iron Man competitions. Some guys chased skirts and others built toys for their kids. You just never knew.

Tactics took up most of my brain bytes. We all knew there would be a reckoning with Iraq. The Air Force closet had been cleaned out, so to speak, and almost all of the older weapons and jets had been retired. What was left was considerably streamlined and there were a lot fewer of us around to fight. The technological advances had evened this up but it was left to us to make the most of these advantages.

Iraq was a relatively simple theater for combat, and the terrain, at least from the air, was fairly permissive. Mountains were only in the far north and east. The far west, near the Jordanian and Syrian borders, was a morass of twisted wadis and rugged low hills. Most of the population was concentrated in Mesopotamia, the land between the Tigris and Euphrates Rivers.

So it makes sense, defensively, to protect the large important focal points rather than the entire country, and this is precisely what the Iraqis did. The cities of Kirkuk and Mosul in the north, Baghdad in the center, Nasiriyah and Basrah in the south were all heavily defended. There were dozens of fortified rings for smaller towns or military complexes, and mobile SAM systems could be anywhere. In fact, the Iraqis had over eight thousand mobile SAMs, not including the thousands of shoulder-launched MANPADS that any soldier could carry. These complimented and overlapped the four hundred larger SA-2s, SA-3s, and SA-6s. Anti-aircraft artillery estimates were in the tens of thousands.

The big stuff was centered around important cities to protect airfields, train stations, communications nodes, and other vital bits of infrastructure. Tracking information from surveillance radars, air traffic radars, and long-range search radars was all brought together in an Integrated Air Defense System (IADS) called KARI. In theory, this would tie all inbound radar tracks on people like me together into a consolidated air "picture." Based on this, the Iraqi Air Defense Commander would then parcel out the interception and targeting responsibilities to the appropriate Iraqi SAM and fighter units.

There were several problems with this. First, KARI was designed by the French, who, though first-class vintners, are usually hopeless as warriors. Ask the Germans or the Vietnamese or the Algerians. Second, Iraqi systems didn't handle jamming very well, and Americans are masters of electronic combat. We could, and did, blank out entire sectors so the Iraqis couldn't see what was coming. Many of our initial targets were long-range search radars that could detect us crossing the Saudi border. We would also destroy telephone relay stations, cell towers, and all other forms of communications equipment. It's a basic concept in any fight: punch out their eyes and mouth so they can't see to react or call for help.

The Russians, who trained most of the Iraqis, are very centralized in their battlefield thinking, and they instilled this in their students. So, cutting units off from their commanders would force independent thought, and this was something most Iraqis didn't handle well. Battles are chaotic enough anyway, and without direction from above many Iraqi units initially did nothing at all.

Then there was saturation. KARI worked okay against the ten or twenty aircraft-strike packages from the Iran-Iraq War, but we had over three hundred aircraft hitting them every day and they were overwhelmed. Throw in the communications disruption and jamming that had them chasing false targets, and it's obvious why we gained air supremacy in two days.

When their MiGs and Mirages did take off to gloriously battle the infidel invaders (that would be us again), none of them ever came back. I helped chase a flight of Mirage fighters into Iran one day as they bravely ran away. Another morning, I watched two MiG-23s fly into the ground as they tried to shake off a horde of U.S. jets swarming in their direction. So, in addition to their technical shortcomings, the Iraqis had a critical morale problem.

We'd gone into this more or less ad hoc in 1991, but by 2003 we'd figured it out. Extreme adaptability is one of the most defining characteristics of the American military, and we adapted. We also function very well as small independent units that don't require a lot of supervision. In fact, supervision is usually highly resented.

Now, with lots of time between the wars, we had the luxury of really picking the threat apart and studying it. Remember, the goal of Operation Desert Storm had been to save Kuwaiti and Saudi oil, not to invade Iraq. But we knew the next war would be different. Next time we'd have to go to Baghdad.

No one liked rotating to Saudi or Kuwait twice per year, but we made the most of it. It was, in fact, terrific practical experience and afforded us a superb opportunity to know the terrain, the weather, and build up our knowledge of a threat we'd face eventually. We still hated it.

The Weasels from the 20th Fighter Wing did this from Dhahran, Saudi Arabia. This base was left over from Desert Storm and sat south of Iraq on the Persian Gulf. Dhahran wasn't too bad for several reasons. First, it was only a hundred miles from the Iraqi border, and in a region so vast this made response times very quick and our missions that much shorter. Second, unlike the rest of the Kingdom, the city of Dhahran actually had a few amenities. The downtown area had been built with petrodollars and boasted good restaurants and even a shopping mall. Because of the oil fields, the locals were accustomed to Westerners and were relatively tolerant.

Last (and most important), there was a causeway across the water to the island of Bahrain. This causeway had been built for Saudis who needed a break from condemning godless Americans and Europeans. They'd race across the narrow highway, shedding robes and headdresses as they drove, to get to the bars and women on the island—apparently, Allah doesn't see them if they're not in Saudi Arabia. We didn't care. We'd go there to eat and shop and sometimes spend the night at a nice beachside resort. No scorpions, camel spiders, or military meals. Bahrain was only a few miles off the coast but was truly another world compared to the Arabian Peninsula.

In 1979, the Saudi government, feeling nostalgic about its desert past, built a complex outside Dhahran for Bedouin tribesmen. This was intended for the elderly, the sick, and those awaiting airtransportation to Mecca for the annual hajj. Over fifty modern condos were built, with four units per floor and eight floors per building. Each unit had a large living room with a kitchen on one end and a window wall opening to a narrow balcony on the opposite side. Four bedrooms, each with a bath and bidet, were accessible from this central area. Everything the modern Bedouin family needed.

Except Bedouins don't live in condos.

They don't put their sick or old in hospitals and they don't fly to the hajj. So, this huge complex stood empty for eleven years until housing was needed for American, British, and French pilots who arrived in 1990 to save the Ghawar oil fields. Sorry—to save the peaceful and progressive Saudi people from their monstrous northern neighbor.

The war ended but the infidels remained. The presence of non-Muslim soldiers in the holy kitty-litter box of Saudi Arabia began to cause great offense throughout the Kingdom and the Islamic world. It was fine for us to fight and even die for them and their oil, but now that the danger was past they wanted us out. Even though Saddam was a genocidal, homicidal butcher, he was, after all, a Muslim and therefore preferable to the bacon-loving degenerate soldiers who had just saved the day.

The temporary solution was to house us someplace out of the way and relatively discreet. Dhahran was chosen, and the 4404th Combat Wing (Provisional) took up permanent residence in the Bedouin compound outside the city.

It was called Khobar Towers—and it was as good as it was going to get.

One humid, sticky night in June changed all that. As the faint mournful echoes of evening prayer floated over our compound, the lights flickered and for a fraction of a second I felt an overpressure in my ears. My brain didn't process the cause until the building shook and I suddenly found myself on the floor in the next room. The glass picture window that made up the exterior wall was gone. It took me a few seconds to realize that I was sitting on most of it. More was in my hair and stuck through my skin in various places. But not my eyes, thank God. As I lay there, legs spread and sticky back against the wall, it occurred to me to inventory my critical body parts.

Testicles first. *Thanks again.*

Then feet, legs, hands, etc. . . . As I was doing this, my suite-mate (each officer got his own room in the four-bedroom suite) appeared in the doorway. The blast had knocked him out of bed and he stood there a moment, scratching himself and peering at me through one open eye.

"Hey . . . I think that was a bomb."

No shit, Sherlock.

In fact, it was an enormous bomb.

Twenty-five thousand pounds of TNT had been packed into a sewage service tanker truck and driven up to the perimeter on the northeastern corner of the compound. A USAF Security Policeman had actually seen the truck and its getaway car approach the fence. Two local Saudis had jumped out of the truck into the car and sped off. Recognizing it for what it was, the cop tried to evacuate Building 131, the closest to the truck—but was too late.

All the American pilots had just finished our nightly fun of cracking skulls during games of roller hockey. I slowly limped upstairs and was heroically drinking milk in my kitchen on the top floor of Building 133 when the bomb went off. Minutes later, as I lay there in the puddle of glass and blood, I remembered a similar blast in Cairo five years before. It had felt more or less the same, just much smaller, and I'd been a bit farther back than the fifty yards that had separated me from the explosion. Staring at my feet, I realized I was still wearing my skates. The other captain saw it, too, and we both laughed.

The laugh of the terminally crazy.

I ditched the skates as sirens began to wail and the shouting began. We made a quick tour of the tenth floor, kicked a few people out, and I limped toward the stairs. I'd gotten a piece of glass stuck in my face and wasn't seeing so well, but eventually we got downstairs and emerged into chaos. All the compound lights were out, but the lights from the surrounding Saudi housing area were shining brightly. Dust hung in the air, thick and nearly motionless. Buildings were burning, people were running, and there was lots of shouting. You see, most of the Air Force is made up of support folks. Essential, of course, but they weren't trained for combat and most of them had no idea what to do. Also, no one except pilots and police had weapons.

Fortunately, the security force reacted quickly, and so did the medical folks. As we rounded the corner, there were already armed cops gathering around the shattered gap in the fence. The wounded were getting triaged on the street. Others were heading toward the tottering building to see if they could help pull bodies out or assist the injured. The police realized the danger and eventually cleared everyone away.

Nineteen Americans died that night. Scores of others were wounded.

"We will pursue this," President Clinton declared. "Those who did this must not go unpunished."

Right.

Well, that didn't happen. The 4404th Wing Commander, Brigadier General Terry Schwalier, eventually even got a second star. Not at first, of course. Someone had to be held accountable, and, quite correctly in my opinion, the blame fell on Schwalier, the man ultimately responsible for the safety and security of the Wing.

Even though this was 1996 and long before 9/11 made bin Laden and al-Qaeda household names, there'd been obvious signs that the situation was deteriorating and that American servicemen in Saudi Arabia were at risk. The previous November, for instance, a car bomb detonated in Riyadh outside the office of the Program Manager for the Saudi National Guard. Five Americans had been killed and another thirty people wounded. All through the winter and early spring of 1996 there had been bombings and violence in Bahrain. In January 1996, an Air Force Office of Special Investigations (AFOSI) report specifically mentioned the threat of vehicle bombs along the Khobar perimeter.

Despite these warnings, Khobar remained exposed and vulnerable in June 1996. Two sides of Khobar were bordered by a Saudi housing area. The north end (where the bomb would explode) was an open park for locals. Schwalier did conclude that the threat of a car bomb necessitated enhanced security so the single gate into Khobar Towers ended up looking like the Maginot Line. Pillboxes, wire, armed guards, etc. . . . all very impressive but what about the *miles* of exposed perimeter around the rest of the complex? Even a simple-minded Saudi terrorist is smart enough not to attack the strongest part of a fence.

Eventually thirty-six of the thirty-nine AFOSI recommendations were implemented at Khobar, but it was too little and too late. For instance, a "Giant Voice" public-address system that could've been used to warn of attacks was incomprehensible to anyone *inside* a building on the Khobar complex. Also, even if one of the rooftop sentries could detect an attack (and one did see the tanker truck pull up on June 25) there was no quick way to sound an alert. There was no siren that could be activated by the sentries, because the wing leadership decided it would offend the local Saudis. Any information or suspicious activity had to be called in to Central Security Control, then passed to the Wing Operations Center and finally to the Wing Commander before a decision could be made. The "system" was, in a word, useless.

I freely acknowledge it was a tough security situation and the likelihood of Saudi cooperation was pretty small, but I never saw evidence that Schwalier tried to press the issues with them. Or with the American chain of command. I contend the root problem was his failure to take a hard line with our so-called hosts to ensure the security of the U.S. servicemen at Khobar. Both the military and civilian leadership seemed to me more concerned with not offending the Saudis than they were with the safety of our people.

Ultimately, the Iranian-backed Hezbollah al-Hejaz (Party of God) was found responsible for the attacks. Thirteen Saudi nationals and one Lebanese man were indicted by the U.S. District Court of Eastern Virginia, but there has been no justice to date. These terrorists remain on the FBI's Most Wanted list.

Although Schwalier was eventually cleared and his actions found not to be culpable for the attacks, my opinion of him remains unchanged. Doing everything possible to protect your people is a fundamental command principle. It can't always be achieved, especially in combat, but a good leader would fall on his sword over conditions like this, and I don't believe Schwalier made the necessary efforts. He didn't make any waves in the interest of our security that I could see, and the result was nineteen dead Americans and hundreds more like me who live with their injuries every day. Remember, we're not talking about a civilian company that makes computer chips or sells fast food. This is the front-line military, deployed on foreign soil. Not doing enough doesn't damage a corporate bottom line—it gets people killed.

More broadly, the Khobar bombing was a warning of just how ominously unprepared the military leadership was to face the post–Cold War security reality, where extremist groups can pose as much of a threat as state-sponsored fighters. (This new state of affairs would, in time, change everything—from training to weapon systems to tactics.) In August 1996, a month after the attack, Osama bin Laden issued a fatwa titled "Declaration of War against the Americans Occupying the Land of the Two Holy Places," referring to the U.S. military presence in Saudi Arabia (home of the Muslim holy sites Mecca and Medina). While bin Laden's "declaration of war" aroused far too little interest among the public and intelligence circles, those who were in the Khobar Towers on June 25, 1996, and were exposed to the savage violence of terrorism knew the road ahead had just become far darker.

Unfortunately, the 1990s gave rise to scores of careerists who filled all the squares, went to the correct staffs and knew all the right people. The problem was that they couldn't fight their way out of a wet paper bag. Our own squadron commander, who bravely ran away from the Khobar fence, had never held any field-grade squadron leadership positions prior to being given a command. And it showed. There are guys who fly fighters and there are fighter pilots. This guy was definitely *not* a fighter pilot.

Some of these men were on decoration quests—either for vanity or career enhancement. Personally, I think most decorations are absurd. Even some of the respected ones can be given away for horseshit reasons. I knew of a major (now, unbelievably, a major general) who put together PowerPoint briefings for generals during Desert Storm and got a Bronze Star for it. He would always say that he'd gotten it during Desert Storm, which was true but disingenuous. Someone would inevitably ask which squadron he'd been with or how many combat missions he'd flown and this guy would always manage to change the subject. The Air Force also permits combat flying time to be logged if you are physically in a designated combat zone, even if there is no fighting going on. This is how some men, like Schwalier, are able to log combat time without ever actually fighting. Again, to me, disingenuous.

My point is not to necessarily pick on men like Schwalier but to illustrate the weaknesses of the system that created them. Loyalty is a fine thing and one of the cornerstones of any combat profession—but so is accountability. I've seen officers fired because their subordinates were having affairs, or had drinking problems or for a score of other things completely beyond a commander's control. It is wildly hypocritical and inconsistent to then permit a commander to be exonerated for loss of life that may well have been preventable.

Anyway, as the 1990s waffled on, we saw more and more of this. Kosovo and Operation Allied Force seem to have been wholly fought to deflect national attention away from Bill Clinton's perennially open pants. That, and General Wesley Clark's narcissistic dream of being considered a latter-day Eisenhower. In any event, neither worked out very well. Clark actually ordered his subordinate commanders to attack Russian soldiers at Pristina airport. Fortunately, the senior British officer, General Sir Mike Jackson, refused point-blank. In fact, he replied, "I'm not going to start the Third World War for you."

Out of the 120-something kills claimed on Serbian armor, we could only find a dozen vehicles destroyed. We did find a lot of destroyed decoys—plywood tanks with little kerosene stoves inside to provide heat signatures, or old World War II relics without treads. The Yugoslavs simply lit fires under the bellies to heat up the metal so we'd see them with our infrared systems.

After the war, a battle-damage assessment team was told to go back in and "find" the correct number of wrecked tanks. The Air Force major in charge of the team came back with twelve confirmed tank kills and refused to inflate the numbers to help Clark's entry into politics. This didn't do the major's career any good, so he transferred to the National Guard. Guys like that get a scotch from me on sight.

As time rolled on, the Vietnam-era pilots eventually retired, and most of us who'd fought the First Gulf War slowly staggered up the ladder. We became flight leads, instructor pilots, and commanders. A very few of us became Weapons and Tactics Officers. We'd spent the years between the wars over Iraq occasionally getting shot at, working out system limitations, and deriving tactics. There were tireless efforts by many talented guys to improve our systems and weapons.

For the F-16CJ, the HARM Targeting System (HTS), thankfully, evolved into something that had less and less to do with lobbing anti-radiation missiles and more to do with precision-targeting. HTS was initially fairly inaccurate, since the HARM didn't require a very tight firing solution. The missile was supposed to "see" the radar signal, called a "beam," and follow that beam back to impact. Think of standing in a dark room with a pistol and shooting at pulsating flashlight beams, and you get the idea. However, shooting at the beam doesn't mean you have much of a chance of hitting the source. You might scare it though, and force it to turn off. That's okay for the moment, but the flashlight is still alive and may get you another time.

So, lobbing HARMs at radar beams and calling it Weaseling is an extremely dangerous notion. Threats rarely do what you expect, and that early version of the HARM, in many opinions, was really a very crappy missile. If the threat didn't emit, then the HARM had nothing to guide on and went "stupid." The concept had worked in the 1960s and 1970s, when SAMs had to actively emit to shoot missiles, but by the 1990s SAMs utilized optics, infrared, or other guidance sources.

The Texas Instrument marketing folks were obviously very good, because I thought, as did many others, that the missile was generally a waste of a weapon station. I shot over thirty of these things in combat and have no idea what they hit except the earth or maybe some poor Iraqi jabbering on a cell phone at the wrong time. So HTS was only initially designed with enough accuracy for the HARM, and the end effect was a targeting solution that wasn't good enough for precision weapons.

Yet.

A very gifted engineer named Gregg helped me rough out a design for what eventually became HTS R7. This would permit much faster targeting solutions with accuracies tight enough to employ precision-guided munitions. We actually drew this up on a napkin (no kidding) at a place called AJ's on the beach in Panama City.

Then there were those of us who passionately believed in suppressing a threat by killing it. I mean, if the thing is in a million pieces on the ground, then it's suppressed, right? Then it won't be back to bother you tomorrow, next week, or in the next war. It's dead. Some of us had seen this in combat and recognized the flaws in the anti-radiation, suppression-only mind-set. This would take almost a decade to change, but HTS was a step in the right direction and the system would undergo dramatic improvements. More to the point, it was all we had.

The pilot was the other reason the CeeJay concept was successful. There was now an entire generation of officers who'd always flown the F-16, and we were very comfortable with fourth-generation technology and doing everything ourselves. Sensor management was, and is, a huge part of a young F-16 pilot's training. To be able to monitor and interpret radars, targeting pods, weapons, and all onboard systems while physically flying a Mach-2 jet is not a common ability. To do it at night, a hundred feet off the ground, while other men are trying to kill you, is extraordinary. I once took an F-15E WSO for an orientation flight in a two-seat F-16. He came back amazed (and worried) that I could do alone what it took his crew to accomplish in a Strike Eagle. Fighter pilots tend to rise to the occasion, whether it's impressing young girls in the O'Club or mastering lethal technology.

So we rose.

AMERICA'S ENTHUSIASM FOR WAR HAD BEEN FLAGGING DURing the 1990s. The world saw through the Kosovo mess, and the general public was, frankly, not convinced that Hussein was much of a threat. Budgets were being cut and drawdowns were looming when the Twin Towers came down on September 11, 2001.

My squadron had rotated home from Southwest Asia two weeks earlier, and that terrible Tuesday morning was our second day back to normal stateside operations. There were mountains of paperwork to catch up on and a myriad of flying currencies to refresh. On September 11, I'd just landed from an early-morning mission when everyone began buzzing about the first plane strike. It was 0846, and I clearly remember wondering how some amateur pilot could end up over New York City and be so stupid as to fly himself into the Twin Towers. We all thought it was an accident. Turned out, it was a Boeing 767 that had the misfortune of being American Airlines Flight 11.

A little after nine A.M., as we stood staring at the enormous flat-screen picture of UA Flight 175 hitting the South Tower, it became obvious this was no accident. The military went through its standard procedure of locking down bases and recalling everyone within a day's travel. Commanders and Weapons Officers were summoned to a hasty conference to get updates on the situation and formulate a reaction. President Bush, in an admirable and unexpected display of courage, continued to read *The Pet Goat* to some elementary-school students.

By 0945, the airspace over America was closed.

This had never been done before and was truly astounding, since normally there are about thirty thousand scheduled flights over the United States at any given time. This doesn't count air cargo, military operations, or unscheduled flights, but by 1215 all aircraft were grounded, turned around, or diverted.

Everyone but military fighters, air tankers, and AWACS, that is. I was airborne by noon, leading a four-ship of armed F-16s over Atlanta's Hartsfield International Airport. There were no rules of engagement, no real idea yet of what had happened, and no one knew quite what to expect. Was this the leading edge of some sort of mass attack on the United States? Was it a prelude to a larger, nastier assault using chemical or biological weapons through, say, a port? Or was it all a diversion for something else?

No one knew.

So the few of us who were old enough to have been alert pilots during the Cold War were ordered to set up a similar program to cope with this new threat. Whatever "this" turned out to be. Never in a million years had I thought I'd be flying combat air-patrol missions over my own country. Usually the sky above America is a vast place filled with contrails, radio chatter, and aircraft, but now there was nothing. It was downright creepy.

The radios were initially very busy, because the five thousand or so flights that were airborne at the time didn't take kindly to being directed to land. However, as the F-16s and F-15s got airborne all over the country, the airliners complained a lot less. One Delta flight that was a bit late in answering air traffic control got treated to the sight of my F-16 flying formation off its nose. Turned out, it was just having standard minor radio issues, but it got escorted down to final approach anyway. I'll never forget the sight of a hundred faces pressed against the windows watching me watch them.

In hindsight, I think it was all handled as well as it could be. Remember, there was no procedure for this and no rules. Add to it the jumpiness of every air traffic controller in the country, and I believe we were fortunate that no one got shot down. It always surprises me how bloodthirsty the ground-pounders seem to be. One controller told me that he'd "give me clearance to fire . . ."—all I had to do was ask. Well, that wasn't going to happen unless I saw an airliner roll over and dive for downtown. Even then, if we'd shot one, where would all the wreckage fall? The 20th Fighter

Wing reacted admirably by only sending up flights led by extremely experienced combat pilots, and no mistakes were made.

When I landed and made it back to the squadron, there were messages from my sisters and, of course, my mother. Somewhat inured to my lifestyle by now, she wasn't openly worried about me but she did say that my father was all right.

What?

It turned out that, unbeknownst to me, my father was in the Pentagon when AA Flight 77 hit. I mean, to survive everything he'd faced and then almost get whacked by a hijacked commercial airliner in his own country? That really *pissed* me off.

He was (and is) a prominent defense consultant, and was in the A Ring to see the assistant secretary of the Army. In an effort to be truly confusing, the building is set up in concentric rings, A–E, with the E Ring on the outside. My dad later told me:

"I'd been walking down the hall to the secretary's office when I felt a tremendous, vibrating crash. I wasn't worried about it, because most of the northwest side of the Pentagon was being renovated and heavy loads were routinely being dropped. However, when I got to the office, the secretary grabbed me by the arm and said, 'Come with me young man . . . we've just been attacked. Look at your suit.' Sure enough, I was covered with a fine gray dust.

"When we got outside, there was a huge column of smoke rising from the northwest side. Turns out that the terrorists had probably seen the helipad there and figured it was near the secretary of defense's office . . . fortunately, their intelligence was as bad as their flying, because the secretary's office is on the river side . . . and the point of impact was mostly vacant."

Still, 189 people died in the Pentagon that morning, most of them trapped in the basement. I wasn't used to worrying about my family—it was their job to fret about me. My dad had quit flying fighters when I was a kid, so I never really had to be concerned about it. I was even less thrilled when I found out that the remains of Flight 77 had penetrated all the way into the B Ring and missed my father by less than thirty yards. That feeling of helplessness sums up the day for me. The fighting end of the military is accustomed to living under threats. That's what we do. America is supposed to be a nice, relatively safe place for folks to go about their lives, and suddenly it wasn't. I felt somehow that we'd let everyone down because these attacks occurred. It's a ridiculous thought, but then again, it was a strange day.

Later that night, a bit after midnight on September 12, the klaxon shook me out of my cot in the alert building at Shaw Air Force Base, South Carolina. Eight minutes later, I was rocketing down the runway in the rain and trying to wake up. As I got airborne in the pitch-black night sky and slapped up my landing gear, the radio broke out on the safety Guard frequency.

"All aircraft within range of this transmission, all aircraft in range of this transmission . . . this is Charlotte air traffic control . . . declaring a free-fire zone for twenty miles around Charlotte."

I blinked. What?

"Repeat . . . Charlotte air traffic control declaring a free-fire zone for twenty miles around Charlotte!"

What the fuck?!

I was fully awake now.

"Charlotte . . . this is FANG 69 . . . flight of two Fox-16s out of Shaw. What's up?"

"Thank God! FANG . . . this is Charlotte!" He sounded out of breath. " . . . we've got . . . unidentified hostile aircraft . . . maybe terrorists . . . I'm declaring a free-fire zone for twenty miles around the Charlotte airport!"

I swallowed, blinked again, took a deep, deep breath, then keyed the mike.

"No you're not."

My air-to-air radar was scanning from the ground up to maybe 30,000 feet. And I saw nothing. "All aircraft on this freq disregard Charlotte's last transmission. FANG 69 is now the on-scene commander in the Charlotte area . . . all aircraft on this freq check in."

No one answered. Big surprise.

Then, on the intra-flight Victor radio, I said to my wingman, "FANG 2 . . . do NOT arm up."

"FANG . . . this is Charlotte . . . we've got suspicious helicopters operating in our area!"

Helicopters? So al-Qaeda had helos now? Didn't think so.

"*Why* are they suspicious?" Leveling off at 20,000 feet, I pulled the power back to hold 400 knots and glanced at the radar. A few days ago it would've been full of contacts, but tonight it was empty.

"FANG . . . uh . . . they're not operating with lights . . . and they won't answer our calls . . . and we've had reports of men . . . uh . . . jumping off to the ground."

I thought I could see where this was going, and I needed to stop the madness. Quickly.

"Charlotte, did you bother calling Fort Bragg?"

The long, pregnant pause said it all, so I switched freqs and called up the Shaw AFB command post.

"Shaw, FANG 69 . . . request."

"Go ahead."

"Get on the landline and call Fort Bragg. Find out what kind of air activity they've got going tonight and don't let 'em give you any covert-ops BS. Tell them there are armed fighters overhead and if they want their helos back in one piece then they need to 'fess up with locations and call signs."

Fort Bragg, just east of Charlotte, happened to be home to the 82nd Airborne Division and the U.S. Special Operations Command. These people got paid to skulk around with no lights and no communications while performing suspicious-looking acts. At least suspicious to the uninitiated, which this guy plainly was. Turned out, that was exactly what was going on, proving again that we are our own worst enemy.

A few days later, the approach controller at Atlanta's Hartsfield airport asked me if I'd make a low pass over downtown Atlanta for morale. A show of force to reassure the folks that all was well. I was astounded. Downtown Atlanta? But we did, at a thousand feet over the skyscrapers, with the speed brakes out so we could plug in our afterburners and make more noise. He asked us to come around again and later told me people were crying and smiling in the streets.

That week affected me in an unexpected way. I mean, *we* were used to taking chances and were prepared, mentally and physically, to fight. But the average American is not, and I saw real fear on my neighbors' faces. All my naive but generous, self-centered but well-meaning countrymen had gotten slapped in the face. Hijackers are cowards. In my opinion, true terrorists are all cowards. That's what the label means: they inspire terror by preying on the weak and defenseless, as they have no chance in a stand-up fight against armed men. Every fighter pilot I knew was extremely angry about this and would've gone to war immediately, given the chance.

This passed. It obviously wasn't our failure, and the wonderful American resilience to catastrophe began emerging quickly enough. The realization that we were not universally loved and admired sank in to our national consciousness, and America seemed to give a collective shrug. Okay, you don't love us, and we don't care. But you did awaken the sleeping giant and now you'll pay for it.

American flags began flying everywhere, stores gave military discounts, and a countrywide "Support the Troops" movement gathered momentum. Many Americans still didn't really understand the military or the larger world around them, but they were trying to learn and show their appreciation. Even those who didn't believe in war protested the government and not those doing the fighting.

The ghosts of Vietnam were finally laid to rest. I think the realization dawned that we were not simply fighting an ideology, as with Nazi Germany or the Soviet version of communism. No, this time we were up against a religious fanaticism that was irrevocably and fundamentally opposed to everything we stood for or valued. Fanatics, of any creed, are dangerous, and there would be no compromise possible with the type of men who would kill helpless strangers. For the first time I could remember, America was more or less united against a common foe and motivated toward a shared cause of protecting the nation. This cause, right or wrong, would serve as the *casus belli* for dealing with Saddam once and for all.

AS THE 77TH FIGHTER SQUADRON THUNDERED OUT OF OUR base in South Carolina on Valentine's Day 2003, more than a month before the invasion, we were ready. Bound for Prince Sultan Air Base, Saudi Arabia, we stopped overnight at Morón Air Base in Spain. Once there, we were sent to a hotel in downtown Seville to catch a few hours sleep. A public-relations officer, an officious little weenie who likely never left the base, told us to stay in our hotel—for our own safety. All thirty of us just looked at him and burst out laughing. What an idiotic thing to say to a fighter squadron on its way to war. Needless to say, late that afternoon I found myself wandering around this most charming of Spanish cities looking for the Cathedral of St. Mary. Strolling through the Alcazar Gardens, I noticed the city seemed remarkably quiet and relatively deserted. I thought I just got lucky. Coming around a corner onto the Calle Vida, however, I heard the sound of drums and the thumping of thousands of feet.

Now, the University of Seville was barely a quarter mile south, and it was a definite hotbed of antiwar protest. But I'd come to see the church and its famous bell tower and had no intention of walking through the university. That would've been like cutting through UC Berkeley in 1968 wearing a uniform. So I ducked into an alley next to the Alcazar—and came out face to face with a marching mob. Like most protesters, they looked young. The majority of them were also waving flags. All red. Banners, too. Hundreds of banners showing caricatures of George Bush and Tony Blair; crossed-out NATO symbols, American and British flags, and one very ugly Uncle Sam with his foot on the globe. They were chanting, too.

"*No a la Guerra! No a la Guerra!*"

"No to the war" . . . and there I was.

I got caught up in the flow, like a swimmer in a strong current, and simply rolled through the dusky old streets with the rest of them. After a few twists and turns we shot out into the bright sunlight, the crowd thinning as it filled the square. Blinking, I slid sideways to put my back against a wall and looked up, startled, at the sandstone-colored tower next to me. La Giralda; a minaret that survived the destruction of the Seville mosque and was now a Catholic bell tower. Glancing around then, I knew exactly where I was—the Plaza del Triunfo in front of the cathedral. The square had filled quickly and I saw news crews scattered about, big cameras panning back and forth over the crowd. What a terrific headline that would make, I thought.

AMERICAN FIGHTER PILOT JOINS ANTIWAR RALLY IN SPAIN.

Then I saw her.

A young girl, maybe twenty, with long, black hair blowing in the breeze. She'd jumped up on one of the concrete piers lining the sidewalk and was holding an immense red flag. The sun was behind her, and the flag was made of thin material, because I could see through it. The girl had on an oversize white blouse, a dark, loose skirt, and no shoes. As I watched, she began waving the flag slowly back and forth. All the people at the base of her piling began chanting and the girl smiled. It was, in retrospect, a true Kodak moment. I watched for a few seconds then turned to slip away— directly in front of a BBC camera filming the girl. Without hesitating, I raised my fist and yelled, *"No a la Guerra!"* before gliding off into the crowd.

I eventually made it back to the hotel and never told anyone about it. As we took off the next day for the bleak, cultural void of Saudi Arabia, the irony was plain. I, who would shortly be leading dozens of aircraft in combat, had taken part in one of the biggest antiwar rallies in Europe. Fortunately, nothing ever came of it, and, in fact, I did get to see the cathedral after all, my last bit of beauty for a few months, which was nice.

I stood outside our operations trailer in Prince Sultan Air Base and breathed in deeply. The heavy Saudi air was very still but I could plainly smell the desert—dust, smoke, and a very faint trace of distant rain. Twilight was always fast in Arabia; the painful, fiery shield of the sun darkened to deep orange, then to blood red as it slid beneath the horizon.

War was here.

Thinking back to Desert Storm, I couldn't recall feeling any fear. I'd stood in my room, listened to the *Phantom of the Opera* soundtrack, and waited for the call. When it had come, I felt a release—no more waiting. A day later, climbing up the ladder into my F-16 before my first combat mission, I was only afraid of screwing up. Of letting down those who depended on me. Years of extensive and unforgiving training had winnowed out the weak and given us all the quiet confidence of true professionals. I knew I could do it—but you never really know.

Dying didn't occur to me at all in 1991. I thought I was invincible back then, so what could happen?

Well, some of that attitude changed over the years. Lots of very talented, skilled guys never came back. Fractions of seconds had separated me from oblivion literally thousands of times. Countless *extremely* close calls have humbled my belief in invincibility. Obviously there's no such thing—maybe my inexplicable survival is God's sense of humor. Or it's just not my time. Or both.

As I stared at the fading sunset in 2002, I'd been tempered with a great deal of hard-won experience. Now, waiting to fight, it was the haunting strains of "Vide Cor Meum" instead of the *Phantom,* and my thoughts were somewhat different than they'd been in 1991. I was responsible for many more lives this time, and any mistakes I made would have implications far beyond my solitary cockpit. This didn't bother me—I was thoroughly accustomed to the responsibility by this point in my career. Still, holding lives in your hands is sobering.

My country had also been attacked. I was well aware that 9/11 was not the real reason we were here waiting to surge across the Iraqi border, but to me it was a vindication nonetheless. This war, I hoped, would be an object lesson to all of those who thought America had received a comeuppance on that September morning. Regardless of the political permutations of this fight, we would show the world again that our political dithering had nothing to do with our military might. Like us or not. Hate us or love us, it didn't matter. If an enemy struck the United States, then they would pay for it in blood and I, along with every fighting man facing north this evening, was here to collect.

Intermission was over.

7

SHOCK AND AWE

March 19, 2003
0530 local time, south of Baghdad

"STOIC 67, SAM IN THE AIR . . . SAM IN THE AIR SOUTHWEST-bound over Baghdad!"

I rolled hard to the right and smoothly pulled back on the stick. The SAM was a flaming dot rising out of the predawn city lights, gathering speed and climbing. I wasn't certain it was locked on me, because my threat-warning display was already alphabet soup. This was hardly surprising: I was just south of Baghdad, and the Iraqis were royally pissed off. We were leading the invasion of Iraq—"the tip of the spear."

"BEEP . . . BEEP . . . BEEP . . ."

The warning receiver woke up, and I glanced at the small screen. It was covered with overlapping signals from SA-3s, SA-2s, Triple-A, and friendly airborne radars from our own fighters. Basically, the entire electronic spectrum was up and running. There were also lots of UNKNOWN symbols, meaning my system couldn't decide whether the incoming signal was hostile or friendly. Based on their northerly direction, I assumed they were all hostile, since there were no friendly aircraft between me and Baghdad.

Terrific.

I immediately pulled the F-16 around to the east and streamed out a decoy just in case. The missile plume stayed visible; it was flying a fairly flat, very fast trajectory. Snapping upright, I pushed the throttle forward to mil power and stared at the SAM. Suddenly, from the corner of my right eye, I saw two more disembodied flames clear the dark horizon.

"STOIC One has two SA-3s . . . westbound out of Baghdad."

If they were SA-2s, they'd have gone much higher, like a shuttle launch, and disappeared. Once the sustainer burned out, the missile dove down from 80,000 feet or so and was completely invisible—until it smashed you to pieces. Very nasty bastards. SA-3s were easier to detect, but they were also much quicker and harder to shake.

"STOIC One, multiple SAM launches, Baghdad . . . heads-up MOXIE!"

Somewhere behind me in the western darkness, I heard the other flight lead zipper his mike. Unlike during peacetime operations, we flew almost exclusively "comm out." That is, without the usual chatter on the radios. Some of this was professionalism but most of it was efficiency. With three hundred airplanes using the same few frequencies, you had to limit conversations to the bare minimum. This meant combat. Missile launches, target locations, or, God forbid, search and rescue.

Modern fighters all had a second, and sometimes a third, radio that was used for inter-flight chitchat. Not that there was much of it. All fighter squadrons had "standards." A hopefully short list of mundane items that we would all do the same way. The Gamblers were very good about this. We'd refined all the extraneous stuff to the point where you only really spoke as an exception. Everything else was just done by the Big Boy Book of Rules.

Then the first SAM stopped streaking west. It hung in space between the city and the stars, and I caught myself holding my breath for a moment. SAM launched. But who was the target? The flames were enormous. I was ten miles away but could plainly see the long, fiery tails; white-hot and fuzzy near the end, the plume became darker and almost red where it touched the missile. The missiles were invisible, of course, but you knew where they were, because that's where the fire stopped. Nothing moved faster across the sky than a surface-to-air missile.

Even after the rocket boosters burned out, the eerie disembodied red flames raced across the black sky looking for targets. You didn't start worrying until you saw the flaming doughnut—a red-orange ring of fire with a dark hole in the middle. This was the SAM and it was pointed right at you.

"Shit . . ." I muttered and thumbed on my Electronic Countermeasures pod. Pushing the nose over, I kept my eyes padlocked on the SA-3 as it turned and pointed at me.

"Heads-up STOIC Two . . . SAM at ten o'clock high . . . stand by . . ."

I thumbed the data-link switch over, heard the "tickle" in my helmet, and saw that my wingman was about two miles behind and to the right of me. Twisting in the seat, I looked back over the tail but saw nothing. It didn't matter. Unlike previous rigid, communications-intensive tactics, we'd evolved into a much simpler mind-set. Modern technology helped—instead of asking where my wingman was, I could send a data-link position request. I also always hated the inflexible, line-abreast formations that we'd been trained with. They didn't work in combat, because if you flew in straight lines you were just asking for a missile up your butt.

In combat, I used a "loose deuce" formation almost exclusively. This puts a wingman on a two-mile string, allowing him to maneuver at will as long as he didn't lose sight of the flight lead and could maintain all of his other responsibilities. These included working his air-to-air radar, visually scanning for MiGs and SAMs and keeping an eye on his aircraft systems. He only spoke when he had something tactical to say. I, as the leader, just flew where I had to and didn't have to think about his position much. In the event we had to react tactically to a threat, we were already spread out nicely. It worked well.

Just then the rocket's flaming trail burned out, so I immediately pushed the nose farther down and began counting, my eyes locked to the HUD. Night-threat reactions while wearing NVGs aren't generally the high-G, aerobatic maneuvers they are during the day. That's because there's a very real possibility of becoming disoriented without your normal flying references. Ten miles south of Baghdad, at night, with a half-dozen SAMs in the air, is no place to lose control of a fighter.

Six . . . seven. . .

Pulling hard back to the right, I pumped out several chaff bundles.

"STOIC One and Two, heading zero-eight-zero . . . defending SA-3 . . ."

The response from the other two-ship was immediate. "MOXIE One . . . Magnum, SA-3, Baghdad."

"STOIC Two is blind at eighteen K!"

Ten . . . eleven . . .

"STOIC Two come south and stay above eighteen."

Twelve . . .

Up on my left wingtip now, I yanked the fighter back toward the city in a constant, five-G barrel roll and punched out a few more chaff bundles. Rolling wings level, I was pointed straight at the city and dropping through 15,000 feet. In the subdued green glow of the cockpit, my eyes flickered to the master-arm switch then to the HUD. A big cross was squarely in the middle, and I used it to point the jet and the HARM at the glowing spot on the ground where the SAM had launched. Shutting my left eye, I mashed down on the pickle button and the jet shook as the 800-pound missile shot off the rail. Instantly cranking up on one wing, I sliced back south in a six-G descending turn.

"STOIC One . . . Magnum, SA-3, Baghdad."

There was so much shit down there that calling out an exact position would be a waste of time. We'd been ordered to stay ten miles outside the city, so I came around heading west to put more distance between us and the threats. If the first SAM had been able to guide, it would've hit me by now.

"STOIC Two is visual." How could he not see me after that HARM launch?

"Fighting wing . . . stay locked." Meaning he'd use his air-to-air radar to stay tied to me. I doubted there'd be MiGs tonight, but the sky was full of F-16s and F-15s if any Iraqi down there had a bravery attack. My four-ship was split into pairs, each operating independently. If you drew a north-south line through Baghdad, my Number Three man and his wingman had everything west of the line, and I had the east. MOXIE was also starting in a higher-altitude block, 25,000–29,000 feet, while I took 15,000–19,000. When the shit hit the fan, all of this would generally go out the window, but you had to start somewhere.

AT FIFTEEN MILES OUT, WE TURNED AND BEGAN ARCING northwest around the city. As we did, like thousands of flashbulbs going off in a dark room, the Baghdad air defenses came violently to life. Angry streams of tracers spurted up against the black sky. Rising from all directions, they flattened out against the stars before curving downward and disappearing. Bigger anti-aircraft fire, 100-mm and above, shot straight up in orange and red clusters before exploding. Yellows, greens, and even a few red tracers spat out from ten thousand guns and covered the city in a pulsating, multicolored net.

Neighborhood by neighborhood, from the outer suburbs in, went black as the power grids shut down. Searchlights waved across the sky, adding white to the Technicolor display, like something from a World War II movie. I could tell where the outskirts of Baghdad were by the SAM launches. Massive white flames briefly illuminated roads and buildings as more missiles ignited.

"Son of a bitch . . ." I whispered.

Yellow flashes began popping all over the city. American bombs. Ugly, mustard-colored detonations immediately changed to red and then faded—or mushroomed into bigger explosions if something flammable was hit.

Keying the Victor radio, I said, "Now we know why we had to stay ten miles outside the city."

"STOIC One . . . this is Two. What the hell is that?" He sounded excited and I smiled. I'd seen this before.

"Cruise missile strike. Tomahawks."

It was over in a few minutes and fires burned bright in dozens of places. Other missile impacts looked like dull red pimples on a black face as they slowly fizzled out. Then the Triple-A and SAMS started up again.

"STOIC One . . . tally missile launch . . . southeast Baghdad," I added.

"MOXIE is tally."

Even as I watched, the fiery plume got stubbier and I realized the missile was turning in our direction. Frowning, I pushed the throttle up and felt the jet accelerate.

"MOXIE One is tally one . . . no, two . . . spiked from the west."

I looked and saw at least two more SAMs lift off from the center of the city.

"STOIC One . . . attacking SA-3 from the south."

I went to full mil power and pointed directly at the launch site. Hesitating a half-second, I saw my camera was on, looked at the switch again, and checked the selected weapon. I closed my right eye this time and pickled.

A brilliant flash lit up the cockpit and left an orange smudge under my right eyelid. The jet kicked a little as the missile accelerated, and I fought the urge to stare. As the anti-radiation missile pitched up, I stared down at Baghdad, opened my eye, and pulled hard away to the right.

Even as I moved, the closest anti-aircraft fire shifted and began shooting in my general direction. They were aiming at the flash, which was precisely why you changed directions as soon as you fired. Another reason not to carry a HARM. But tonight it was all we had.

"MOXIE One . . . defending . . . uh . . . west. SA-3," he added.

MOXIE One had never seen combat but was an experienced F-16 flight lead. In fact, none of the other members of this flight were combat veterans. Surprisingly, there were very few of us remaining who'd fought in either Desert Storm or Kosovo, though half our pilots had been into Iraq before, between the wars. So each four-ship was at least led by a combat veteran.

"STOIC One . . . Magnum SA-3 . . . Baghdad south."

I dumped the nose and picked up speed. Northeast-bound now, I was slowly arcing around the city. The 100-knot wind from the west actually helped, because it was trying to push me away from

Baghdad, not into it. Up off the nose, there were lights on the ground from little towns, so I knew I was approaching the Tigris River.

"MOXIE One . . . updating three-zero-zero . . ."

"MOXIE Two is blind . . ."

I pictured it in my head. MOXIE was continuing to defend himself and was passing through northwest, or 300 degrees. His wingman had just lost sight of him—not uncommon at night, when you're getting shot at—and was "blind." I zippered the mike, then spoke, twisting around in the seat as I did.

"STOIC Two . . . Slapshot SA-3 bearing two-nine-zero . . ."

In the greenish-white circles of my night-vision goggles, I saw a gray shape glide across my tail and point northwest. Looking forward again quickly, I came around to the same heading, so we were running parallel to each other about three miles apart. From the corner of my eye, I saw the flash as my wingman fired another HARM at the site that was shooting at MOXIE.

"STOIC Two . . . Magnum SA-3!"

"Come off south," I commanded immediately and watched him reverse his turn away from me. We ended up in trail, me behind him, heading away from the city. I crossed his tail, sent a data-link, and weaved back to the west.

"STOIC Two . . . come back right . . . one's at right, two o'clock . . . three miles, low."

I heard the tickle from his radar a few seconds later and saw the familiar Viper spike behind me. With radars, data-links, and night vision, I wasn't too concerned about my guys getting lost. Looking back between Baghdad and the western blackness, where MOXIE was, I couldn't see the missiles. I wasn't optimistic that the HARMs had actually hit anything, but they might've forced the SAM targeting radars off the air.

"STOIC and MOXIE, push back to Alex."

"Alex" was a pre-briefed rejoin point beyond the reach of most of Baghdad's air defenses. I always briefed such a point in case we needed a safe place to get together. It was also used as a fallback position in the event of an aircraft emergency or radio failure. Floating comfortably between the unfriendly earth below and the stars above, I stared up through the canopy at the sky. The stars were brilliant, like millions of wet diamonds on a black quilt. Beyond number.

0535 IN THE MORNING OF MARCH 19, 2003. WE HAD JUST started the Second Gulf War.

STOIC 67 and MOXIE 71 were four F-16CJs originally tasked to be on station in Killbox 87 Alpha Sierra south of Baghdad. The old demarcation was called the Line, the 32nd Parallel, and this had just been rescinded so we could roam all the way up to Saddam's front door. The main idea of this was to divert the Iraqi air defenses, including any MiGs, onto us, because we knew something the Iraqis had just figured out. The war was officially beginning tonight. In fact, it just had. Operation Iraqi Freedom. I realized I was breathing a little hard, and chuckled.

Flying at night was the best time to Weasel, in my opinion. Seeing the stuff that was being shot at you was the biggest advantage. Nighttime also made optical launches nearly impossible for the bad guys. Of course, defensive reactions were much more difficult, because you lacked the normal daylight visual cues. A pilot could fly through the green world of night-vision goggles, but that picture was often washed out by too much light. Oil fires, the moon, and any explosion would ruin an NVG picture for a few seconds.

There was also really no air threat at night. At least not in Iraq. Their MiGs were doing well to get off the ground during the day,

Undergraduate Pilot Training graduation, 1987. Welcome to the USAF.

TopGun clipping. All fighter wings have these competitions, and this was my first win.

Lt. Hampton earns F-16 Topgun honors

Lt. Dan Hampton of Rockwall was recently named F-16 Topgun in the 23rd Tactical Fighter Squadron's air-to-air dogfighting competition. The competition encompasses every ACT (Air Combat Training) flight during the previous six months. Each pilot's missile and gun shots as well as tactical ability is evaluated and rated.

Each fighter pilot must meet certain qualifications every six months to remain in combat ready status. This includes all air to air and air to ground attack events.

The fighter pilot who scores the highest in each category is named his squadron's Topgun. Each squadron Topgun then competes against other squadron's winners to become the fighter wing Topgun.

In September, in addition to winning the Topgun trophy, Lt. Hampton was promoted to the rank of Captain, USAF. He is currently stationed in Germany and is the son of Mr. and Mrs. Dan Hampton of Rockwall.

Lt. Dan Hampton

Germany, 1990. Every bachelor fighter pilot should have a fast car. This Porsche became my favorite toy—next to an F-16, of course.

Inbound SCUD missile being destroyed by a Patriot battery at the start of Desert Storm, 1991.

23rd Tactical Fighter Squadron "Fighting Hawks" Hunter Killer team ready for takeoff in the first Gulf War. (See chapter 3.)

French-built "indestructible" bunker used by the Iraqis and destroyed courtesy of the U.S. Air Force.

After the first daylight raid into Baghdad during Desert Storm.

Self-portrait during a surface-to-air-missile (SAM) hunt in northern Iraq, 1991.

Blood chit. If we were shot down over enemy territory, these were used to tell any locals that we were the "good guys," and if they helped us to safety they'd be well paid.

Beni Suef, Egypt, 1992. A shot of me during my exchange with the 242nd Tactical Fighter Wing of the Egyptian Air Force. (See chapter 4.)

Left: Leading a mission into Iraq, 2003. We were the first over the border in Operation Iraqi Freedom. (See chapter 7.) *Right:* Inside the F-16 CJ cockpit.

A shot of me leading a four ship following a strike into Iraq, 2003. Note the empty weapons pylons under the wings. The picture was taken by a friend from inside the air-refueling tanker.

Air refueling is absolutely essential for fighter combat operations, as we burn up fuel very quickly.

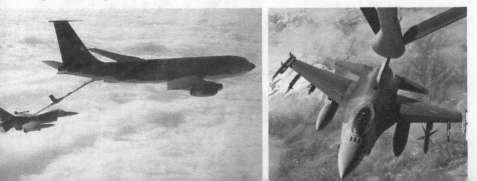

With my favorite SAM-killing weapon—the cluster bomb. This one is personalized for my wife and daughter; it killed an anti-aircraft artillery nest.

Baghdad reeling from Shock and Awe, 2003.

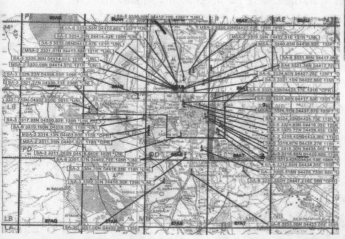

A map of the known SAM sites around Baghdad in the early days of the second Iraq War. There were at least as many "unlocated" sites. In any event, it was our job to kill them all.

In Kuwait following the Nasiriyah mission. I tried to save some surrounded Marines by strafing an Iraqi armored column that had cut them off. The haze is left over from a gigantic sandstorm. (See the prologue and chapter 8.)

Me and LTC Scott "Zing" Manning—call sign ELI 33—after we destroyed Saddam Hussein's escape helicopters in Baghdad, April 7, 2003. (See chapter 11.)

77th Fighter Squadron "Gamblers" at Prince Sultan Air Base, Saudi Arabia, 2003. We were going home the next day! That's the Gamblers' patch in the upper left: "All Aces, No Jokers." Along with the 23rd Fighting Hawks, with whom I served in the first Gulf War, these were the finest fighter squadrons in the USAF.

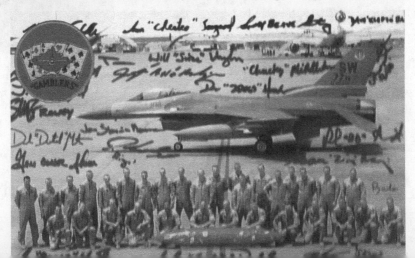

After the SAMbush mission in Baghdad. Note the dark stains around the 20-mm cannon port over my head from repeated strafing. (See chapter 10.)

Like father, like son . . . Me and my dad, Colonel Dan Hampton, USMC (Ret.), A-4 Skyhawk attack pilot.

It's impossible not to look good next to a hot fighter jet and a hot woman—my beautiful wife, Beth.

and if they did fly at night, they'd be completely dependent on ground radar control, which we had targeted and decimated. Night was also better for escape and evasion. If you ejected, then at least you weren't floating down in plain sight of every armed peasant within 50 miles. Tonight, 200 miles deep into enemy territory and trying to attract SAMs, this was a real concern.

Twelve years earlier, I'd been in these very skies, getting shot at by the same people. Economics, geopolitics, national defense, revenge . . . you could take your pick of any number of reasons why I was once again ordered north of the 32nd Parallel to kill Iraqis. The real reason was that both sides wanted a war.

Saddam Hussein, beset within by rebellious Kurds and increasingly disillusioned military officers, opted for the time-honored strategy of solving domestic troubles through an external threat. He figured that if he could provoke the United States into action, then other Islamic countries would fall in line and fight to throw us out. This was a predictable and naive approach. But then, Saddam was basically a street punk who'd risen to power by animal cunning and sheer ruthlessness. As with most dictators, he lacked a real grasp of the world beyond his own little arena and mistook his domestic dominance for global significance.

I'd always thought that the First Gulf War must've shocked Saddam. He'd been a U.S. ally during the 1980s. The Reagan White House had even removed Iraq from the State Sponsors of Terrorism list in 1982 so we could transfer dual-use technology to Baghdad. "Dual use" means it can be, and usually is, used for peaceful or military purposes. For instance, the same nuclear reactor that provides power also generates plutonium as a by-product. Plutonium is fissile and can be then utilized to produce nuclear weapons. Dual use.

Saddam Hussein had also received agricultural credits, weapons, and intelligence from America to support his war against Iran.

His vicious rise to power had been generally ignored beyond the Middle East until the shah of Iran fell. The United States needed a new proxy to counter Soviet-supplied Arab nations, and Saddam wanted to be the man. He was even made an honorary citizen of Detroit in 1980—not bad for a fatherless thug from an ugly, dusty town in Iraq.

EARLY THIS VERY MORNING, THE CIA HAD BELIEVED SADDAM Hussein and his two sons were spending the night at a secure complex in southeast Baghdad. Dora Farms lay just below a horseshoe-shaped bend of the Tigris River and less than ten miles east of the international airport. So, the detailed war plan that we'd all studied (OPLAN 1003V) was thrown entirely out in favor of this "hot" last-minute intelligence. The rationale was that if the Iraqi leadership was wiped out, then there would be no war.

Now we were past all the theorizing. My four-ship had been cleared north past The Line (the 32nd Parallel), and we were jabbing at the fringes of Baghdad's air defenses. Armed with HARMs, we'd charge in by pairs at the outer ring of SAM batteries. As soon as we got spiked, we'd split apart and both run perpendicular to the SA-2s and SA-3s. By turning sideways, we made it harder for their radars to hold their locks so they had to stay on-air longer. This gave our systems a better chance of ranging them in and providing a targeting solution. It also decreased the SAM firing range considerably, as we weren't closing the distance by flying directly at the site.

When we'd taken off four hours earlier, no one had a timeline on the Dora strike, since no final approval had been given. So we just hung around 200 miles inside Iraq, air-refueling every hour, until Washington and the Pentagon made up their minds—which they did at 7:12 P.M. Eastern Standard Time. Minutes later, a flight of F-117s, based from al-Udeid in Qatar, crossed into Iraq, awaiting clearance to drop four tons of bombs on Saddam's head. A CIA asset inside Baghdad passed the word that the Iraqi dictator was inside his bunker, and at 5:31 A.M., Baghdad time, the southern suburbs rattled as the Dora complex suddenly disappeared. Utterly undetected, the stealth fighters headed back south, leaving the angry and bewildered Iraqis shooting at empty sky. And the Weasels.

Since then, armchair generals, strategists, and the "think-tankers," who analyze things to death, have all gone back and forth on the Dora Farms operation. The supporters contend that a "decapitation" of the Iraqi leadership would have caused great confusion and likely prevented the war. I think they're half-right. There would have been great confusion, but I think the Iraqis would've still fought. In fact, it might have even been a harder fight, with professional soldiers running the war and Saddam out of the way. Not that the outcome would have changed.

Detractors say that the attack forfeited the element of surprise and made the initial phase of the invasion more difficult. Again, half-right, in my opinion. I would suggest that our 450,000 troops and several hundred combat aircraft had somewhat clued in the Iraqi High Command that we were coming. Exactly *when* was problematic. And irrelevant. I couldn't have cared less if the Iraqis knew the exact minute of our opening strike, because there wasn't anything they could do to stop it.

In fact, after the Dora Farm strike, British and American ground forces moved north into Iraq and captured the Rumaila oil field. Splitting up then, the Americans moved northwest toward Nasiriyah, and the Brits headed northeast into Basra. More than thirty American special-ops teams, with their British and Australian counterparts, infiltrated Iraq that day.

It's also possible that the strike generated enough confusion to disrupt whatever plans Saddam and his generals had made. These plans certainly included launching Scuds at Israel. If that had occurred, followed by Israeli retaliation, who knows what kind of a mess would've ensued. I really don't think Syria and Egypt would've attacked Israel. At least, not with all of us deployed to the Middle East. This was Saddam's big hope, of course, but, like so many of his other thoughts, it was nonsensical. Whatever else might have happened, the air strikes immediately following the Dora blast did knock the Iraqis off balance and put them on the defense from the beginning.

This is always a good thing to do to your enemy at the start of a fight.

"BEEP . . . BEEP . . ."

I glanced down and saw the "3" blink on my scope. But there were about six of them, and they were far enough away to not worry me.

Suddenly a string of explosions ripped through the darkness of downtown Baghdad. Maybe B-52s or more Tomahawk missiles from the Navy in the Gulf—I didn't know, but the anti-aircraft fire became positively surreal.

Tens of thousands of Triple-A rounds shot angrily upward. The large-caliber stuff made it level with me and exploded. But they even fired the smaller guns—rapid-fire hoses of yellows and oranges that arced low over the ground and detonated. Most of it was firing for effect and rage. No doubt tomorrow Radio Baghdad would declare hundreds of American warplanes shot down. It was all bullshit, of course, but it boosted Iraqi morale.

Zippering the mike, I came around to the right and snapped wings level. We were now directly south of the city by twenty-five miles and heading east. Searchlights were sweeping overhead in a vain attempt to catch a fighter or a B-52. Running my eyes over the cockpit, I saw I'd used about a third of my chaff and my wing tanks were empty. The decoy was still with me, and the warning receiver looked like a Scrabble board. I took a deep breath and exhaled. It could be a lot worse. It—

"BEEP . . . BEEP . . . BEEP . . ."

My eyes locked on the display. SA-3. Close!

Reacting instantly, I rolled inverted and pulled straight down into the blackness, pumping out chaff bundles.

"STOIC One . . . defending SA-3 . . . close!"

Iraq was black—except for the parts that were burning, that is. There I was, upside down, at night, over enemy territory. The Viper's nose was pointed straight down and I was hanging in my seat facing the brightly lit Iranian border.

"STOIC One . . . break! SAM under you . . . break!"

Slapping the throttle to IDLE, my right wrist strained against the stick and the fighter pirouetted. Spinning 180 degrees in about two seconds, I pulled hard on the stick while smacking the chaff button with the back of my left hand and began counting.

"C'mon . . ." I muttered as the jet fought gravity to come back up through the horizon. Slamming the throttle forward, I kept pulling and looked back for the SAM. As the F-16's nose came through the horizon, I pushed the throttle into full afterburner.

"STOIC 2 . . . Ma . . . Magnum SA-3!"

Poor kid sounded like he was being strangled, but he got the HARM off. I caught an absurdly bright flash, and for a split second I saw the pointed nose of an F-16 before the darkness swallowed it again.

Two. . .

My head swiveled like it was on a stick. But without seeing the launch, I didn't know what direction the damn thing had gone, and so I had no real idea where it was coming in from.

"STOIC Two . . . any posit on the missile?"

Four. . .

"Negative . . . lost it . . . Two is blind!"

Perfect.

Sixty degrees nose high, I was pointing back up at the stars. Pulling the throttle back to IDLE, I again flipped onto my back and stared at the sky. Nothing. Pumping out more chaff, I glanced at the HUD. Nineteen thousand feet and 390 knots.

"STOIC Two . . . come south above twenty K."

"MOXIE are southbound . . . Bingo."

Pirouetting again, I pulled the fighter around to the south and leveled off at 17,000 feet, panting hard. The RWR mercifully shut up, and I dropped my mask to let the cool air hit me in the face. Glancing at my multifunction display (MFD), I decided not to thread the needle down the MiG bases along the Euphrates River. Not because of the Iraqi Air Force, but because the air bases all had SAM rings. So MOXIE and STOIC came around southwest and headed in the shortest direction to the Saudi border. Maybe, I thought, if we refueled we could go back in and go MiG-hunting.

Wiping my face, I sat back in the seat and looked at the rapidly graying sky as sunrise approached. The more I thought of it, the more I believed that last SAM had been a false alarm. Rocking my wingman in for a battle-damage check, I keyed the mike. "STOIC and MOXIE . . . cut the Dog loose." Meaning, sever any decoys. Looking in my HUD, however, I saw that my decoy was already gone, and I took a deep breath.

That last SA-3 had been real after all.

AFTER LANDING BACK AT PRINCE SULTAN AIR BASE, WE IMME-diately began planning to continue the Shock and Awe campaign.

Contrary to popular belief, this neat little phrase wasn't invented in 2003. In fact, it had been formalized in 1996 as a military doctrine based on the use of "overwhelming decisive force," "dominant battlefield awareness," "dominant maneuvers," and "spectacular displays of power" to "paralyze" an adversary's perception of the battlefield and destroy his will to fight.

Okay.

Every battle or firefight I'd been in was like that, but someone now had to put a name to it. I think it appealed to the self-perception of American military and political leaders. They correctly saw our military capability as overwhelming, ultimately unstoppable (if utilized properly), and downright frightening. What they screwed up, and seem to always get wrong, are enemy reactions to our force. American leaders assume whoever we're fighting will simply lift their skirts and run away. This doesn't always happen, however. Chances are, when your nation is attacked, you'll forget about everything else but defending your country and your family. Unless, of course, you're French. Then you surrender and eat cheese. (Good cheese, I must say.)

If the United States was invaded, I don't think people would give a damn how the guy next to them voted in the last election—they'd simply fight. American reactions to the September 11 attacks are a perfect example.

Planning on the other guy's capitulation is also a dangerous way to start a fight.

In any event, the war was rolling. The following day, the ground invasion began in earnest as U.S. Marines, Brits, and Poles attacked the port of Umm Qasr. The 3rd Infantry Division and the 1st Marine Expeditionary Force would enter southern Iraq on their way north. The heavy air campaign resumed on March 21.

Shock and Awe. In a twist of fate, it was the shock and awe of 9/11 that had provided the outward legitimacy for this war. We named it counterterrorism. Neighboring Arab countries would now call the invasion of Iraq an act of terrorism. Just goes to show you, the battlefield winner gets to write the slogans regardless of who triumphs in the end.

SHOCK AND AWE HAD BEGUN IN EARNEST, AND I WAS GLAD. The sooner it started, the sooner we'd win and could all go home. Walking outside our operations trailer, I stood there in the morning sun. My sweaty flight suit had long since dried, and I smelled stale. I yawned and rubbed my fingertips against the stubble under my chin. The door slammed behind me and the Gambler squadron commander, my good friend Storm'n Norman, stepped out.

"Breakfast?" I asked.

"Rather not. Been sick today already."

I chuckled. The Wild Weasels were at war again.

8

SANDSTORM

SOUTH OF NASIRIYAH, I PASSED 20,000 FEET, NOSED THE fighter over, and gratefully pulled the throttle back. The steering was already called up to the Dog air-refueling track, and as the airspeed dropped, I selected the maximum-endurance mode. This would give me an ideal altitude and airspeed to arrive at my selected point with minimum fuel. We used it a lot, because F-16s were always running short of gas. I continued pulling the throttle back until the airspeed matched the little V-shaped caret next to my airspeed readout in the HUD.

Two hundred and five knots.

So slow it felt like stalling. I ran my eyes over the cockpit and quickly flipped the master arm to SAFE and also switched off my flares. Not that it mattered, since I'd used them all up long ago. It was March 24, and I'd just come out of the blowing, sandy mess around Nasiriyah. I didn't know if the Marines were safe, but I'd shot up the Iraqi convoy and stopped their reinforcements.

I wiped my face, took a deep breath, and ignored the flashing FUEL symbol in the HUD. Twelve hundred pounds of gas left. Under normal conditions, that's what you shut down with after landing. But I was nowhere close to landing. Even without the SAMs, Triple-A, and MiGs, all flying is dangerous. This is particularly true with bad weather in fighter jets that burn fuel at appalling rates. During "normal" operations, with a hundred or so fast movers all trying to take off or land from the same piece of concrete, situations can get out of hand very quickly. However, years of training and experience took over again and I immediately began flipping through steerpoints and checking distances. Keying the mike, I said, "LUGER . . . this is ROMAN 75."

Nothing.

I tried the other radio. "ROMAN Two . . . ROMAN One on Victor."

Nothing.

I sent a data-link, but if he'd changed radio frequencies, he'd never get it.

Running my air-to-air radar out to eighty miles, I stared at the screen. There were little white squares drifting across the top, but no way to tell if they were tankers. Glancing at my kneeboard, I punched in the air-to-air TACAN channel for the refueler that was supposed to be in the DOG South track.

Nothing.

This really wasn't my day. Rummaging through the disorganized bag of mission materials was useless. Pages and pages of radio frequencies and even a copy of the *Laws of Armed Conflict*, in case I wanted a little light reading. You've Gotta Be Shittin' Me.

"If I get out of this, I swear no one else will have to deal with this *horseshit* . . ." Muttering disgustedly, I stuffed all the paper back into my helmet bag. Maybe I could start a fire with it after I ejected.

The sun had disappeared into a really nasty wall of sand that was growing along the horizon. The orange glow had faded fast into the haze, and soon it would be dark. Rejoining on a tanker, assuming I could find one, at night, in a sandstorm, with no gas, was enough to pucker anyone's sphincter.

"Fuck it."

Bringing the F-16 around in a slow turn, I headed for Kuwait. There were two big air bases in that country, plus Kuwait International Airport. I'd find a piece of concrete. Just then, of course, my VHF radio came alive.

"ROMAN One, this is Two on Victor!"

"Go."

"One . . . Two is Bull's-eye one-six-zero for two-seventy, Angels 22 . . . tanker in tow."

Immediately reversing, I came back heading southwest and slewed my radar cursors to the position he gave. There! About fifty miles off the nose. I locked onto the brightest return and was rewarded with an aircraft symbol at 22,000 feet, heading directly for me at 300 knots.

"ROMAN One is radar contact. I'm off your nose, fifty miles, Angels 20."

"Two is contact. The tanker is TENDON 31 on Carmine 33."

"Just give me the frequency." Radio freqs were always color-coded and you had to have the daily communications list to break the code. I didn't feel like tearing through the bag again and, frankly, couldn't care less if the Iraqis heard me air-refueling.

"Copy . . . that's 310.6." He sounded a little abashed. But the boy had done good work by somehow persuading the tanker to come north toward me. Tankers were understandably reluctant to venture into Indian Country, and who could blame them? Switching frequencies, I stared through the HUD at the distant contact. I couldn't see the tanker, but the radar could. Close enough—this just might work.

"TENDON 31 . . . this is ROMAN 75."

"Loud and clear, ROMAN . . . we're northeast-bound at twenty-two . . . Bull's-eye—"

I cut him off. "ROMAN is radar contact and visual."

"Copy that." He sounded relieved. "Starting a right-hand turn back to the border."

"Negative." I eyeballed the radar and did the geometry in my head. "Repeat, negative. Come ten degrees right and continue. I don't have the gas to maneuver or chase you down."

In fact, I'd be lucky to rejoin and take fuel before flaming out, but I didn't say that. "TENDON copies. We'll come to you." To the tanker pilot's everlasting credit, he added, "We always wanted to see Iraq."

In fact, coming across the border into what was definitely hostile territory, with potential MiGs and certainly some SAMs, was a ballsy thing to do in an unarmed, non-maneuverable flying gas-can.

So I held my breath, flew silky-smooth, and willed the few remaining pounds of jet fuel to remain in my nearly empty tanks. At about twenty miles, I stared through the HUD and picked up the edges of the fat-bodied tanker emerging from the fuzzy orange background. A truly beautiful sight; I actually sighed with relief.

To execute a midair refueling, the idea is to end up about a half-mile behind the tanker and a little below. As the tanker's boom extends, you then ease up into the pre-contact position—about twenty feet back from the tip. You're then cleared to "contact" and you ease the jet forward very, very slowly, until the boom operator, called a boomer, can plug the end of his receptacle into your jet. In peacetime, there's lots of talk back and forth between the boomer and the receiving pilot, but in combat, there's none.

Once you're plugged in, there is a double row of lights on the tanker's belly that indicates your vertical and horizontal position relative to the boom, and you just "fly the lights" to keep your aircraft in position. Think of your wet tongue stuck to a frozen pipe being towed behind a car at 300 miles per hour, and you get the idea. It's even more fun at night.

Anyway, there wasn't time for any of that now. I also didn't have the fuel to overcome any maneuvering mistakes, which is why I told the tanker to just continue straight ahead. At about eight miles, I was pointed directly at him and pushed the throttle back up to mil power. By three miles, I was directly off the tanker's left wing, and I could make out my wingman flying formation off the big KC-135's right wing.

Without looking down, I carefully felt along the left console and toggled a big, square switch that opened the air-refueling door behind my cockpit. At a mile, I was about 100 knots faster than the tanker and still pointed directly at him. Squaring the corner, I brought the F-16 around directly behind him as the airspeed bled away from the turn. The boom bounced down then and fully extended. Another lovely picture.

Sliding in the last fifty feet, I fanned the speed brakes several times until my airspeed was just high enough to move forward. I was at eye level to the boom now, and it was about ten feet in front of me. Using the boom's position as a reference, I flew straight at it. When it seemed as if it would shatter the canopy and spear me in the face, the boomer nudged it sideways and I saw the tip disappear behind me. Finessing the throttle, I matched the tanker's airspeed and stopped in position.

For several long moments, nothing happened. If he couldn't pass gas, or I had any type of receiver issue, then I was truly screwed. I'd be lucky to make it back across the border to eject in friendly territory.

But then came the gentle push of the boom against my jet and, staring up at that wonderful wide belly, I saw the director lights come on. Of the hundreds of times I'd done this, it had never felt so good.

"GOOD AFTERNOON, SIR! WELCOME TO TENDON 31. WILL this be leaded or unleaded?"

Everyone's a comedian. I realized I'd been holding my breath, and I exhaled with a relieved chuckle and made my voice sound calm. I got paid to be calm and, no matter what, you had to sound good.

"Premium please. Check the oil, too."

He laughed. "You should be taking gas now, sir. Looks like you've had quite an afternoon."

I didn't want to look away to see if my fuel counter was increasing, so I just flew. After a few moments, I wriggled my fingers and toes to relax the death grip I had on the throttle and stick. After a couple more minutes, I risked a glance and saw the fuel had increased to 3,000 pounds. Enough to make it to Kuwait. I swallowed and exhaled again.

"Mind if we take a few pictures, sir?"

"I missed my bikini wax this morning." See, I'm funny, too.

"None of us have ever seen the burn marks from the cannon."

With that, there were some flashes from the bubble turret beneath the tanker, where the boomer lay. I squirmed my completely flat butt around and shrugged a pair of very tired shoulders against the harness. A few minutes longer, I'd be full up, and we could go home. I thought about the Marines in Nasiriyah and wondered if they'd gotten out. I had passed the last target area coordinates to the AWACS, and maybe a flight of night fighters could scope out the area.

As the tanker came around heading west, the last rays of sun were vanishing and the ugly haze looked a lot closer than it had before. Above me, the sky was already dark, but since we were still in Iraq we all kept our lights off. My jet was comfortably heavy with fuel again, and when we rolled out, the boomer said, "All full, sir." He whistled softly. "Fourteen hundred and seventy gallons."

I jotted it down and did the math in my head. More than 10,000 pounds of fuel.

Clicking the disconnect switch, I slid slowly back and down away from the boom, and waved to the boomer. Closing the refueling door, I added a little power and took up a loose formation on the tanker's left wing. We'd stay with him until he got back across the border then we'd head south to Prince Sultan Air Base near Riyadh. I wanted a gallon of water to drink, and an enormous, hot meal. What a day.

"ROMAN 75 . . . this is TENDON." It was a different voice. Probably the tanker pilot.

I clipped the oxygen mask back over my face. "Go ahead."

"Ah . . . AWACS just passed that KKMC, al-Batin, and Rafha are zero-zero, due to blowing dust."

Zero-zero. Slang for "zero ceiling and zero visibility." Another way to put it would be *complete shit*. No way to land. Those were all bases in northern Saudi along the border with Iraq. Glancing ahead of us there was nothing but a rolling carpet of dust and I wasn't surprised. All 1.4 million square miles of Saudi (about one-third of the continental U.S.) could disappear under blowing sand in a matter of hours, and I'd been busy that long. This was worse than I'd ever seen it; picture an undulating, brown sea stretching as far as you can see. The haze generated by this monster was so high that the stars were dimmed. It was like staring through a brown frosted glass.

"TENDON . . . can you get the weather for Prince Sultan and Riyadh?"

"Already got it. Riyadh is a quarter-mile vis, blowing dust. Prince Sultan is still at one mile."

"Good enough, TENDON. We're RTB at this time. If you get any updates would you pass them on Victor 130.225?"

"Wilco."

"And TENDON . . . thanks for coming to get me."

"We heard what you were doing down there . . . how could we say no?"

I chuckled drily. "You could've said no . . . so thanks again." I could barely make out the tanker pilot's outline in his cockpit, and he waved.

"Be hard to sleep at night if I did that. Best of luck, ROMAN."

I gently pulled up above the tanker, and my wingman followed from the other side. We were over a point called Customs House, on the Saudi-Iraq-Kuwaiti border, although I couldn't see it. Beginning a gentle left turn, I automatically switched to the AWACS coordination frequency. This was a standard procedure over Customs House, and I knew my wingman would be there, too.

"LUGER, LUGER . . . this is ROMAN 75."

Normally, jets coming out of Iraq would do a battle-damage check for holes, leaks, hung weapons, and generally anything bad that would keep you from getting home. But tonight it seemed the least of my problems. Centering the steering on Prince Sultan Air Base, I switched on the autopilot, pulled the night-vision goggles from their canvas bag, and clipped them on my helmet.

"ROMAN 75 this is LUGER. Go ahead."

"ROMAN is two by Fox-16s, five hundred rounds of twenty mike mike expended, checking out, RTB."

"Ah . . . ROMAN . . . confirm you're RTB to PeeSab?" Prince Sultan's identifying letters were PSAB—get it?

"Affirm."

"PeeSab latest observation is one half-mile, sky obscured. Winds are three-zero-zero at thirty gusting to fifty."

Nice.

I said it again—what a shitty day. The storm was moving west to east toward the bases along the Persian Gulf and in Kuwait, so there wasn't much time.

"Copy that LUGER. What's currently open?"

He had more good news. "Sheikh Isa is a half-mile, blowing dust, and Dhahran is one mile but falling."

Sheikh Isa was in Bahrain and Dhahran was on the coast. Terrific. So the only reasonably clear air was where I was now flying, and it was disappearing fast. When I looked outside, it didn't look that clear anyway. The lights from Kuwait and the big cities down the Saudi coast were usually visible, but now there was nothing. I couldn't even see the oil fires through the goggles, and a tiny sliver of uneasiness poked up through my belly. I'd been in countless bad situations before, right? Right.

I keyed the Victor radio. "ROMAN Two . . . say gas."

"7.1. Tanks dry." I had 10,500 pounds, so fuel wasn't the issue. Still—go where the gas is.

"LUGER . . . call TENDON 31 and see if we can RTB with him to al-Udeid."

This was a big tanker-and-logistics base in Qatar on the southern end of the peninsula. I called up the steerpoint and came around, heading southeast.

"ROMAN . . . this is LUGER. TENDON 31 has no further gas available."

I looked at the steering information: 355 miles. With all this fuel, that would be no problem. But the good news kept coming.

"Ah . . . ROMAN, be advised that al-Udeid is now reporting a half-mile and blowing dust. TENDON is diverting to Diego."

Diego? I blinked. That was the tiny island of Diego Garcia in the

Indian Ocean. Oh yeah, this was just getting better and better. I zippered the mike to wake up my wingman and began a slow left turn back to the north. There was only one choice, since Iran didn't count.

"LUGER . . . get me the current weather for Kuwait."

I pulled my Smart Pack off my leg and found the correct page. Flipping up the goggles, I turned on the white eyebrow light beneath the glare shield and squinted at the Divert card diagram. This was a depiction of the entire theater of operations, showing all suitable emergency airfields, their various frequencies, and other basic information. This annoying situation had just become an emergency, since the entire Middle East was vanishing beneath the dust. Al-Jaber would be my top pick. A-10 Warthogs and F-16s were based there. The food was okay, too.

I tapped the chart, then reached into the G-suit ankle pocket for my approach plate-book. This is a compilation of all the airfields in a given region and the instrument approaches available at each one. Instrument approaches are precise procedures that use specialized equipment on the ground and in the aircraft. The pilot then flies off his instruments through the weather down to a predetermined vertical and horizontal point. He either sees the runway or he doesn't and executes a missed approach. Military pilots were rated to a half-mile visibility with 200-foot ceilings under normal conditions; this isn't much when you're landing at 150–175 knots.

"ROMAN . . . Al-Jaber reports a quarter-mile vis, intermittent to zero-zero."

Swell.

Before I could ask, he added helpfully, "Kuwait International is closed. Say intentions."

Say intentions? How about London or Madrid?

"ROMAN 75 is diverting to Ali al-Salem." Apparently, the only place to land in friendly territory on this side of the planet.

"Roger that . . . Salem weather is three-quarters of a mile, blowing dust, wind is two-four-zero at twenty knots gusting to thirty."

"ROMAN copies all." I switched steerpoints and checked us a little right. Ali was about 110 miles from my present position, so I eased the throttle back to slow down while I studied the approach.

Approach? What approach? I thumbed through the book again. Nothing. Checking the four-letter airfield identifier, I looked again. Nothing.

So, there was no published instrument-approach to the only field in this hemisphere where I could land. If the weather was better, day or night, we could simply fly in and land using eyes instead of instruments. But the weather sucked.

My luck was holding.

Nor could we divert anywhere the weather was better, because that meant Iran. In any event, all this crap was moving that way anyway. Three-quarters of a mile. I figured we had less than an hour before Ali went down, too.

"ROMAN Two, go to two-mile trail and call tied. Descent check."

I scribbled down the Ali tower frequency from the Divert card and ran my fingers quickly over the switches. Since my wingman and I both had enough fuel, there was only one option. I'd fly us down to the end of the runway using GPS guidance and take a MARK point, a precise latitude and longitude for whatever piece of ground I chose. It could then be coupled with the aircraft's Instrument Landing System and would generate horizontal and vertical steering to that point on the ground.

There were problems with this. Each jet's system accuracy was a little different, so when I passed the point to my wingman, it would vary to a small degree. Normally, this was acceptable, but *normally* we weren't a few hundred feet above the ground, at night, in a sandstorm, trying to land from the information. Real instrument approaches use highly tuned, ground-based systems and painstakingly certified procedures. But aside from ejecting, we didn't have a choice.

"ROMAN Two is tied."

I saw the F-16 spike on my Radar Warning Display signifying that my wingman had fallen back several miles and locked me with his radar. This was the safest and most accurate way to bring a wingman down through the weather. His radar would tell him my heading, altitude, airspeed, and lots of other things. He just matched my airspeed, kept the radar locked, and maintained whatever distance I wanted all the way down. Piece of cake, as they say.

"Ah . . . ROMAN 75 this is LUGER."

I couldn't wait to hear this. "Go ahead."

"ROMAN . . . we've got several other flights of fighters holding in the air-refueling tracks who also need to divert."

I had thought I was the last flight out of Iraq, but apparently not. "ROMAN copies . . . how many?"

"Ah . . . four two-ships."

"Shit," I muttered yet again. Eight other fighters that needed to get down, and I just got elected.

"ROMAN you were the Alpha mission commander this morning so you're the senior pilot airborne."

Perfect. Well, this is where all that experience was supposed to pay off. I took a deep breath and looked at the Situational Awareness display, getting a handle on everyone's relative position.

"ROMAN copies. Have all strays contact me on Victor 130.225."

"ROMAN that's a clear frequency."

I really hated AWACS sometimes.

This guy was really worried that some Iraqi might hear us talking about diverting to Kuwait. "Just pass it," I somehow managed *not* to bark at him. Slowing down to 250 knots, I adjusted my internal cockpit lights for the NVGs. I also turned up my exterior NVG lights to full bright. Only someone looking through goggles could see them—in any event, the Iraqis on the other side of the border weren't a concern at this point.

I was about forty miles south of Customs House when the first flight checked in.

"ROMAN 75 this is HEIST 36."

"ROMAN reads you . . . say numbers, low man's fuel, and posit from Customs House."

"HEIST is a flight of two. 6.7 in Twitch south."

I jotted it down. "Copy. Stand by HEIST. Any other flights on this Victor, check in with ROMAN and say fuel."

Turned out, there was also a DERBY, a MONTY, and a WARDOG—all F-16 two-ships led by junior flight leads. They were each part of the afternoon strike package that had fallen apart due to weather. By the time I reached Customs House, I'd figured it out. MONTY was lowest on fuel, followed by HEIST, WARDOG, and DERBY. I jotted it all down on my kneeboard by flight, fuel, and position. The flight low on fuel would be the lowest in the stack and first in to land after my two-ship. I planned to drop off my wingman on short final and low approach to come back around for any stragglers.

"MONTY flight, you are now ROMAN Three and Four . . . HEIST is Five and Six. WARDOG you are ROMAN Seven and Eight and DERBY you're Nine and Ten. Acknowledge."

They all checked in with their new call signs. It was easier to keep things straight this way, and established one flight lead—me.

"ROMAN Three flight proceed to Customs House and hold at 21,000. ROMAN Five hold at 22,000, ROMAN Seven at 23K, and ROMAN Nine at 24,000. All ROMANS depart your current positions at assigned altitudes, standard east-west holding pattern at 250 knots."

They all acknowledged. Holding in line with the wind would

simplify things, and all the flights now had different altitude, so they wouldn't be a conflict to each other. I'd also stacked them up from the bottom, low flight with the lowest fuel, in the order they'd descend to the base. This way, they'd just peel off like layers from an onion and not fly through each other's altitude blocks.

"ROMAN Two you're cleared to hold at 20K . . . One is dropping down to get the mark point for our approach. All ROMANs stand by."

THE IMMEDIATE PROBLEM WAS TO DESCEND THROUGH THIS shit and get an accurate mark without killing myself. I pulled the power, popped open the speed brakes, and slid down into the dark brown mess below me. Holding 250 knots, I dimmed the lights and started a gentle right turn. With the steerpoint for Ali al-Salem set in the HUD, I planned to align myself to the runway ten miles out and fly in to take the mark.

The jet began to buffet when I passed 10,000 feet, as the winds near the surface increased and shifted. Eyeballing my displays, I played the stick, throttle, and speed brakes to roll out on a ten-mile final at 3,000 feet. Instrument approaches "stepped down" an aircraft in altitudes based on terrain and obstructions like towers. There was also a Minimum Safe Altitude (MSA) that would keep you clear of all dangers within twenty-five miles of the field. Since Ali had no approach, I was using the 3,000-foot MSA for Kuwait International. Hope it worked. I switched the UHF radio to Ali Tower and turned up the cockpit heat. Slowing to 200 knots, I lowered the gear handle.

"Ali Tower, ROMAN 75."

No reply. Of course.

Feeling the welcome thumps, I saw three green lights indicating the wheels were down and locked. "First good news tonight . . ." Like all single-seat pilots, I talked to myself a lot. "Ali Tower, ROMAN 75."

It didn't matter if he answered, because we were coming in anyway. But it would be nice to talk to someone and maybe confirm the runway wasn't full of holes or covered with Iraqis.

At five miles, I leveled off at a thousand feet and checked my fuel. 6.4 and my wing tanks were dry. Thank God for that tanker pilot, I thought. Hope he made it to Diego Garcia.

"Calling Ali Tower . . . say call sign."

A voice. A wonderful, flat, unemotional American voice. I squeezed my eyes shut a moment and replied, "Ali . . . this is ROMAN 75, four miles, gear down, low approach . . . runway three-zero right."

"ROMAN . . . the right runway is closed due to cratering. Three-zero left is open but no runway lights are available. Be advised, current visibility is a half-mile and blowing dust."

And the hits keep on coming. I slowed down to a bare 160 knots and said, "Tower, do you have approach lights on the left?"

"Affirmative . . . but no edge lights and only a few centerline lights." Edge lights outlined a runway and the centerline lights were a useful guide to keep big jets oriented in the middle of the concrete. We'd make do.

"ROMAN copies the weather. Lights to full bright on three-zero left, please, and say winds."

"Ali winds are two-eight-zero degrees, twenty gusting to thirty-five."

I ran my eyes around the cockpit one last time, then called up the MARK symbology as I passed two miles and 500 feet. Turning on the landing light, I got a face full of brown, blowing crap, and quickly switched it off. I peered through the goggles at the fuzzy wasteland off the nose. It was like a tan snowstorm.

There! Off to the right, I saw a whitish glow from some lights from the ground. Tilting my head back to see under the goggles, I saw the faint yellow blob of the air base. Adding a little rudder, I crabbed the jet to the left to stay aligned and stared to where the runway had to be.

"ROMAN . . . call runway in sight. You're cleared the option." Meaning I could land or low-approach.

"75 copies . . . I've got nine other fighters to bring back so this'll be a low approach."

Assuming I can find the runway, that is.

"Tower copies, standing by. Good luck," he added.

And there it was.

The flashing sequencer lights came pulsing out of the darkness at one mile. I instantly slewed the little diamond symbol in my HUD to the point where the lights ended. At a half-mile, through the goggles, I could make out the runway threshold and one or two centerline lights farther down. Good enough. I put the diamond about a thousand feet down the runway and stabbed forward with my right thumb. The F-16's computer did its magic, and a little block of green numbers appeared, telling me the latitude, longitude, and elevation of the diamond.

Adding power, I pulled the nose up slightly and closed the speed brakes. As the fighter accelerated, I slapped up the gear handle and keyed the mike.

"ROMAN 75 is on the go. Ali, I'll stay up your freq and please let your TOC know that we're inbound with ten fighters."

"Ali copies all. Wilco."

Wilco meant "will comply." It was always nice to deal with professionals. Passing 5,000 feet, I ran out the air-to-air radar and keyed the VHF radio.

"All ROMANS, stand by to copy."

Normally, the mark point could be data-linked, but I just read out the coordinates as I climbed, and they all acknowledged.

Locking onto my wingman, I angled in toward Customs House from the Iraqi side of the border and hoped our Patriot missile batteries knew I was a friendly. Breaking into the clear at 19,000 feet, I squinted through the NVGs at the greenish-white outline of the other jet. Searching left and right across the sky, I saw several others orbiting above in different places.

"All ROMANS, Christmas tree . . . Christmas tree."

"Christmas tree" meant to light up like one, and I caught the twinkling and flashing of F-16 exterior lights as they came on against the black night sky. I should've thought of that sooner, but over here, it was just habit to fly without lights.

"All ROMANS . . . we'll penetrate in flight order from Customs House. Two minutes between flights and two miles between aircraft. Outbound heading is zero-eight-zero at 250 knots. Hold this until the final approach fix at ten miles and 3,000 feet for runway three-zero left."

I paused and let them scribble that down. "At ten miles slow to 180 knots with the gear and intercept the glide slope inbound."

There. I'd just created an instrument approach. Several key points had to be spelled out so everyone would do it the same way and not overrun the jet in front of him. Air-to-air radars made it nice, but I'd still seen it chowdered up in the past. This way, everyone would leave Customs House at identical airspeed and head to the same location. At the next point, called the final-approach fix, everyone would slow to another set airspeed, and put the gear down. Then they'd fly the approach course to the left runway until the vertical steering, called a glide slope, indicated a descent.

"Slow to final approach speed at three miles and call full stop with Ali Tower. All ROMANS acknowledge."

And they did. All nine of them, with no questions. It was good to fly with fighter pilots.

"Ali Tower copies all." Ah. A sharp controller.

I glanced at my HUD and it showed eleven miles to Customs House. "Ali Tower ROMAN 75, flight of ten, will commence the approach in three minutes. We'll need a follow-me truck in EOR and confirm transient alert has been notified."

"ROMAN . . . affirmative on all."

I crossed Customs House heading east at 250 knots. Fanning the boards, I dropped the nose ten degrees and said, "ROMAN One flight, pushing. 5.1."

"Pushing" meant I was outbound from the briefed point, and the low man on fuel in my flight had 5,100 pounds of gas. Somewhere behind and above me, the next flight of two should be lining up to "push" in two minutes. "ROMANS . . . check course three-zero-zero set . . . altimeter two-nine-nine-one."

Three hundred degrees was the final approach course to the runway and 2991 was the latest altimeter setting. Everything was done, except for the flying, so I shut up and flew. Sliding back down in the thick dust, I shook my head and stifled a yawn. Despite the heat blowing in my face, I was still cold and I had a headache. Later, I told myself. I could yawn after landing.

"ROMAN Three flight—pushing."

I looked at the time, and it was exactly two minutes after I'd called. I didn't know any of these pilots but we all spoke the same language and had the same basic skills. Otherwise, this wouldn't have been possible.

By the time the next two-ship called, I was about twelve miles from Ali and beginning the turn to final. At ten miles, I abruptly pulled the power, fanned open the speed brakes, and lowered the gear. The fighter slowed in a hurry, so I retracted the boards and added power to hold 180 knots.

"ROMAN One, ten miles, gear down for two."

I knew nine other sets of eyes were squinting at their displays, gauging positions and timing. The tower replied, "Copy ROMAN, continue. Winds are two-eight-zero at thirty knots." He didn't say the visibility and I didn't ask. What was the point?

I concentrated on holding the approach course dead-center at 180 knots. If I jackassed it, then the accordion effect would ripple down the line and screw everyone over. At about eight miles, the little horizontal bar on my ILS symbology fluttered and began its slow drop. This was the glide slope, the controlled descent, that I had to maintain to the runway. The other bar, a vertical one, would keep me lined up on the runway. I checked the HUD against the larger, old-fashioned round-dial instrument on the console, and they showed the same indications. Wriggling my fingers to work out the stiffness, I shifted around in the seat a bit.

At three miles, I could see nothing but swirling dust. Easing the power back, I slowed to 160 knots and let my eyes flicker between the ILS steering and the radar altimeter.

"Ali, ROMAN One is three miles, gear down, low approach. All other ROMANS will full-stop."

"Tower copies . . . confirm you'll be coming back?" Was there anywhere else to go?

"Affirmative . . . ROMAN One will land last."

This way, if a wingman missed approach or had instrument trouble, I'd still be airborne to bring him back down through the weather in fingertip formation. Passing two miles and 700 feet, there was still nothing in the HUD. Less than twenty minutes ago, I'd been able to pick up the base from here, but not now. Despite my confidence, my mouth got a little dry. It wasn't like we had a lot of other choices here.

There! I thought I saw a faint flash off the nose and strained forward against the straps. Again! And again. I glanced at the ILS steering and saw it had drifted slightly left, but it was close enough. Fighting the urge to nose over toward the runway, I continued flying the approach until the lights disappeared beneath me, and I could see the runway threshold.

Shoving the throttle forward, I pulled the nose up and closed the speed brakes. Leveling off a hundred feet above the concrete, I left the gear down and keyed the mike.

"ROMAN One had the runway at one mile and 300 feet. One is missed approach. All ROMANS wait in EOR."

"Three copies."

"Five copies."

"Seven copies."

"Nine copies."

As I darted past the end of the runway (EOR), I saw a small white truck with flashing yellow lights, waiting. Flipping the gear handle up, I added more power and began to climb. As the ground disappeared beneath me, I turned northwest into a thick black wall of sand. The turbulence had increased to the point where it could buffet my jet, and I glanced at my fuel. Forty-five hundred pounds. Still plenty.

Number Three had just called his gear down so Number Four was behind him on final. I'd just heard Number Seven call "pushing," so that put Number Five and Six somewhere in between. Turning left, I was now paralleling the runway and heading southeast. At 5,000 feet, I cracked the throttle back to hold 250 knots and stared at the air-to-air radar. Two aircraft were off my left side, heading northwest—that would be Number Five and Six on final. So the flight that was perpendicular to me and ten miles off my nose had to be Seven and Eight on their way to final.

"ROMAN Nine . . . pushing."

Cranking back right about thirty degrees, I ran the radar out to pick up the last two fighters but I couldn't find them. Too much altitude difference, or a bad angle, or gremlins. It didn't matter. I simply pulled away, stayed at 5,000 feet, and continued toward Customs House for another minute. This would build in enough spacing between me and Number Ten and, sure enough, it did. He was sixteen miles in front of me when I turned back to the east.

One by one, I heard the tower clear the others to land and no one called missed approach. *This'll work,* I thought as I lowered the nose and descended back to 3,000 feet. Dropping the oxygen mask, I rubbed the stubble on my cheeks and the aching bridge of my nose. The cockpit was toasty, and I'd finally quit shivering, so the heat came down a notch. Shaking my head back and forth, I fought back another yawn. God, I was *tired*. Every time I blinked, it felt like two pieces of sandpaper rubbing together.

At eleven miles, I began the easy turn to final, and Number Ten was cleared to land. The gear handle came down as I called up the ILS steering one more time. But as I stared at two green landing gear lights instead of three, the tower controller said, "ROMAN One . . . current visibility is now a quarter-mile. Say intentions."

I blinked, still staring at the unsafe gear indication. Intentions? Let's see, how about ejecting over Bahrain, checking into a five-star hotel, and drinking all night in a casino?

"You've gotta be shitting me . . ." I muttered again. This was like an emergency simulator scenario that had gone ape-shit.

"Confirm all other ROMANS are on deck."

"Affirmative. State intentions."

That word again. I really hated that word.

"ROMAN One is six miles, gear down full stop, three-zero left."

I opened the speed brakes and dropped the nose to catch the glide slope. Normally, with a gear problem, you'd just orbit around in clear airspace and work through the checklist. But with a deteriorating quarter-mile visibility and no place else to go, that wasn't happening. I pushed the little round green gear light in to check the electrical circuit. Maybe the bulb had just burned out. No such luck.

Five miles. Twenty-two hundred feet and 160 knots. Sometimes cycling the gear solved minor problems, so I cycled the handle up and watched the red "in transit" light illuminate. The two green lights went out. Fighting the aircraft's upward surge and 30-knot crosswind while flying the ILS, I added power again and lowered the handle. The fighter yawed a bit as the gear came down, and this time I actually heard three thumps. But still only two gear lights.

Fuck it.

"ROMAN . . . Ali Tower reporting gusts to forty knots."

Terrific.

Still, you have to sound good no matter what. "ROMAN One copies," I replied calmly. "Short final with the gear, full stop." I think.

"Cleared to land."

I was crabbing almost thirty degrees into the wind, and the jet was bouncing in the unstable air like popcorn in a popper. Again, there was nothing in front of me but blowing sand and blackness. At one mile, I was dead on the approach centerline at 300 feet. A normal ILS approach has a minimum altitude of 200 feet, so I continued down and leveled off at 100 feet. Ignoring the gear issue, my burning eyes, and sweaty hands, I concentrated every ounce of consciousness on the ground before me. Risking quick glances left and right, I could see nothing but billowing gray clouds of dust.

The distance counter in the HUD said 0.1, so I had to be directly over the threshold.

"Shit." I shoved the throttle forward to go around. I had no real hope of flying another instrument approach and finding the runway, but if you can't see you can't land.

A light!

Just disappearing beneath my left wingtip.

There! White painted runway markings and an enormous 30L. I'd been blown slightly right by the wind, but there it was. Cobbing the power back, I opened the speed brakes and dumped the nose. Dropping through the dust, I kept my eyes glued to the pale ribbon of concrete. As it rose up, I pulled the stick back and angled left as much as I could to favor the unsafe left gear. With about ten feet to go, the runway seemed to just reach up and grab me, as if to say, "Enough . . . just fucking land."

The fighter slammed down and I winced.

But nothing collapsed, and I didn't flip off the runway in a cloud of sparks and flame. With the throttle in IDLE, I lowered the nose immediately, thumbed the speed brakes to full open, and concentrated on staying in the middle of the concrete. Fortunately, this runway was 9,000 feet long. As I slowed to taxi speed, I realized I'd made it.

"ROMAN One . . . taxi to the end. Turn right to join your flight. The FOLLOW ME will take you to parking."

I swallowed and took a deep breath. Then I saw them. A row of flashing strobe lights and the red-and-green wingtip lights of the other F-16s. They were beautiful.

"ROMAN One copies. Thanks for the help."

"Ali Tower . . . no problem. And welcome down."

Relief washed through me. Slowly approaching the turnoff, I closed the speed brakes, checked my lights on, and lifted the ejection seat lever to SAFE. Turning off carefully, I flashed my landing light at the follow-me truck, and he pulled away. The visibility was horrible now, and we literally crawled along the taxiway amid the blowing tumbleweeds and trash. Imagine driving through a dark car-wash and being sprayed with sticky brown foam while garbage hits your windshield, and you might get the picture.

We taxied around a maze of ruined aircraft shelters and several other twists and turns before eventually arriving at a narrow strip of concrete just east of the other runway. Easing through the dust, I saw half a dozen little glowing wands and managed a smile. These were crew chiefs waiting to "catch" the jets and get us all shut down. Someone was on the ball out there. Following the first set of wands, I stopped at the crew chief's signal, set the parking brake, and looked back at the rest of my strays. As the last one rolled to a stop, I keyed the mike.

"All ROMANs . . . check switches safe, tapes off, and secure all your classified." Squinting down the row of dirty-gray fighters, I added, "We're all tired so let's not goon up anything simple."

Our tapes and mission-planning materials were all classified, so we all checked each other after each flight to keep screw-ups from happening. It was even more important in a situation like this, on an unfamiliar base, at the end of a *very* long day.

After one more look around, I slowly pulled the throttle to CUT-OFF and felt the engine gratefully wind down. Unstrapping, I took my own advice and jammed everything classified into my helmet bag. Switching on the flashlight clipped to my harness, I then shut off the aircraft battery and everything went black. As I flipped the switch to raise the canopy, a wave of cold air hit me in the face, and I flinched. The crew chief hooked up a ladder, and I gingerly unstuck my ass from the seat for the first time in over ten hours. Wincing a little as my legs straightened, I swung out and sat on the top of the ladder for a moment, taking gasps of frigid, dusty air and looking at the small crowd below.

I've known pilots who've slipped on the way down after long flights and ended up sprawled on the concrete. You lose style points for that, so I came down very slowly. To my surprise, one of the guys waiting for me was a full colonel in a flight suit.

"Welcome to Ali!" He grinned and shouted at me over the

wind, "You did a helluva job getting in here tonight."

I slowly stretched my aching neck and tried to grin right back. "Thank you, sir . . . there was nowhere else to go."

"What? We weren't first on your list?" He laughed.

"You were the list."

The dust, by the way, was much worse. Like someone was dumping boxes of yellow cake mix into huge fans and blowing it in our faces. He clapped me on the shoulder and pointed off into the gloom. "I know. We've got another four F-16s over there." He looked me up and down and said, "When you're ready I'll take you to chow. It's not exactly linen tablecloths and Waterford crystal but it's hot!"

"Good enough, sir . . . we'll be ready fast."

The local maintenance guys had already chocked the wheels and were busying themselves taking oil samples and other post-flight stuff. I found out later they were all F-16 mechanics from al-Jabber Air Base to the south. Apparently, the Vipers there used Ali as a forward refueling and divert base, so they kept some of their crew chiefs here. Bad for those poor bastards but good for us.

Lugging helmet bags, harnesses, and weapons, the ten of us stiffly piled into several pickup trucks and headed straight to dinner. The colonel drove one of the trucks himself and got us into the chow hall.

I stood there in the door, blinking against the light, and inhaled. Rice, chicken, and burned bread—but it smelled heavenly. A chubby little mess sergeant hurried over, smiled broadly at the colonel, and nodded politely to us.

"Everything's ready, sir. Hot line, cold line, and the snack bar."

"Help yourselves." The colonel waved an arm. "Just coffee for me. If you want to drop your stuff here I'll watch it while you get food."

I found out later that he kept the chow hall open for us when he heard we were coming in. Meeting us and driving us around was also something most Operations Group Commanders didn't do. He was quite a guy. I'm embarrassed to say that I've forgotten his name, but I never forgot his leadership example.

Later that night, rolled up in a groundsheet in the corner of a tent, I shivered myself to sleep colder than I'd ever been in my life. I was wearing everything I had, including my G-suit, helmet, and harness, to try and stay warm. In the morning, the colonel showed up again, with two big plastic bags. At his own expense, he'd bought razors, soap, and towels for us. The sandstorm had mostly blown itself out, but there were still thunderstorms, and the air was thick with residual, hanging dust.

Nevertheless, the war was still on. The Marines were fighting along the Saddam Canal, trying to get past Nasiriyah and cross the Euphrates River. When they did this, they could push up Highway 8 to al-Kut and pincer Baghdad from the east. The 3rd Infantry Division, which had bypassed Nasiriyah, was stalled out near Samawah, about sixty miles south of Baghdad. Having escaped Baghdad, Saddam Hussein had declared March 25 as a "day of sacrifice," and Iraqis took this to heart. The fighting was heavy and casualties were mounting. More ominous was the revelation from Coalition Intelligence that large ammunition convoys, accompanied by chemical decontamination vehicles, were moving out of central Baghdad. The Iraqi plan was to take advantage of the bad weather to launch sustained counterattacks. They figured if they could slow up our advance, then the general Iraqi populace would arise to fight off the invaders. It was a good gamble on their part.

Unfortunately, they didn't account for the tenacity of U.S. ground forces, nor the ferocious attacks from American fighter aircraft—despite the weather. The next day, the fourteen F-16s on the ground at

Ali al-Salem were fragged to attack various targets in the Nasiriyah-Najaf-Kut triangle with whatever weapons we had remaining.

The weather was still horrendous. One good friend of mine got caught in a thunderstorm just south of Baghdad. The downdrafts were so powerful that his F-16 fell from 30,000 feet before he was able to regain control and recover 800 feet above the ground.

When we eventually returned to Prince Sultan on the afternoon of March 25, yet another unwelcome surprise was waiting. Unbelievably, I had been grounded.

ALL THE FIGHTER ASSETS AT PeeSab, INCLUDING THE 77TH Fighter Squadron, were part of the 363rd Expeditionary Operations Group, 363rd Air Expeditionary Wing. In my opinion, shared by many, many others, the senior commanders were not the varsity lineup. One of them would loiter outside the chow halls to prevent folks from dropping orange peels on "his desert." Another would actually hang around parking areas making sure people used spotters when they backed their cars up. The Operations Group (OG) was commanded by an unpleasant, pedantic colonel who was a holdover from the peacetime, No Fly Zone world between the wars. He had two female, tanker *navigators* for deputies—hardly an ideal command structure for a wing at war.

According to their directives, our big priorities during the war included the correct disposal of piddle packs (there was a Power-Point slide for that one) and proper wear of the desert "boonie" hat. There was a slide for that, too.

The day after my Nasiriyah mission (to save the Marines) the OG read the Mission Report and it must have busted his under-sized genitalia. He was absolutely mortified that one of the "cowboy" Viper pilots—that would be me—had dared go below 10,000 feet during the execution of a combat mission. Since his knowledge of Close Air-Support was confined to a lecture he'd heard once at Air War College, this wasn't surprising.

So after saving those Marines, rounding up eight stray fighters, *and* getting them safely down in that nightmare sandstorm this guy tries to ground me. I was flabbergasted. Everyone else was shocked and my squadron commander was positively apoplectic. I've never seen him that mad, even when we gave him wasabi one night in Vegas and told him it was guacamole. Sorry Storm'n.

Somehow, and I've never really known how, Colonel Bill "Kanga" Rew found out about it that very evening. As it happens, Colonel Rew was the 20th Fighter Wing Commander, our parent unit in South Carolina, and was currently serving as the Director of the Combined Air Operations Center there at PSAB. He was (and remains) a first-rate fighter pilot and Patchwearer. Basically, he ran the combat flying operations for the entire Coalition Forces Air Component Commander (CFACC).

Now the Coalition Forces Air Component Commander (CFACC) was a bull of a general named T. Michael Moseley, also a fighter pilot and a Patchwearer. That particular day he happened to be totally pissed off because his Marine counterpart had been publicly chastising the Air Force. The Marine general had a perception that Moseley's pilots weren't adequately performing close air-support for his ground troops because the Air Force didn't want them to fly down into the SAMs and Triple A. So Moseley is steaming about this when along comes Kanga Rew with a story. A story about at least one Air Force pilot who did what it took, in abysmal conditions and at great risk, to *save* Marines. Moseley is apparently thrilled and wants to meet this guy. Well, says Kanga, the pilot's got plenty of time now that the 363rd EOG has grounded him for saving those Marines.

What?

Actually, the way I heard it was "What the *fuuuck* is going on down there? Get those pinheads over here on the *double*." Or something like that. In the end, my grounding lasted about ten hours which was okay because I was asleep anyway. By the time I stepped out to fly the next combat mission, the in vogue expression at PeeSab was to "take an OG" instead of taking a shit. Everyone was saying it. Fighter pilots don't cut much slack when there's shooting going on.

I didn't see the OG again. He remained at PeeSab but stayed safe in his office with his computer and coffeemaker. Must be a little embarrassing to get a first-class ass chewing by a four-star general *and* manage to be wrong, too. He also received the following official email that used small enough words so he'd understand, telling him what an important mission ROMAN 75 had flown.

From: MCGEE, MICHAEL B. LCOL
Sent: 5/25/2003 12:32 PM
Subject: Roman 75

  Sir,

  I wanted to pass some information regarding a Roman 75 flight that did some pretty incredible work for the MEF on 24 MAR. His actions stropped an enemy reinforcement that was about to overrun some Marines separated from their main unit.

  On 24 MAR 03 at approximately 1345Z, Warhawk (V Corps ASOC) received a request for emergency CSA from Chieftan (MEF). 3rd BTN/2nd Marines had a unit that was stranded North of An Nasiriyah, and Iraq reinforcements were coming toward their position from the North along Highway 7, ivo 38RPV17525557. A flight of

F-15Es was sent to engage the enemy threat. The F-15Es were unable to find or engage the target due to the very poor weather in the target area. The MEF then sent a flight of A-10s that again were unable to find or engage the target due to worsening weather. Ceilings were estimated at 8000' and visibility was down to a couple miles. Since it was an emergency situation as passed by Cyclops (controller), we then sent Roman 75, flight of F-16CJs. The flight of F-16CJs was able to find and destroy the target. Due to the poor weather, Roman 75 had to execute a low altitude strafe against the target, the only way at the time to destroy the target.

Two other flights were unable to find or engage the target after many attempts under these very difficult wartime conditions. The flexibility, tactical expertise, and calm under intense pressure demonstrated by Roman 75's flight was above and beyond the call. This professional action of the flight lead under very poor weather conditions and in direct contact with the enemy ground forces saved 3rd Battalion from the reinforcing enemy forces.

Lt Col Mike McGee
V Corps EASOC Airboss
Dep Cmdr for Joint Integration
4 EASOG

This guy didn't even have the balls to come see our squadron depart for home after the war ended. Fortunately, these types of people were rare and a marked contrast to officers like Kanga, Storm'n, and Ops Group Commander at Ali-al Salem. True professionals, they focused on combat missions and using their positions to actually help those doing the fighting. I'd love to see that colonel from Kuwait again, to shake his hand and buy him a drink.

But the war didn't stop for the weather. This was a reality the Iraqis were slow in grasping, and it cost them dearly. They hoped to use the dust to obscure their movements and move into position for coordinated counterattacks. It's a good thought, and worked in 1944 for the Germans, but it wasn't going to stop a military that could see through bad weather and had satellite tracking.

In the end, after marching bravely out of their fortified positions with flags waving, the so-called elite Iraqi troops got the hell beaten out of them.

I believe that the sight of the arrogant, goose-stepping Republican Guards limping back into Baghdad convinced other military units, and, above all, the civilians, that Saddam's grip on Iraq was loosening. Consequently, there would be no mass uprising of the people to throw the hated invaders (that's us) into the sea. The military, however, did stay, and dug in tightly to fight the coalition forces as we approached the capital.

And approach it we did. The Army's V Corp moved up from the south, and the Marines, mad as hell about Nasiriyah, were blitzing northwest from al-Kut. The SAMs and Triple-A around Baghdad were warmed up now and waiting for the attack helicopters and close air-support aircraft that would support the attack on their capital.

But they wouldn't have to wait for long—the Wild Weasels were coming to get them.

9

The Valley of
the Shadow

March 26, 2003

THE WINGMAN CAME OFF THE TANKER'S BOOM AND SLID BACK-
ward away from the big KC-10. I zippered the mike and pulled up
and away, toward the north. I saw the flash of WICKED 24's wings
as he turned with me out of the Twitch air-refueling track. Eyes
out now, we transited the other tanker tracks, looking for pods
of big jets surrounded by little jets. I lit the burner momentarily
and climbed up above 25,000 as we headed north across the Iraqi
border.

The tankers usually refueled at 25,000 or below, and the surveillance jets, like AWACS and JSTARS, were normally above
30,000 feet. So 27,000 to 28,000 feet was generally a safe haven as
we crossed into Iraq. It always amazed me how, with such a big sky,
jets gravitated toward each other. Of course, up here, really only
F-16s and F-15s roamed about. The Navy F-18s were much farther

to the east, and the A-10s couldn't get this high. Even so, we kept our eyes out until well north of the border.

Twenty miles farther we FENCEd in. FENCE was originally a mnemonic of things to complete prior to combat: F (flares) E (electronic countermeasures) N (navigation aids—off) C (camera—on) E (emergency beacon—off).

We'd added to it over the years. Seat straps got tightened, exterior lights came off, weapons systems were set up, etc. I also ran my seat up a bit higher to better see any SAMs farther over the canopy rail, and turned the threat-warning volumes up as high as I could stand. I usually also removed my gloves so I could manipulate switches better, and almost always flew with my helmet visor up. Each pilot had his own system and it didn't matter as long as everything was done prior to getting too deep into Indian Country.

"You've gotta be shitting me . . ." I muttered and looked at the mess below me. My flight of two CeeJays was roaming around Killbox 88 Alpha Sierra just south of Baghdad. This is what was left after the Mother of All Sandstorms had passed through. The winds may have died down, but the visibility was still terrible and Iraq was completely covered by a nasty mixture of fuzzy brown dust and low gray clouds.

"WICKED 23, this is RAMROD." The orbiting AWACS had been unusually quiet today, which was a welcome change. Unfortunately, I wasn't far enough north to pretend I couldn't hear him.

"Go ahead."

"JEREMIAH directs . . . repeat . . . JEREMIAH directs armed reconnaissance of the area around North three, three, oh, three, point five . . . West four, four, one, one, point three . . . how copy?"

Now right there I should've experienced inexplicable radio difficulties. JEREMIAH was the daily call sign of the general commanding all coalition air forces. He was sitting 700 miles away in an air-conditioned, carpeted tactical operations center, probably eating a doughnut. This duty rotated among senior officers, who got to sit back and watch the war on the big screens.

Since Operation Desert Storm, our command and control technology had improved—and I use that word sarcastically—to the point where all our aircraft could be tracked electronically. This was then projected on a movie-theater screen in the TOC. There were ascending rows of amphitheater seats, which wrapped around the room. Computer stations were interspersed around, manned by majors and lieutenant colonels whose main function at the moment was to be there and breathe. They had little paper name-cards on their cubicles that said things like FLTOPSMAIN, MPCFIDO, and AAR-DETCO. Alphabet soup to anyone other than one of them. Anyway, the general got to sit at the very top, in a little glassed-in room, like the bridge of a ship.

However, when JEREMIAH spoke, we had to listen—or fake radio problems. I jotted the coordinates down on my kneeboard and made the mistake of replying.

"Copy that, RAMROD. Say items of interest." Meaning, what do you want me to look for?

"WICKED—possible armored vehicles and personnel moving south out of the city along Highway One."

I zippered the mike, looked outside, and sighed. It was a normal request under ordinary circumstances. However, I wasn't wild about flying down through all that shit, not to mention the still-undefeated Baghdad SAMs and Triple-A, just to locate a stray Iraqi patrol. Especially since our own ground units were still fighting their way north and were currently about fifty miles to the south of the capital. So again, despite space intelligence, satellites, and aerial platforms like JSTARS, it came down to human eyes on a target. My eyes, in fact.

Still, if the Iraqis were going to move, it would be now—precisely because the weather was atrocious. Their own air force didn't fly in bad weather, and they never seemed to grasp that we could and did.

I knew without looking that my wingman would be floating around behind me about a mile away, so I flipped on the autopilot, pulled the throttle back to hold 300 knots, and unfolded my map. In the twenty-first-century Air Force, it was old-fashioned to carry a map, but I always did, precisely for times like these.

The coordinates AWACS had plotted were out along Highway 8, barely ten miles south of Baghdad, just north of the small town of Iskandiriyah. Tactical maps have lots of good information on them, and I tapped my finger over a huge lake southwest of Baghdad. Milk Lake, we called it. Besides the purpose of this reconnaissance, my other concerns included not knowing what was actually beneath me and not being able to see whatever was there. If I came in from the west over the lake, then those two problems would be temporarily solved. At least, long enough for me to get in and get out.

That is, until I popped back out over the land on the eastern shore of the lake. But the ability of an unsuspecting Iraqi patrol to acquire, track, and shoot at a target rocketing along at 550 miles per hour was a chance I'd take. I stuck the map under the kneeboard as my hands and eyes moved smoothly around the cockpit. Chaff and flares were armed, seat was up, threat-warning volume was up. The jet was ready for combat.

"WICKED Two . . . One on Victor."

"Go ahead."

My wingman today was a lieutenant named Ian Toogood. Really. We called him "Notso." Get it? Notso Toogood. Actually he *was* good. A typical brainless lieutenant (just like I'd been) but utterly fearless.

He'd heard the whole exchange, but I explained what I was going to do and that included leaving him up in the clear air. He wasn't happy about being left behind, but there was no reason to risk his life, too. Also, a combat flight lead is just that—a flight leader—so wingmen do what they're told. Especially if the flight lead is also a Weapons Officer. So I zippered the mike and sliced away below him, heading west. Pulling my power back, I glided down toward the thick brown fuzz and squinted at the ground.

Nothing—no holes or breaks in the clouds.

Leveling off at about 15,000 feet, I left 5,000 feet between me and the clouds in case of a SAM. Eyeballing the HUD, I continued west until I was thirty miles—less than four minutes—from the point on the highway.

Taking a deep breath, I pushed the power back up, raised my visor, and began another slice back to the east. Dropping the nose, I centered the steering and gradually slipped down into the dust. As the horizon disappeared, I rechecked the radar altimeter and kept descending. According to the map, I would be over the western edge of the lake and there shouldn't be anything hostile below me except water.

Passing through 10,000 feet, I flipped the master-arm switch to ARM. I had the standard air-to-air missile load of two AMRAAMs and a pair of Sidewinders. We always had a full load of 20-mm cannon shells, and I also was carrying a couple of CBU-103 cluster bombs.

By 5,000 feet, I was twenty miles from the road. The sky around me had turned chocolate-brown. Tilting my head back, I caught the weird sheen of weak sunlight filtering through the dust—like lying on the bottom of a muddy pool and looking up. At 1,000 feet, the jet began to buck and suddenly pitched sideways. I swore and tightened my grip on the stick. Dropping out of the clouds at about 800 feet, I stared down at the angry waters of the lake. Whitecaps flecked the gunmetal-gray surface, and that surprised me. It meant strong winds and unsettled weather.

I felt a twinge of uneasiness. There had been no way to predict what was under the clouds, but I didn't expect violent weather. It was also dark and, even as I watched, lightning suddenly ripped a gash through the blackness up ahead and to my right. Then again, to the left. Apparently, there was still a very nasty storm hidden here beneath the dust. Swallowing hard, I angled away from the thunderstorm and pushed the throttle to full mil power. The ragged cloud layer pressed down from above and I had no choice but to continue descending. Or abort. I really had no choice.

Eight miles from the highway, I crossed the Euphrates River heading northeast at 510 knots and 200 feet. Maybe it was a premonition, or just faith in my own instincts, but as the water changed to hard, brown earth, I released one of my Little Buddies.

Technically called the AN/ALE-50, the Little Buddy was a towed decoy that was intended to attract hostile tracking radars and missiles to it, not the aircraft. Since it streamed out behind the jet, anything that locked onto its signal would be guided to the decoy and not the fighter.

Hopefully.

Shredded, tattered clouds hung down on all sides and I could see nothing but the ground below. It was the middle of the afternoon, yet the sky was a menacing mix of greens and blacks against a dirty-brown background. Very weird. Even at over 500 knots, the jet was bouncing and pitching in the unsettled, turbulent air.

Still, it was just a flying situation. I mean, low altitude in shitty weather less than twenty miles from Baghdad wasn't exactly a walk in the park. But neither was it MiGs and SAMs and Triple-A. So I wriggled backward against the seat and concentrated on holding the fighter steady.

The highway!

Appearing beneath the ragged cloud curtains, a dark gray slash of paved surface ran away to the north and south. The earth was greener here, and hundreds of shabby little huts and brown boxlike houses dotted the landscape. Leaning forward, I squinted through the canopy but couldn't make out any vehicles or anything that looked like a convoy.

The jet was skidding sideways from the wind, and I booted the rudder to hold it steady. I felt the tremendous power of the engine through my fingertips as it fought against the weather. My right hand was slick from sweat, and I wished I'd put my gloves back on. Highway 8 was about a mile off the nose, and I rolled up on one wing and looked north. There was nothing moving on the road. This was a waste of time, I thought. Well—

Suddenly the sky changed color. The clouds turned coal-black and colors exploded everywhere. Crimson reds and oranges and yellows. Tracers everywhere, reaching out for me and zipping past the cockpit.

This is it, my shocked mind clicked. *I'm dead!*

Flying by sheer instinct and ingrained habit patterns, I jinked. I pulled Gs violently left and right. I pulled up and shoved down. I pumped out chaff and flares. I didn't dare use the afterburner, because the few Iraqis that hadn't seen and heard me would see me then.

The fighter rocked sideways and my head hit the canopy. Huge red-orange mushrooms tore aside the gray sheets of rain and lit up the darkness beneath the clouds. It was like being inside a bag of fireworks that had suddenly erupted. Who knows what hell looks like, but I think this was close.

"BEEP, BEEP, BEEP, BEEP . . ." The threat-warning receiver went ape-shit.

Blinking rapidly, I caught a glimpse of 6s and 8s and Triple-A on the little saturated screen. Flashes from thousands of guns lit up the ground like sparklers. Light gray fingers of smoke shot upward from all directions.

Mother of God!

Reacting instantly, I shoved the nose down, slammed the throttle forward, and slapped out more chaff bundles. The adrenaline shooting through me went straight up from my gut, through my heart, and out the top of my head. Shoulder-launched SAMs or big stuff, I couldn't tell and it didn't matter.

The ground was rushing up, so I reversed and began to pull as the jet bottomed out at a hundred feet over the highway. Looking back to the right as the fighter slowed, I instinctively shoved the throttle into full afterburner. Everyone would surely see me now. It didn't matter—everyone already saw me. There is actually a difference in the way men shoot at you. It feels different if they're merely reacting or frightened or defensive. Or angry.

This was *very* angry ground fire. These men were unbelievably frustrated that they'd been held back for five days and not allowed to fight. Now they had a target—me.

The Iraqis below were on the move with the intention of catching our ground forces with a surprise counterattack. They were thoroughly pissed off to have been spotted by this lone American fighter pilot. And they wanted me dead. It was like being rolled in honey and tossed into a hornet's nest.

Green tracers shot past the cockpit; all around me the clouds changed color, from red to orange to pink, as lightning mixed with explosions. Then time compressed and I saw the vehicles. Patrol . . . *my ass*. There were hundreds of grayish-tan vehicles all up and down the road. A brigade or more, at least. I hadn't seen them, because they were exactly the same color as the highway and they weren't moving. In a moment of stark, unreal clarity, a few tank barrels swung around and I actually saw men in the armored carriers firing machine guns my way.

Dirty-white smoke trails lifted off from the throng of soldiers and snaked up at me. Shoulder-launched SAMs! Lethal little fuckers, with infrared seeker heads and very, very fast. With less than two seconds to react, I rolled back nearly inverted and pulled at the ground.

"Sonofabitch!"

I stabbed the countermeasure-dispense switch with my left thumb as fast as I could move it. This put out a sequence of chaff and flares that was designed to defeat infrared and radar-guided missiles. But it did nothing about Triple-A. Or about the fifteen thousand Abduls and Mohammads hosing their AK-47s at the sky.

Rolling wings level to the ground at less than a hundred feet, I pulled straight up. Grunting against the Gs, I forced my head around toward the SAMs and puked out a few more flares and chaff bundles. The jet was still fast, maybe 400 knots, but zooming uphill and slowing down. So I barrel-rolled back toward the road, eyes straining against the dust, and tried to see the missiles.

Then the horizon disappeared!

I had a moment of sheer terror that only a pilot knows when all his visual flying cues suddenly vanish. For an eternal half-second, I didn't know which way was up, down, or sideways. This wasn't good, a few hundred feet above the ground in a dusty cloud over thousands of angry enemy soldiers.

Get out of the damn cloud, my brain screamed. Over-pulling and slicing back toward the earth was the only way to do it, so I tugged the throttle out of afterburner and did just that. Problem was, without a horizon, at that altitude, I was about three seconds away from becoming a permanent part of Iraq.

Suddenly the dust peeled back, and I had a face full of earth. Scrub brush, tires, and even an old car chassis registered in my head as I dropped out of the clouds.

Holy shit!

Instantly pulling back hard on the stick, I felt the F-16 mush toward the ground. Shoving the throttle into burner, I caught sight of the road about a hundred yards off my left wing. I was more or less heading northeast, *away* from that mess.

They saw me.

Once again, everything that could shoot swung in my direction and opened up. Green tracers arced through the dark air like whip-cords. Orange blobs from heavier anti-aircraft pieces floated past, and ground fire sparkled all around me. But the F-16 responded, and as I came up through the horizon, rolling away from the threat, I hit the pickle button and felt the cluster bombs kick off.

Immediately snapping the jet hard over to the right, I avoided the clouds this time, pointed east, and dove back toward the relative safety of the earth. Passing a hundred feet, I twitched my tail to the left, pulled out of burner, and raced away northeast. Looking back, Highway 8 was still lit up like Times Square. In fact, so many vehicles were shooting at me that the column appeared as if it was burning. More SAM trails streaked out beneath the clouds, and I snapped back right and plugged the burner in. I did this three or four more times, until the road disappeared.

Throttling back to mil power, I swallowed hard and realized that I'd been thumbing the countermeasures switch the entire time. It was empty, of course, and, glancing at the HUD, I saw that all my towed decoys had been shot away.

Thank you, Raytheon.

I also saw that Highway 1 was eight miles behind me and receding fast. Easing up to a hundred feet, I stared through the HUD. Off to my right, somewhere in the gloom, was the Shaykh Mazar

MiG base, but they'd never fly in this crap. It did have SAMs and Triple-A though, so I angled away to keep clear.

There.

Straight ahead was the metallic gray-green snake of the Tigris River. Little brown villages lined the banks and I saw boats in the water. The men in the boats had seen and heard me. They were standing up, shaking their fists, and grabbing their undersized crotches, so, with a touch of bravado, I waggled my wings as I flashed past.

"I should've kept the cluster bombs," I muttered, rolled up on a wing, and gave them the finger.

Once the Tigris disappeared, I began a smooth pull up through the dust and turned away from Baghdad toward the south. Initiating a data-link, I heard the little cricket noise as it found my wingman and displayed his position on my MFD. Passing 2,000 feet, I glanced at the display and saw WICKED 2 was actually about twenty-five miles due south of me.

Angling southeast to give Shaykh Mazar a wide berth, I broke into the clear at 8,000 feet and stared up at the sun. Taking a deep breath, I dropped the mask and leaned my head back against the ejection seat. I had the same feeling I'd had a few days earlier, at Nasiriyah, when I broke out safe above the mess. It was beautiful. For a few seconds, as I continued to climb away from the city, I just stared up at the powder-blue sky.

But even at only 400 knots there isn't much time for reflection, so I ran the air-to-air radar out and locked onto my wingman.

"WICKED Two, One is Bull's-eye one-five-zero for fifty-six . . . passing ten thousand for twenty."

After a few seconds, I saw the familiar F-16 radar spike on my RWR.

"Two is contact."

"Cleared to join . . . fighting wing. One is 5.1, tanks dry."

"Two is 8.7 . . . feeding."

So, I had about 5,000 pounds of fuel remaining, and my wing tanks had been sucked dry. I glanced at the digital time in the HUD. From the time I'd passed the shoreline of the lake headed inbound, the entire thing had lasted less than six minutes and taken almost 7,000 pounds of fuel. And four towed decoys and 120 chaff and flare bundles. And two cluster bombs. And a partridge in a pear tree. I wondered if I hit anything. Sighing, I pulled out my gloves and wiped my face. It didn't matter. They hadn't hit me.

"RAMROD, RAMROD . . . THIS IS WICKED 23." I FIGURED I might as well give them the good news.

"WICKED . . . stand by for update."

A flash caught my eyes and I looked to the right and slightly high as my wingman swooped down from the south, crossed overhead, and slid into position off my left wing. Waggling my wings to bring him in close, I punched up the steerpoint for the nearest refueling track.

I looked over at the other fighter and the pilot's helmeted head. He had his visor down and his sleeves rolled up. I grinned. Just a chip off the old block. Giving him a quick sign with my thumb and forefinger, I saw him nod and begin the Battle Damage check.

"WICKED . . . this is RAMROD . . . vehicles and armored units at passed coordinates are possible RPG units . . . repeat . . . RPG units."

RPG. Republican Guard tanks and mechanized infantry. *That* would've been nice to know. Saddam's elite force. Elite compared to the other Iraqis—or Iranians or the French—but certainly not to us. They were still all going to die, they'd just die better-dressed. However, Republican Guards also had their own attached air-defense units, as I'd seen up close and personal. Shaking my head, I watched Notso slide beneath me and appear on the other side as he looked my jet over for holes, leaks, and missing parts.

"WICKED . . . exercise extreme caution."

Gee, thanks. I wondered what he thought I'd been doing for the last ten minutes.

"WICKED . . . how do you hear?"

I took another deep breath. If I answered now, I'd say something unprofessional, snide, and completely called for. So I waited until Notso finished his battle-damage check and flashed me a thumbs-up. Kicking the rudder, I watched him peel away, giving me a glimpse of the bombs and missiles slung under his wings.

Keying the mike, I managed to sound bored and said, "RAMROD . . . WICKED 23 . . . armed recon complete. RPG units confirmed . . . armor, mechanized infantry, and air defense."

"WICKED . . . can you estimate numbers?"

I saw it in my mind's eye. The road. Hundreds of vehicles pulled off to the side as far as I could see. The flashes from the guns.

"RAMROD . . . division-strength. Several hundred vehicles . . . all southbound on Highway Eight."

"WICKED . . . can you say type of vehicles?"

"The shooting type."

"Say again?"

This went on for a few minutes while we headed back to the tanker to refuel. They plainly wanted more information, but from the few seconds I'd had to make an assessment and survive, that was all there was. Then he said it.

"Ah, WICKED . . . we'd like a second pass over the target."

Now, second passes are always dangerous, because whatever you flew over and attacked is now fully aware, awake, and angry. But we do it when we have to. In critical situations, like close air-support or search-and-rescue, no one would hesitate, but this wasn't one of those situations. Besides, I had no more chaff or flares or decoys. And I wasn't sending Notso down there. The boy had a long life ahead of him and it wouldn't be fair to all the women who hadn't met him yet.

"RAMROD . . . does JEREMIAH direct this?"

There was too long of a pause. Finally, he came back with, "Ah . . . negative WICKED. This is a RAMROD request."

You've gotta be shitting me.

I wasn't going back down there simply so those bozos could fill in a few missing spaces on whatever form they were working up. I'd seen everything that needed to be seen. And I told him that. And that we were heading to air-refuel, then going home.

As it turned out, those Iraqis on the road were not simply relocating, and they definitely weren't just a patrol. They were, in fact, armored and mechanized infantry units from the Medina and Nebuchadnezzar units of the Republican Guard. They were moving south to counterattack the American advance at the Karbala Gap. The Iraqi High Command had concluded that the American advance was stalled and, in fact, the 3rd Infantry Division had slowed about fifty miles south of Baghdad due to continuous harassment. North of Nasiriyah, the Marines were heavily engaged and very slowly fighting their way up the Tigris River.

With the sandstorm as cover, Saddam ordered the Guards to move out of their positions in Baghdad and head south to fight. Unknown to me, another RPG brigade was also moving southeast out of Baghdad to strike at the Marines.

U.S. airpower had literally beaten the fight from the Iraqi frontline combat forces, but Saddam's generals reasoned that the current bad weather would impede American air support. And without air support, the Iraqis felt equal to confronting the American Army and Marines. They'd obviously forgotten the First Gulf War. It also slipped their minds that American fighter jets would attack in any weather. We didn't like it, but it certainly didn't stop us. So, as with so many battle plans, it was gutsy from one point of view and utterly stupid from the other.

About fifty miles past the refueling track, we crossed the border into Saudi Arabia and I actually started to relax a little and slow down mentally. A fighter pilot gets accustomed to thinking at 500 miles per hour, and, as anyone who's ever lived with one can attest, this is really annoying. But it's an occupational hazard. My brain began settling back to relatively normal levels, and I could feel the muscles in my back stretching out a bit.

Removing my helmet, I ran my fingers through my sweaty hair and poured water on my head. As I scratched my scalp and took a long drink of warm plastic-tasting water, I noticed something strange. My thumb and forefinger were twitching slightly. Very slightly, but twitching nonetheless.

Now, I'd had more close calls in my career than I could count, and I'd been seeing the Elephant on and off since 1991 without flinching. I stared at my hand a few more seconds, snorted once, and tugged at my glove.

But I knew that I'd just come closer to Death today than ever before. I hadn't attacked anything or done anything heroic. This mission would never get written up, nor did I ever mention it. But I just knew.

I knew that I'd found a place where even the Elephant doesn't go.

10

SAMBUSH

April 6, 2003
1104 local time, north of Baghdad

"DAMN IT!"

One eye burned as bits of dust floated under the visor and hit my eyelid. Rolling over until completely inverted, I pumped the stick forward and snapped the F-16 upright. Keying the mike, I squinted over the wingtip. "ELI Three and Four . . . defending Triple-A over Baghdad."

Dirty-white smudges suddenly appeared where we'd been, so I shoved the power up, climbed a few thousand feet, and pulled away from downtown. The newly christened George Bush Airport (formerly Saddam International) passed behind me to the left as we hit the western suburbs of Saddam's battered capital city. Bunting over, this time blinking fast to keep out the specks, I stared back down at Baghdad. Saddam's capital was a bit beat-up; the pea-green Tigris River was visible beneath the brown smudges hanging over downtown. Like black commas, hundreds of smoke trails rose over the buildings and streets. Tracers arced and sporadic explosions blew more debris into the dirty air. Apparently, the Iraqis still had some fight left down there, even after the arrival of the Army and Marines.

Today was a motorcycle-gang mission. Basically, we roamed around different killboxes and looked for a fight. The threat was unknown, the weapons were our choice, and our only objective was to kill whatever the Iraqis had left.

On this day, we had two four-ships of F-16CJs—ELI 31 and LAPEL 77. I led the second element of ELI and we'd split up the area around Baghdad. ELI One, Zing Manning, was southeast of the city somewhere, beating up the Iraqi defenders along the Tigris River and dodging F/A-18s. Hornets had been everywhere the past few days as the 1st Marines fought their way into the capital from the east.

The 3rd Infantry Division had attacked and taken Baghdad International Airport on April 4, during some of the toughest fighting of the war. On April 6, the Army had initiated Operation Thunder Run from the suburbs toward the airport, and that section of the city was essentially safe. But the center of Baghdad, plainly, was not; the place was a mess. Lines of frightened civilians tried to escape to the north and west, while the military threw up defensive positions downtown to counter the American advance.

Iraqi armor moved through the northern outskirts of town, and fierce street fights broke out everywhere. Tanks are hard to distinguish anyway, and without the targeting pods that we'd pushed so hard to add to the CeeJay, it was nearly impossible for a pilot to tell friend from foe. So we'd decided to leave inner-city tank-busting to the A-10s and F/A-18s. We were trolling for any SAMs, particularly the remaining Rolands and SA-8s, which would kill helicopters and Warthogs.

—⁓—

ARCING AROUND THE CITY FROM THE WEST, I DROPPED DOWN
to about 10,000 feet to stay well beneath the increasing cloud cover.
The city was a kaleidoscope of grays—gray earth, darker gray concrete, and gunmetal-gray roads. Shafts of sunlight lanced through
the clouds and softened the hard background in mottled dove-gray
patches. Lines of black smoke rose straight up from countless bright
red fires. Orange and yellow tracers occasionally shot upward and
exploded beneath the clouds.

I rolled up again and flicked a wing hard to the right. Obediently, my wingman floated to the outside, my left, as we continued
around the city. This put me between him and any threats, but
still allowed him to fly formation off of me and observe Baghdad. I
heard the crinkling sound of a data-link in my headset and glanced
at the MFD. He'd data-linked me a Flap Wheel radar and an SA-3.
The Flap Wheel was a fire-control system, and that meant Triple-A
guided by radar—much tougher than the stuff they shot visually. I
angled away from the location and looked again at the SA-3. It was
about fifteen miles north of us, just off Highway 1. There was a big
MiG base up that road, called Balad, so no doubt the SAMs were
there to protect it from people like us.

I grinned. Fat fucking chance.

Arcing about eight miles from downtown, we crossed Highway
1 on the northern outskirts of Baghdad, heading east at 450 knots.
I methodically scanned the ground ahead on both sides of the jet's
nose. The RWR was turned full-up, the jamming pod was on auto,
and we'd both streamed decoys. I also was bobbing and changing
my altitude randomly every five or six seconds. We were in full-up
Wild Weasel mode.

Passing over Highway 2, I glanced back over my left shoulder to check on the wingman. He was right where he should be, and I exhaled. Everything was okay and—

"BEEP . . . BEEP . . . BEEP . . . BEEP!"

My eyes riveted back to the RWR, even as I instinctively rolled away from the flashing "3" on the display. Pumping chaff with my left fist, I keyed the mike and yanked the fighter upright, heading due north.

"ELI Three, defending SA-3, north Bull's-eye eight . . ."

Shoving the stick forward, I floated off the seat and slapped the chaff button again as a voice yelled, "ELI Four . . . missile! Ah . . . ELI Four, missile in the air!"

Where??

Snapping my head around to the right, I kept the power up and pulled sideways to hold the city in sight. Nothing. Opening my mouth to ask him, I saw a flash out of the corner of my eye.

There!

Almost directly off my nose, at twelve o'clock. The billowing gray smoke was hard to see against the nearly universal gray background, but the flaming trail of the missile was plain enough.

"ELI Three . . . tally missile launch, SA-3, right two o'clock, close." I began a level, six-G turn away from the smoke to put the missile off my right wing. Lifting above the Baghdad skyline, the long plume was now visible against the clouds. But where had the first one gone?

"ELI Two . . . posit of the first SAM?"

"Two . . . uh . . . No joy on the SAM." He couldn't see it.

Rolling out, I bunted forward again as the RWR continued shrieking at me. There's never just one threat, so I kept rapidly scanning the ground as we passed over the ramshackle neighborhoods and canals that spiderwebbed across northern Baghdad. Triple-A bursts were noticeable over downtown, and I saw the telltale fingers of other SAM launches farther south. The missile I had originally seen disappeared into the cloud deck, but its Low Blow radar was still locked to me.

Yanking the fighter around, I pointed directly at the patch of ground where the SAM site must be. Calling up the mark function, I nosed over again and slewed the little diamond over the general area. Luckily, there wasn't much wind, so the smoke trail was still hanging in the air over what looked like a junkyard. The coordinates popped onto the HUD, and I pulled away hard to the left. Being belly-up to a threat that can shoot you isn't a great idea for long, so I rolled out, checked for bad stuff coming at me, then rolled and pulled again.

Northbound now, with the SAM battery directly behind me at six o'clock, I saw my wingman float overhead to a wide loose-deuce position. Vapor streamed from his wingtips as he dropped into formation.

"ELI Four . . . stand by data." And I zapped him a data-link with the SAM coordinates as we headed due north along the Tigris River. Zippering the mike, I brought us around the right, heading northeast. This would keep us well clear of Highways 1 and 2, which were full of retreating Iraqi military units. We'd also skirt south of Baqubah, a good-size and undefeated town north of Baghdad. The terrain was better out here, too—there was much more room to maneuver. The ground was low and wet, with fewer roads, so there'd be less of a mobile SAM or Triple-A threat.

LAPEL 77 was the other four-ship with us that morning, so I changed to his Victor freq. "LAPEL One, this is ELI Three."

"Go."

"ELI Three flight is engaging an SA-3, Bull's-eye zero-two-zero for nine. Posit?"

"LAPEL One and Two are southeast Bull at twenty-five thousand, headed for the tanker. LAPEL Three flight is coming off the tanker in DOG South."

I zapped him the SAM coordinates. "LAPEL One, have LAPEL Three ingress from the south and stay west of the river until we sort this out."

"Wilco."

My two-ship was on a twelve-mile arc due east of Baghdad. We were now heading north at 8,000 feet and directly abeam the SAM site. It was a good position. Operating on the fringe like this made us a tantalizing target, something you can almost reach. So they'd be watching and waiting. If the tracking radar got nervous or tried to lock on us, then our own systems were in the best place to locate it exactly.

The LAPEL flight would also be in area, so if I was attacked and wriggling around, he could find the SAM and put a bomb through it. Or vice versa, if he got targeted. The biggest problem with Weaseling were unknown threats, and this was a graphic example of that point. We really didn't know what was down there. It could be a more deadly SAM, or a Triple-A nest, or an entire battery.

Turned out, it was all of that.

"ELI Three's 6.4."

Sixty-four hundred pounds of gas and no reply from my wingman meant he was within five hundred pounds himself. I touched the RWR volume, countermeasure panel, and tightened my harness a bit. Glancing outside, I saw the two snub-nosed cylinders beneath my wings and called up the weapons display. Today, in addition to the normal cannon and air-to-air missiles, I had two CBU-103 canisters—cluster bombs. These things are terrific Weasel weapons, because they can be used for area targets and are easy to use under fire. It's like using a shotgun instead of a sniper rifle.

Each canister had about two hundred softball-size bomblets inside. The number of bomblets per thousand square feet is called the pattern density, and was mainly decided by how far above the ground the canister opened. This was controlled from the cockpit and varied according to the target. You'd need a greater bomblet density to knock out tanks versus unarmored targets like SAM sites.

Wheeling around to the right, we came back to the south on a fourteen-mile arc. The "3" was glowing softly on the RWR at about my two o'clock position. Orange-colored tracers shot up several miles off the nose and slightly right. They were aimed in our general direction but too far away to be a threat. I remembered that there was a small auxiliary airfield in that area and angled away slightly. As the next stream of tracers passed well behind my tail, I keyed the mike. "ELI Four . . . Slapshot SA-3, bearing two-two-zero."

The other F-16 turned, vapor streaming from his wingtips, and pulled hard across my tail to point at Baghdad. I checked to the right far enough to keep him in sight and stared at the target area. The Diyala River twisted out from the city like a dirty green snake. East of it, where we were, the khaki-colored ground was deserted. Past the river, toward the SAMs, the earth became a mottled quilt of sage-green fields, gray roads, and scattered villages.

"ELI Four, Magnum SA-3 . . . Bull's-eye zero-two-two for nine."

A huge plume of white smoke mushroomed beneath his wing as the HARM came off. We both pulled away to the south, away from the missile's path as it flattened out and sped toward Baghdad.

More Triple-A arced upward from the downtown area and the southern suburbs. This had to be directed at the Marine Hornets beating up on the Kut Highway and bridges over the Tigris. So much the better, as it would be a distraction to the Iraqi Air Defense units.

The target I'd marked was now directly off my right wing at twelve miles. Zippering the mike, I rolled almost onto my back and pulled to center the steering in the HUD. Popping upright, I brought the throttle back to hold 450 knots and quickly searched the ground. At my left, ten o'clock position, the downtown Triple-A had opened up again and the Tigris River was nearly fluorescent green in the weird light. A big canal ran along the Madina slums on the northern edge of the city, and I was surprised that one entire section was bright red. Iron in the water or sewage—either way, it was strange.

"ELI Three, attacking."

With my right thumb, I called up the SMS display and checked the CBU settings one last time. The CBU-103 was a vast improvement over older cluster bombs. It could correct for winds, and in Iraq the wind was a very real variable that could easily mean the difference between an effective attack or a miss. Fins on the tail would also cant to spin the canister, and once it reached a pre-set rate, the canister would open and the bomblets would deploy. I confirmed all these settings, pulled the power back to hold 425 knots, and kept a slight descent as I passed 10,000 feet.

Black smoke continued to rise from the south and east, and my radar was speckled with contacts. Occasional flashes along the river caught my eye; it looked like the downtown fighting was still very heavy. Farther west, I saw the hanging gray fingers from more SAMs but hadn't seen them launch. The RWR was saturated and useless, so my eyeballs were everything at the moment. The Strike frequency was alive with close air-support chatter, so I turned the UHF radio down.

At seven miles, I was in the sweet spot. The jet was throbbing perfectly, I was dead on-target, and everything was working. The HUD symbology for this particular weapon was called a "staple," because that's what it looked like. The top and bottom represented the maximum and minimum release ranges for the CBU based on my altitude, airspeed, and winds. There was a smaller staple for the optimum zone, and this is usually where we tried to release—

situation permitting. I watched the little caret slowly slip down the staple and squinted through the HUD. The TD box was sitting firmly where I left it, but I was still too far away for fine-tuning.

"ELI Three . . . break right. Now!"

My throat clutched, but my hands instantly moved. Instinct and training habits took over again and I shoved the throttle forward, over-pulled to the right, pumped out chaff, and yanked the fighter sideways back toward the north. I was directly over some shitty little town on Highway 5 with a perfect four-way canal-road inter-section. Rolling out directly over the road, I slammed the stick forward, felt my helmet smack the canopy, and blinked as the cockpit dust floated into my face.

"Missile in the air! Missile . . . ah . . . north Bull's-eye ten."

I twisted in the seat and looked back over my left shoulder, bringing the jet along, too. There! I picked up the smoke trail as it cleared the horizon line. Actually, there were two.

"ELI Three's tally two missiles. Left eight o'clock . . . they're climbing eastbound and correcting north."

That's why I hadn't seen them. They'd come from the edge of the city just past the main canal and everything down there was some shade of gray.

"ELI Four is blind."

I kept my eyes on the SAMs. The wingman would be fine. It was hard to say which of us was targeted, since the RWR was still saturated. Flying by feel alone, I pulled the power back a bit and brought the nose up. Still looking back past the tail, I checked left and thumbed the decoy on again just in case. I also sent a data-link.

"Four . . . stay above ten thousand until visual. One is re-attack-ing from the north."

Cranking up hard on one wing, I swung around in the no-man's-land between the highways and put Baghdad on the nose again. With the target in the HUD, I pushed over and called up the CBU symbology again.

Even as I watched, another immense cloud of light smoke billowed up against Iraq's greenish-gray background. Slewing the diamond left, I put it directly over the smoke and stabbed forward to make a new steerpoint.

"ELI Four's visual."

I zippered a reply and squinted through the HUD. Like tan warts, I could make out several raised berms in a flat area just north of the canal. But without a better picture, I'd have to get a lot closer.

Where's the fucking targeting pod when I need it?

Up the Pentagon's ass.

Suddenly, several glowing streams shot upward from the site, and I flinched. The heavier Triple-A looked like fiery tennis balls as they rose quickly, hung in space, then fell back toward the earth. These seemed to be aimed right at my forehead, and for a long moment, I pressed ahead directly toward the ground fire. Descending through 9,000 feet, I was in range of anything down there except a kid with a slingshot.

That was probably next.

Leaning forward, I followed the last hanging smoke trail back to the ground and . . . there! In front of the center earthen berm were four horseshoe-shaped revetments. Where the smoke trail began, I could plainly see the light-colored, pointed tips of missiles. Triple-A began flashing from the top of the center berm, but I ignored it and concentrated on refining my aim just a hair. As the white-hot balls whizzed up past the nose, I put the tiny pipper on the center of the revetment, bunted forward slightly, and mashed the pickle button.

One CBU canister kicked off, and I instantly pulled straight up and shoved the throttle to mil. They'd been leading me with the anti-aircraft fire, so I had to change position now. As the jet came through the horizon, I snapped over onto my back and sliced back toward the farmland north of the city.

Slapping the throttle back, I was now passing through 5,000 feet and 500 knots, and I yanked violently right, then rolled out. Bunting again, I came back to the left in time to see the puffy white bursts overhead. Pulling back hard on the stick, I popped some chaff and zoomed up a few thousand feet, adding power as I climbed. Twitching my tail like this would hopefully defeat the stuff I couldn't see but knew they were shooting.

Glancing back over my shoulder, I saw a large, dirty-brown cloud rising from the center of the site and knew the cluster bomb had hit.

"ELI Four . . . see any secondaries?" Secondaries were one very visible indication that you'd hit something. But even without them, my CBUs could still really mess up a SAM site. Close detonations can knock launchers off their mountings and put fatal holes in things that don't burn, like radars or people.

"Four . . . negative."

Well, I hadn't, either.

But I also hadn't seen any more missile launches, so maybe the Iraqis were dazed or hiding in shelters with their skulls ringing. Maybe not. Didn't matter. What did concern me was the fact that there was an entire SAM site down there no one had known about. A missile battery that could kill our attack helicopters on their way into Baghdad to support the Army and Marine ground units.

AT 10,000 FEET AND TEN MILES FROM THIS NEW TARGET, I crossed Highway 2 and pulled the power back to hold 400 knots.

ELI Four had reappeared and was hanging fairly close off my left wing. I smiled. It was always disconcerting for young wingmen to get separated from a flight lead, especially being shot at while over enemy territory. But it happens, and he'd managed to rejoin without garbaging the radios, hitting me, or getting himself shot down.

"ELI Three is 6.1."

"ELI Four . . . 7.2."

I nodded. I'd done a lot more maneuvering than he had, so I'd be shorter on fuel and it was better that way. Beginning a wide, right-hand turn, I looked back at Baghdad, and switched over to the AWACS.

"LUGER . . . this is ELI 33."

The Tigris was a sage-green ribbon against the darker green fields on either bank. A good-size suburb known as Taji lay just west of the city. As a vital rail depot for Baghdad, this place was supposed to be a nest of SAMs, including a few SA-6s, so we'd give it a wide berth. Shaking my head, I tried to see the railroad tracks but could not. (I'd actually bombed the Taji railway station in 1991 to keep the Republican Guards from moving. Small world.)

LUGER wasn't talking, so I scanned my comm card and found the frequency for HYPER. Iraq was divided into north, center, and south sections, based on latitude. HYPER was the AWACS that controlled north of the 35th Parallel, so maybe I'd have better luck with him.

I didn't.

"ELI Three . . . LAPEL One."

"Go."

"Ah . . . LAPEL One has a stuck refueling door and I need to RTB. I'd like LAPEL Two to join up with you."

"Where's LAPEL Three?"

"They came off the tanker ten mikes ago . . . probably inbound and close by."

"LAPEL Three is Bull's-eye two-five-zero for eighteen. Just west of the airport," he added.

I looked over the wingtip at Iraq. Baqubah was off to my north-east and that little auxiliary field was just off the nose. This was as good a place as any.

"ELI Three flight and LAPEL come up on Cobalt Eight." This was LAPEL's frequency but if their flight lead was going home he wouldn't need it. Now we could all talk and data-link together. "LAPEL Two you are now ELI Five."

"Five copies. 10.6."

Good—he had plenty of fuel. ELI Five was a young, cool-headed captain named Dave Brodeur, otherwise known as Klepto. I slewed the diamond over Baqubah, took a mark, and data-linked it. Several bends in the Diyala River were heavily irrigated and looked like big green testicles. It was the perfect rejoin point for a bunch of guys with more balls than brains.

"LAPEL Three, cleared overhead above fifteen thousand. ELI Five stay overhead at twelve K and head's up for Taji."

They all acknowledged. I had one can of CBU-103 plus a full load of 20-mm for the cannon. Number Four had a HARM left and the gun, while ELI Five had two cans of CBU with his gun. Glancing at the lineup card, I saw LAPEL Three had CBUs and his wingman had HARMs.

I'd sketched out a rough picture of the compound and figured, based on the northerly winds, we should hit the southern revetments first, so the smoke and dust wouldn't obscure the rest of the compound.

"ELI Three this is LUGAR."

Of course it is.

"LUGAR, ELI Three . . . come up Zinc 14 and stand by for data."

Zinc 14 was a secondary strike frequency. This way, I could pass him the information without trashing the radio for the other fifty jets listening in. I peered at my scribbling and diagram. "North three-three . . . two-five . . . four-one. East four-four . . . two-seven . . . two-nine."

Staring south at Baghdad, I saw more missile launches toward the southeast, and I wondered about ELI One. But Zing was a big boy and knew what he was doing. I'd never get down there and get involved quick enough to make a difference. These situations all had a "flow" to them, and it was difficult to mesh with flights that were already on station and involved in attacks.

"LUGER . . . this is an SA-3 complex . . . at least three batteries observed. Fifty-seven mike mike Triple-A." I remembered the last bunch of shit whizzing by the cockpit and added, "Probably Zooce as well."

"Zooce" was slang for the ZSU-23-4. This was a very small, very mobile anti-aircraft gun. A four-barreled, high rate-of-fire system, it was nearly impossible to defend against and was a really nasty piece of work.

"LUGER copies all. Say intentions."

That word again.

"LUGER, keep all friendlies clear of the northern half of Kill-box 88 Alpha Sierra. ELI and LAPEL are working the target from the north and east. Will advise."

I came through my third orbit and saw Triple-A over the little tan airfield to the south.

"LAPEL Three is on station."

I looked up but saw nothing. The upper-level clouds seemed a bit lower though, and much thicker. All the more reason to destroy this site today so they wouldn't try to move it under cover of bad weather.

"LAPEL . . . when I call 'Attacking,' you arc southeast of the target. Turn in and attack when I call 'Rifle' or 'Defending.' Any defensive call gets a HARM from LAPEL Four."

This was a Hunter Killer attack I'd personally developed and re-fined over the years. One pair attacks from one axis, while the other pair arcs on another side of the target. This forces the SAM to react to both threats and usually resulted in shots fired. If the attacking flight is fired on, then they simply abort, turn sideways, and begin to arc. The other pair immediately turns in and attacks. HARMs are fired to distract, and eventually someone works in close enough to kill the SAM. If all went well, which rarely happens, when the first pair released weapons, the second pair would begin their at-tack. "Rifle" was actually a term for shooting a Maverick missile, but I'd always hated extra words. In a perfect world, we'd use three pairs, called a six-pack, to overwhelm and nail the site. These guys all knew the attack but it felt better to reiterate the major points.

Incidentally, attacking and killing a SAM site is at least as dif-ficult and dangerous as killing an enemy fighter jet. These days, I believe, it's harder, because modern missile technology is deadlier than the quality of any enemy pilot who might face us. During the Vietnam War, over eleven hundred fixed-wing aircraft were shot down from SAMs and Triple-A; seventy-seven were shot down by MiGs. The U.S. military had lost just one fixed-wing aircraft to air combat in Operation Desert Storm and Kosovo, but eighteen were downed from ground threats. Yet, despite this, there was still no such thing as an air-to-ground "ace." Makes you wonder.

"Copy all," LAPEL Three replied. "What target?"

I glanced at the diagram. "If I abort then take my target. If not, I'll zap you a DMPI."

Designated munition point of impact. Proof that whenever pos-sible, the military will always use four words when one would suf-fice. DMPI meant "target."

"LAPEL copies . . . ready." He sounded eager.

"ELI Five, stay put here. We'll pick you up for the next attack."

"Five copies."

"ELI Three . . . attacking SA-3, Bull's-eye zero-two-two for eight. Check switches."

Looking left, I cranked over in a five-G turn and put the SAM site on the nose. Following my own advice, I ran my fingers and eyes over the countermeasures and weapons display.

Paralleling the Tigris River, we were pointing southeast directly at Baghdad. My wingman was on the east side, about two miles away and slightly high. The cloud cover had settled in, but it stayed up around 20,000 feet and didn't affect us yet. Dark gray smudges from large-caliber Triple-A also hung over the city. More appeared, popping open like grotesque red and orange mushrooms, as the Iraqis fought back against the American jets.

Several streams of white anti-aircraft fire hosed off in our direction as we passed the little airfield. I couldn't see anything on the runways or taxiways, and the Triple-A looked to be small-caliber stuff that couldn't hit us unless we were stupid.

At eight miles, I nosed over slightly and watched the TD box settle on the SAM complex. There were two sprawling neighborhoods just south of the canal, separated by a triangular swath of ground that looked like a trash dump. The SAM site was just north of the canal and the dump. I was going to hit the southern edge of the complex where I'd seen the other revetments. The wind behind me would blow the smoke over Baghdad and leave the target area clear for the others. Even as I watched, I saw the familiar rolling cloud of a missile launch; lucky for me, it came from the south corner of the site.

"ELI Three, missile in the air, Bull zero-two-two for seven."

My wingman jumped on it. "ELI Four, attacking . . . SA-3!"

"Negative." I looked over at him. "Negative. LAPEL Four . . . Slapshot SA-3, target area." Five miles from the target area, the last thing I wanted was a huge ball of HARM smoke showing our position. Might as well hang a big neon SHOOT ME sign overhead.

"LAPEL Four, Magnum SA-3!"

My hands were light on the stick and throttle, ready to slam sideways and get the fuck out if the SAM showed any signs of having been corrected in my direction. But it didn't. The missile headed west in a slight climb, leaving a wobbly gray trail across the skyline. It also left an excellent visual cue for me—again, I followed the smoke to its launch point. The revetments were a bit farther west than I remembered, but there was an algae-covered irrigation ditch pointed directly at the SAM cluster. It looked like a nasty green finger.

Pulling the power back, I passed through 7,000 feet. That weird, bright-red section of canal caught the corner of my left eye while Triple-A sparkled off to the right toward Taji. Leaning forward, I hung in space for a moment and took in the target area. There were four big revetments and several smaller ones. The one where the smoke had come up from was next to a road, and I could see the familiar pencil-shaped missiles sticking up from the earth. The other revetments had missiles, too, but the Iraqis were big believers in decoys.

This one was real.

As the pipper touched the lip of the emplacement, my thumb came down on the pickle button. For a half second, I did nothing till the bomb cleared the wing. Pulling straight up to the horizon, I immediately rolled hard right and shoved the throttle into mil power.

"ELI Three, Rifle SA-3!"

As I came around, heading west to parallel the canal, every gun on the complex opened up. Flipping upside down, I pulled toward the ground and headed north as tracers cut through the sky.

"ELI Four . . . Triple-A over the target . . . don't overfly it!" I was breathing hard now and looking back over my shoulder for him and for any missiles. "Go north for the rejoin."

"Four copies . . ."

"LAPEL Three, attacking SA-3."

"ELI Four . . . ah, secondaries to . . . at the south end!"

Snapping upright, I took a couple of breaths and twitched my tail again. Nothing. I was hauling ass north again at 3,000 feet just on the east side of Highway 2. Immediately zooming up to get above small-arms firing range, I bunted at 5,000 feet and looked back. The southern revets were obscured by dust and smoke. Too much damage from one can of CBU, so I must've hit something else—fuel or maybe a few spare missiles. I thumped the canopy rail and grinned.

"LAPEL Three . . . hit the center of the complex. The largest berm in the middle of the empty area . . . has four missile revets on the north side and at least three radars on top. Kill the radars."

"Three copies . . . main berm and radars on the top."

"Affirm. Drop both cans in a pair."

He zippered the mike while I pulled the power back to save some fuel. Tactically, I should've hit the radars first and blinded the SAM site, but I didn't think my one remaining CBU would cover enough area for that. But his two cans, dropped as a pair, would impact about 500 feet apart, completely shred the top of the berm, and send a few more Iraqi gunners to paradise.

"LAPEL Three . . . Triple-A from the target. Defending north."

I bumped my air-to-air radar out to twenty miles and saw a solitary white square about twelve miles in front of me at 15,000 feet. Locking on him, I listened to LAPEL's attack.

"LAPEL Three is in for the re-attack . . . Four continue arcing north at ten thousand."

I nodded. That was smart. He was leaving his wingman up where everyone could see him, then he'd swing around and attack from below. The gamble was that the Iraqis would think both fighters were together and arcing along just out of range. A distraction would help, so I keyed the mike. "ELI Four . . . Slapshot SA-3, target area."

We weren't back together yet, but the defenders would plainly see the HARM launch and either duck or search around the smoke. Either way, LAPEL Three had a good chance of getting in unobserved.

"ELI Four, Magnum SA-3 . . . Bull zero-two-one for eight."

Tilting my head back, I scanned the sky where I thought he should be and was rewarded by a thick line of smoke streaking southeast toward Baghdad.

"ELI Four . . . continue to the rejoin point and hold at twelve thousand. ELI Five . . . One is radar contact on your nose, nine miles at eight thousand."

"Five is radar contact . . . visual."

"Fighting wing. ELI One is 5.8."

Overflying the rejoin point, I began a sweeping left turn and caught a flash of sunlight on metal. Looking up, I saw Klepto float overhead, then invert and pull himself into a loose fighting-wing formation.

"LAPEL Three . . . Rifle, Rifle. Off east. Lapel Four come east of the river at eight K or above."

"ELI 33, this is LUGER."

"Stand by." Perfect timing, as always.

I heard the data-link cricket and looked at my MFD. Both LA-PELs were south and east of the target. ELI Five and I were superimposed together northwest of the SAM complex, and ELI Four was directly over the rejoin point. The Tigris disappeared under the wings, and off to the west I could barely make out the pale green smear of Tartar Lake. It was actually Buhayrat ath Tharthar, but Tartar Lake was easier to say. Thirty minutes ago I'd seen it clearly, but it was now vanishing in the haze, suggesting we'd have weather problems to contend with very soon.

"ELI 33, this is LUGER."

I shook my head and reversed the turn slowly to the left. "Go ahead."

"ELI . . . ah . . . TOGA 76 is going to RTB early for mechanical problems so we have no one available for your final refueling. Suggest you come south now to catch TOGA 24 before they leave."

"Why is TOGA 24 leaving?"

"Ah . . . ELI, they're leaving at the end of their fragged station time."

I took a deep breath and swallowed the various remarks that bubbled up to my lips.

"LUGER . . . pass to TOGA 24 to remain on station to cover TOGA 76's refuelings. Also ask TITUS 33 if he can remain a bit longer. ELI 33, flight of three, will be off target in ten minutes."

"ELI, we'll try to work it out. They're pretty tight on their times."

"And I'm pretty busy at the moment," I replied tersely. I mean, these guys were sitting in a safe orbit over Saudi Arabia—why did *I* have to think of the plan? "Tell TOGA he can move to DOG South if it makes him feel better and we'll pick him up on the way out."

I turned down the radio volume to avoid hearing his verbose reply. On Victor, I zippered the mike, then said, "ELI Three, attacking." I then sent a data-link so everyone would have the picture.

The fighter surged ahead as the throttle hit the mil power stop, and I once again ran my eyes and fingers over the cockpit. I did a double take at the HUD when I noticed my decoy had been shot away. Deploying another, I checked the chaff and flares and noted about half remaining of each type. It was enough.

"ELI Five, your targets are revetments in the northern section of the complex." I could see it in my head, but this kid hadn't been over the area yet. "You'll need to come north from your TD box about one klick toward the northwest corner. There are four revets grouped together."

"ELI Five copies."

I hoped so. Angling left a little, we were skirting Taji to the north, and I fervently hoped there really wasn't an SA-6 there. But there was no other way to attack in the time and gas we had left. Besides, I'd attacked from the north last time, and Weasels *never* came in the same way twice if it could be avoided.

Ten miles out, we crossed the Tigris heading southeast toward Highway 2 and Baghdad. Pulling power and nosing over, I put the target in the HUD just as the FUEL warning popped up. I toggled it off and quickly typed in a lower number.

Six miles out and passing 8,000 feet, the first wispy tendrils of low-lying clouds were thickening, and I knew we were running out of time. I also saw dust hanging over the center of the SAM site— LAPEL had done his work.

"ELI Five, call tally on the complex."

"Five . . . I . . . wilco."

It was time. "Five, you've got the tactical lead on the left . . . ELI Three is floating to cover."

It would be easier for him to find and drop on the target without having to fly formation off of me. Besides, I didn't have anything left to shoot except the cannon. He zippered the mike and I smoothly pulled up until he passed me, then I barrel-rolled over to his left side so I'd be looking through him toward the SAM site and Baghdad. If anything bad came off the ground, it would come from there.

Five miles from the target, the other F-16 nosed down and ramped toward the ground. Bright streams of anti-aircraft fire arced over downtown Baghdad but Klepto never flinched. Not until the SAM came off the ground in front of us.

"ELI Five . . . break right with chaff! SAM at twelve o'clock low, close!"

I caught a quick glimpse of the Viper's belly before he rolled away to the west. Tiny gray puffs of chaff popped out behind him as he sliced toward the Tigris River. I yanked hard to the left and headed out east with Highway 5 in my face, with missile symbols covering the RWR display.

"LAPEL Four . . . Magnum SA-3, north Bull eight."

That was our last HARM, but now was as good a time as any. Cranking up on one wing, I stared back at the SAM site and eyeballed the missile's smoke trail. It was heading due west, and I saw no curve to indicate it had turned. Still, who really knew?

"ELI Five, come north . . . check decoy."

"Five is northbound. Walking the Dog."

Good man. I pulled the power back and leveled off at 6,000 feet. Glancing at the HUD, I did the math. We'd defended and aborted at about five miles, and LAPEL Four fired his HARM a few seconds later. Assuming he was ten miles away at the shot, the HARM would take about thirty seconds to get to the general area of the SAM complex. According to the clock, it should be impacting about now and—I eyeballed the distance from the target—we were about eight miles away. Less than a minute out to hit the site. Far enough.

"ELI Five . . . turn in now and re-attack. ELI Three will stay above 6,000 feet."

"Ah . . . ELI Five was no-joy on the target."

No joy. He hadn't seen it. LAPEL Three had already dropped his bombs, and I didn't have the gas to wait for another flight of fighters.

"Copy that. Distance?"

"Five is nine miles to the north."

Instantly beginning a hard left turn, I put the target directly off

my left wing at seven miles. "Five, turn in now and call five miles."
As he zippered the mike, I grunted against the Gs and continued to
turn until the SAM site was directly before me.

"ELI Three, attacking from the east below three thousand. At
your five-mile call, I'll mark the target with the cannon."

"Five copies. Will look for smoke."

Actually dust, but why split hairs? I took a deep breath, dumped
the nose, and pushed the power back up. With only 4,500 pounds
of gas, this was definitely the last pass, and if we didn't kill it
today, then it was highly likely that no one would. Dropping fast, I
pumped out a few chaff bundles and rolled out, heading southwest
over the Diyala River.

"LAPEL Three . . . Magnum SA-3, northwest Baghdad."

I grinned under the oxygen mask as the airspeed touched
500 knots. God love the boy. He didn't have any HARMs to
shoot, but called it anyway for the benefit of the Iraqis listening
to our frequencies. Maybe it helped, maybe not. Made me feel
better though.

Punching up the cannon symbology, I watched the circle with
the dot in the middle wobble a second, then I stared outside. Another decrepit town that had languished under Saddam's rule
flashed under my wings as I roared southward. Several belated
Triple-A bursts shot out of the rooftops, but they were too late.
I was flying at better than 900 feet per second, and without radar
guidance, I doubted anything would hit me. I was also counting on
surprise and being a lot lower than the gunners were accustomed
to seeing.

Passing the highway, I immediately racked the jet over about
twenty degrees to the left, snapped upright, and began to count.

Two.

"SAM launch . . . SAM in the air over Baghdad. Two of 'em

heading east!" I had no idea who called that but, sure enough, there were missile trails emerging over the downtown skyline and climbing upward, toward the southeast. I hoped ELI Five didn't abort.

"ELI Five is five miles." Good man.

"LAPEL Three . . . Magnum SA-3, northwest Baghdad." More spoofing.

Three. Slamming the throttle back to mil, I pulled straight up. The ground dropped away beneath me and the horizon rapidly expanded. When the F-16's nose touched about fifteen degrees above the horizon, I rolled smoothly to the right and sliced back until the steering lined up in my HUD. As I flipped upright, one glance took it all in. I was 1.9 miles from the SAM complex at 470 knots, passing 3,200 feet on my way down.

If the target was the center of a clock face, I would be at three o'clock pointing inward, and ELI Five would be at twelve o'clock heading toward the six position. The big green canal was plain to see, and there wasn't any smoke remaining from the previous attacks, but I quickly found the center berms.

Twenty-five hundred feet now and almost 500 knots. Too fast. Tugging the power back, I fanned the boards a moment to slow down.

There! A shark-tooth protrusion in the perimeter fence and, a bit farther west, was the northern corner of the compound. Squinting through the HUD, I called up the cannon symbology again and put the pipper just inside the fence.

Fifteen hundred feet and about a mile away at 440 knots. If my timing was right, then ELI Five would be around four miles from the target. I came over the outer fence at a thousand feet and saw tiny figures of men scurrying over the berms. There were three revetments in the north cluster, with equipment and people in two of them. Kicking the rudder, the F-16 slipped sideways and lined up on the center of the three emplacements.

"Stand by, Five." This would be close.

"ELI Five is four miles . . . TD box is on the north corner."

I slid through 500 feet and let the green pipper settle on the base of the revetment. Pointed missiles were plain to see, and there were men running back and forth. Flashes suddenly caught the corner of my left eye, and I knew we'd missed some of the Triple-A pits around the complex. But it was too late to worry about now, so I held the pipper rock-steady and squeezed the trigger.

"BURRPP."

The fighter shuddered as the cannon spat shells at the revetment. I let up for a half-second to let the symbology settle out, bunted over, aimed again at the missile launcher, and squeezed the trigger again.

"BURRRPPPP."

The picture froze in my mind for another half-second when I stopped firing. The first burst of a hundred cannon shells hit a bit short and chewed up the entrance into the berm. Men were scattering left and right as the second burst hit the dirt inside the revetment that held the missile launcher. Everyone around it disappeared in a cloud of dust.

Rolling violently away from the emplacement, I shoved the nose back down in a wild-porpoise maneuver. This banged my head against the canopy but got me clear of any frag and spoiled the aim of anyone stupid enough to have his head up.

But there must've been at least one gunner with some balls down there, because streams of bright dots arced over my canopy. Sideways to the ground, facing back toward the SAM complex, I also saw half a dozen dirty-white popcorn puffs from 57-mm Triple-A. Spitting out some chaff, I snap-rolled upright, savagely pushed the nose down again, and headed west like a striped ape in a jungle fire.

"ELI Five is visual your smoke!"

Bright orange fire suddenly lit up the ground behind me and I twitched my tail to see. Twisting in the seat, I flipped the visor up and saw a black cloud envelop the emplacement I'd just strafed. Flaming bits of metal burst out in all directions followed by a SAM that shot out of the top. I was keying the mike to call it, when it fell over and dove into the Baghdad suburbs just across the canal. *I'll bet my wingman sees the damn thing now,* I thought. Yanking the Viper around to the north, I said, "Drop on the revet just north of the explosion."

"ELI Five, Rifle SA-3 . . ."

I sent a data-link, turned hard to the north, and threw up the SLEWABLE mode of my radar. Looking back again over the seat at the SAM complex, I saw more Triple-A from the center area, but it was anger-management, not the tracking type. My radar didn't lock but the RWR lit up with an F-16 spike from behind me.

"ELI Five is tied, visual."

"Join to fighting wing. ELI Four, come south above ten K and you're cleared to join to one-mile trail. LAPEL Three, the target area is yours. Stay east of the Tigris for five minutes till we get clear."

"LAPEL copies . . . nice mess you made back there!"

I chuckled. "The scraps are all yours. Heads-up for at least two active Triple-A pits."

He zippered the mike as I hit the Tigris and headed southeast between the river and Taji.

PASSING 15,000 FEET, I SLOWED TO 350 KNOTS AND PUT THE long, brown ribbon of Highway 1 on my tail. A beautiful gray F-16 appeared a mile off my left wing, and ELI Four was dutifully a mile behind me and a little high. I waggled my wings to bring them both in and unclipped my sweaty oxygen mask. Wiping my face, I called up the steerpoint for the DOG South refueling track and stared down at Baghdad.

While my two wingmen slid into formation, I idly noted that my second decoy had disappeared somewhere over the SAM site and my chaff buckets were nearly empty as well. After battle-damage checks and fuel checks, we loosened up and headed down to refuel. The weather was getting worse, so I was happy to be done for the day. By my tally, we'd expended six cans of CBU cluster bombs and at least five hundred rounds of 20-mm cannon shells. And four HARMs, if you can count them. I passed all of this to LUGER as we checked out, and he replied, "A relay from JEREMIAH . . . shit-hot work today for ELI and LAPEL."

Well, I thought, doesn't that just put the cherry on the parfait. But I was nice and thanked him. JEREMIAH today had to be Kanga Rew. He was the only guy who bothered to talk to us.

"By the way, ELI . . . Air supremacy has just been declared over all of Iraq."

I also found out later that the SA-3 complex was indeed a brigade-level headquarters and had contained at least four missile batteries along with twenty anti-aircraft guns for support. ELI and LAPEL had destroyed all four batteries plus the early-warning and search radars. Our attack had rendered the site useless. More important, it wouldn't be threatening any of the American close air-support aircraft or helos working over the city as the fight for Baghdad intensified.

Skirting the Abu Ghraib section west of downtown, I could see the twin parallel runways of Saddam International Airport. Smoke still rose from the area to the east of it and downtown. On a whim, I flipped over my comm card and typed in a frequency.

"Baghdad Tower . . . Baghdad Tower, ELI 33."

A male voice with a Southern American accent immediately answered. "ELI . . . this is Baghdad. Go ahead."

"Afternoon Baghdad . . . flight of Vipers overhead, goin' home. Just wanted to see if we'd won the war yet."

"Waal, y'all are talkin' to me and ah'm sittin' in their tower eatin' ice cream and wipin' my ass with their prayer rugs. Guess we're winnin'," he drawled.

Air supremacy indeed.

11

ELI 33

April 7, 2003
1046 local time, Baghdad, Iraq

"Son of a bitch," I MUTTERED INTO THE SLIPPERY OXYGEN
mask as sweat ran down my forehead, through my eyebrow, and
into my left eye. Then I saw it.

In front of a rolling cloud of dirty white smoke, the surface-
to-air missile came up off the ground. The SAM was twenty feet
long, weighed a thousand pounds, and was accelerating to 2,300
miles per hour. Its speed exceeded a half-mile per second, and it
was locked onto me.

There wasn't much time.

"BEEP . . . BEEP . . . BEEP . . ." The radar-warning receiver,
called RWR, screamed into my helmet, telling me enemy radars
had locked onto my jet. "BEEP . . . BEEP . . . BEEP . . ."

I hesitated a long moment to make sure the thing was actually
tracking *me.* I shoved the nose of the F-16 down, my butt came off

the seat, and I blinked rapidly as cockpit dust floated into my face. The long white plume behind the missile flattened out as it leveled off a thousand feet above the Baghdad rooftops.

Not me, I briefly thought. It's onto something else. Not me.

But then it pitched upward and the smoke trail shortened as the enemy radar fed tracking corrections to the missile, and it turned to kill its target. Me.

Shit . . .

Flipping the Viper on its back, I deployed one of my towed decoys. This little thing would stream out 300 feet behind me on a cable and generate a nice fat signal for missiles to track instead of my jet. I hoped so, anyway, since the SAM was gathering speed as it arced around in my direction. Staring down at central Baghdad, I swallowed hard, counted two of my heavy, thumping heartbeats, and then smacked a bottle-top-size button on the bulkhead above the throttle. As bundles of radar-deflecting chaff shot out behind the tail, I pulled straight down toward the city.

Instantly reversing the pull, I snapped the jet around to keep the missile in sight and pulled the throttle back. I dropped out of the sky on the tip of a wild corkscrew with the horizon crazily spinning before me.

Down!

Down toward the gray earth. Down toward the buildings and the muddy-green Tigris River.

Down through the hole in the clouds to the guns of Baghdad.

A gap in the clouds was called a "sucker hole" for a reason. Usually a rough tear in an overcast cloud deck, it was a way to get down below the weather and visually see your target. Sometimes it was a large gap and sometimes it wasn't. But it was always dangerous and this one was no exception.

The problem with a hole in the clouds was that everything on the ground that could shoot was generally aimed up *through* the hole. Waiting. Waiting for some fighter pilot with more balls than brains to try and sneak down through it. A sucker.

But sometimes it was the only way. If a friendly got shot down, then you went through the hole and did whatever you could to save his skin. Sometimes you were forced through it after evading the SAMs. Or you were given a special mission, like emergency close air-support and had no choice.

That would be today.

There was no choice. ELI 33, two F-16s from the 77th Fighter Squadron, had just been given a critical mission in Baghdad. And to stay high and slow, silhouetted against the clouds, meant a messy explosion and bits of me floating into the Tigris River.

As I slammed the throttle back to IDLE, my eyes flickered to the HUD in front of my face. I was now at 450 knots and accelerating. Fanning open the speed brakes to slow down, I shoved my helmet visor up and stared at the missile. The SAM corrected its flight path and was beginning to turn north directly toward me. As the smoke thinned out, I could actually see the long, pointed body of the missile against the gray buildings and wispy clouds.

Then the second SAM lifted off.

"ELI One, tally the second SAM, right one o'clock . . . west of the river . . . One is defending!"

The radio clicked three times in my headset, meaning my wingman heard my call, understood I had seen another SAM launch, and was looking for the missile himself. ELI Two was Scott Manning and, like me, he was a veteran lieutenant colonel and instructor pilot. He just happened to be flying a wing position today, and it was good to have someone along who didn't need babysitting.

The smoke plume from the second SAM was visible, streaking over the rooftops. Long, colored fingers of anti-aircraft artillery clawed upward. Some were obviously tracking and others just fired for effect. It made the Iraqis feel better to shoot their guns, and they had plenty of ammunition. Twisting and weaving, I flew south along the Tigris River, trying to work east and away from downtown.

The first SAM had disappeared. After an almost slow-motion start, it quickly accelerated past the sound barrier, gaining altitude and speed. My RWR gave an electronic depiction of all the radars and missiles tracking my aircraft, and it was completely saturated. There was so much jizz, or radar emissions, in the air that the display looked like a Scrabble board. At last count, there were still more than fifty SAM sites in Baghdad alone.

New flashes erupted from the right, and I winced as a stream of fireballs arced up in my direction. Then another. And another. Crazed streams of glowing beads that crisscrossed the sky on all sides of my jet. Anti-aircraft artillery. Triple-A. There were ten thousand guns down there.

"ELI One . . . Triple-A . . . defending east."

Yanking the jet sideways, I booted the rudder pedal and glanced to my right. As the fighter skidded through the air, I took a breath and glanced at the suburbs. Lots of glowing, white-hot pellets shooting upward from the rooftops.

Too many.

"ELI Two . . . come in from the west . . . don't follow me in."

"Unable," came the terse reply.

Shit. Again. He was already committed.

Everyone in Baghdad was awake now and looking up at the two American fighter jets who were insane enough to come down low over their capital city and basically flip the bird to every SAM and anti-aircraft gun on the ground. I think it *really* pissed them off.

Down . . . down . . . down. The fighter was shuddering from the speed and the weight of the cluster bombs under my wings. Five hundred and twenty knots now . . . 600 miles per hour. What a way to spend a birthday. Today I was thirty-nine, and I'd really rather be on a beach with a pitcher of margaritas.

Fanning the speed brakes again, I cranked the jet back to the left, twisting eastward to put some distance between myself and the anti-aircraft fire. Berserk garden hoses, spraying streams of glowing droplets and leading me like a duck on the wing. I pulled up and felt the F-16 jump. Holding it a long moment, I bunted forward again and forced the nose down. The gunners tried to keep up but they liked straight and level bombers—not jinking, gray targets like me.

Target? . . . screw that. *I'm* the predator. I whipped my head around toward the south and east.

Little fuckers, I swore to myself. If I've got any extra bombs, I'll be back for you.

The SAM . . . where *was the damn thing* . . .

Of course, you rarely saw them anyway, and you almost never saw the second or third one. Situational awareness, that elusive sense of what's happening around you, was easily overloaded. In combat, time really can slow down at critical moments. That, combined with training and experience, at least gave you a fighting chance.

I was still staring directly down at the city. Like someone had hung me in a chair facedown on the horizon. Pulling back hard on the stick and fanning the boards again, I dropped through 8,000 feet with vapor streaming from the wingtips. Snapping the jet left and right, I strained to see the threats.

The first SAM had disappeared. At this range, I had less than ten seconds before it hit me. I began to count.

Two . . .

The second missile had pitched up, too, following the first one with the same arcing flight path. My breathing quickened, and I rolled the Viper slightly right toward the SAMs and pulled hard.

Six times the force of gravity, about 1,200 pounds, slammed me back into the seat.

Three . . .

Ignoring the sweat on my face, I snapped the fighter upright, shoved the throttle into afterburner, and pulled straight for the sky. Though I couldn't see the missiles, I knew the effect this had. Each time my jet moved, the tracking radar on the ground had to detect it, measure it, and transmit that movement to the SAM. Microchips interpreted my position, moved the fins, and the missile changed course to keep up with me. All in fractions of seconds. But each movement cost the missile incremental time, distance, and energy. Each movement could also save my life.

Four . . .

Grunting against the tremendous force of gravity and 500 knots of pure jet power, I let the nose come up through the horizon, then rolled again. This time, away, so my butt was pointed at the missile's general area. Holding the pull a moment longer, I then shoved forward—or bunted—the fighter again and tugged the throttle out of afterburner. This time, I floated weightless against the seat straps. Inverted now, ass to the missile, and hanging in space, I hoped my maneuvers confused the tracking radar as much as they hurt me.

Six . . .

The second missile had disappeared, too. The motor had burned out and the damn thing had shot up above somewhere and was now dropping down on me like a malignant spear. The Triple-A pits around the river had also opened up, since I was well below 10,000 feet and in range. The Iraqis were using a sound tactic. Fire the SAMs and get a fighter to defend itself until it was low enough to be engaged by the guns. It worked, too.

Eight . . .

Almost . . . almost . . .

Now!

Pulling back hard to the right, I began a huge, deep roll shaped like a barrel. A barrel roll was wide, fast, and powerful. The idea was to give the missile too many changing variables to overcome in the limited flight time it had left. If you could force a SAM to overshoot, you'd won, as it couldn't maneuver and come back like a fighter jet.

Pulling up, I smoothly brought the F-16 over on its back, but instead of rolling out I let the nose continue to fall down past the horizon, toward the smoky earth. Soon I was lying completely upside down along the horizon. It wasn't a high-G maneuver nor was it particularly violent. The idea was to get through the horizon inverted, pull the power to slow down, and then roll your way back to your starting point. Graceful and powerful, it played hell with older radar-tracking systems. Too many oblique angular corrections, and it would run the missile out of airspeed. It was effective against the SA-2 and SA-3. It didn't work at all against the newer SA-6 and SA-8.

And usually you could only get away with it once. The second SAM, or other types of missiles and Triple-A, would catch you by then.

And that's exactly what happened.

The city slowly spun upright as I came through the bottom of the roll. Blending in a smooth pull, the nose came up, and I was slowly and heavily pressed against the seat. Every four to five seconds, I smacked the chaff button; my head constantly swiveled, looking for other threats. The Triple-A had disappeared behind me for the moment, and I knew the first SAM must've overshot. Too much time had elapsed. Stealing a quick look at the HUD, I saw the target was behind me and about six miles away to the northeast.

At 550 knots, I zoomed up through the horizon and reversed

to come back around toward the target. As I did, my eye caught a flicker of movement. Instinctively, I pulled straight up, rolled, and slapped the chaff button.

It saved my life.

The deadly shape of another missile passed behind me on its way into the clouds. It had come *up* . . . it couldn't have been one of the SA-3s. The "X" in the bottom of my HUD told me the decoy was still alive and transmitting. So, it had been an infrared-heat-seeking SAM . . . not a radar-guided missile.

Son of a bitch . . . where there was one there were two. Still zooming upward, I turned sideways in the seat and tried to look down over my shoulder. But I stared a second too long and lost the picture of the world around me. Blue changed to gray and the horizon disappeared as I sliced into the cloud deck.

"ELI Two . . . defending, Triple-A!"

Perfect . . . there was nothing I could do for him at the moment—he was on his own.

Suddenly the jet bucked wildly under my hands and my stomach came up through my chest. I'd been hit!

But the F-16 kept flying and my eyes flickered to the warning-light panel. Nothing. *What the fuck* . . .

My eyes darted around the cockpit at the warning panels and engine gauges.

I must've flown through the disturbed air from the missile. I twisted my head back and forth, trying to find the horizon. Up was down and down was sideways. This sucked.

"WARNING . . . WARNING . . ." Bitching Betty rang through my helmet as the fighter shuddered and ran out of airspeed.

Eighty-six hundred feet over Baghdad, out of airspeed, and falling out of the sky. Not good.

Staring at the attitude indicator on my front console, I gave up on the outside world for a moment and flew the jet out of the cloud using the big round instrument. As my wings fell through the horizon, the jet picked up speed, and my breathing slowed a bit.

I'd come back down to 5,300 feet now, heading north and accelerating past 350 knots. I still had a target to hit.

"ELI One is ten miles south of the target, northbound at 5,300 . . . 6.9."

Ten miles. Barely a minute and a half. Sixty-nine hundred pounds of fuel and 5,300 feet above the gray, smoky earth. Still high enough to keep me clear of Iraqis with AK-47s but in range of every anti-aircraft gun and SAM in Baghdad. No choice, really. To climb up would take time and make me slow, and that was not a good combination over a heavily defended city.

"Two is 6.1 . . . thirteen south . . . uh . . . eastbound."

Thirteen miles southeast . . . he must've defended himself over there to stay clear of downtown. Sixty-one hundred pounds of fuel. That gave us a bit more than two thousand pounds to play with before he was BINGO (out of fuel) and we'd have to return to the tanker for gas.

I pictured it in my head as if I was looking down from above. God's-eye view, we called it. If the target was the center of a clock face, I was at six o'clock and my wingman was at four o'clock. I'd turn north toward twelve o'clock and attack. Number Two would circle up toward three o'clock and then turn in for his own attack. The time it took him to do that would keep him clear of my frag. ("Frag" was short for *fragments*—the bits of my bombs and whatever I'd hit that were on their way back down after being blown up. It was critical not to fly through the crap, since engines didn't agree with pieces of metal passing inside them.)

"ELI Two . . . arc east at ten miles and call in from the east."

Hopefully, this would work. With any luck, the Iraqis would be looking in the direction I'd come from and my wingman would hit them from the side. You never both attacked from the same direction if you could help it.

He zippered the mike, and then said, "Check cameras on . . . Green it up."

I checked my switches again and made sure the camera was filming and the master arm was on, or "green." That was another advantage to flying with another highly experienced pilot. He was thinking ahead, too. Zing was a good man. It made things easier when you didn't have to keep track of several young, inexperienced wingmen.

My headset gave me a cricket-like chirp, and I glanced down at the right-hand display above my knees. Multi Function Displays (MFD) were an amazing bit of situational awareness. As the name implied, they could be set up to show almost anything related to the jet, the weapons, or the area you were fighting. On the right MFD, I had a screen up that presented known SAM rings, several routes of strike aircraft, and my current target. The left display was used for my air-to-air radar.

A tiny symbol appeared, accompanied by another chirp, as my wingman data-linked me his position. He'd avoided the unmarked SAM and Triple-A belt that I'd found and was angling around to attack from the east.

I looked down and saw the northeast Baghdad suburbs disappearing beneath the left wing. It was time.

"One is in from the south."

Rolling and pulling, I brought the fighter around to the north and shoved the throttle up to full non-afterburning power. The F-16 surged forward immediately, and I checked the HUD.

9.1 miles to the target.

Attacking a target in a modern fighter is a bit like playing several musical instruments at the same time. My left hand constantly adjusted the throttle. My left fingers worked the radar, fanned the speed brakes, and managed my electronic countermeasures. I also changed radio frequencies and accessed any of the hundred different functions of the up-front control head with my left hand.

I flew with my right hand. The F-16 has a side stick mounted on the right side of the cockpit, not coming up from the floor like older fighters. My right fingers danced along the Display Management and Target Management switches on the stick while I flew. I also dropped bombs, launched missiles, and shot the cannon with my right hand. I really never needed to take my hands off the controls to do anything. It was a very well-designed cockpit. It had to be, for one pilot to keep up with five or six types of weapons, fly, navigate, and fight.

8.0 miles.

I glanced at my fuel displays and saw that they agreed with each other. Satisfied, I shoved up my visor again and peered at the solid green line running from top to bottom in my HUD. Called a "continuously computed release point," or CCRP, it provided steering to a release point that was calculated based on the selected weapon and selected target.

7.0 miles.

My eyes flickered around the cockpit again. Master arm was on. The jamming pod was transmitting against every threat it could sense. My towed decoy was out and also, theoretically, transmitting. The altitude readout was rock-steady at 5,000 feet, and I walked the throttle back to hold 500 knots.

Leaning forward, I stared around the HUD at the target area. Khan Bani Sad airfield. Saddam Hussein's back door.

There! The runway lay in a cleared patch of tan earth just west of the green banks of the Diyala River. Unlike on a planned mission, I had no photographs or diagrams of the target area. All that had been passed to us fifteen minutes ago were the coordinates and vague info about a helicopter pad on the northern end of the airfield. Earlier today, a B-1 bomber strike had leveled a city block in the al-Mansur neighborhood of Baghdad, trying to kill Saddam. He hadn't been there, and, knowing the war was lost, was now trying to escape the city via the helicopters.

And that wasn't happening, if I had anything to do with it.

Scanning up the runway, I could see the taxiway and a large concrete apron. If there was a control tower, I couldn't find it. If there were helicopters, I couldn't see them yet, either.

6.1 miles.

I leaned back and centered the steering again. I'd have to drop my cluster bombs on the coordinates if I couldn't see the copters with my eyes. Thumping the console in frustration, I bent forward one more time. Dropping on coordinates might work for a bridge or building, but the chance of hitting several small helicopters was . . .

"I'll be damned."

Tendrils of vapor were spinning in circles like an old-fashioned water sprinkler. Rotor blades . . . stirring up the heavy, humid air. There they were. Four helos, about a hundred yards apart.

Instantly, I tapped the button on my stick that changed aiming solutions. Continuously Computed Impact Point (CCIP) relied on my eyeballs, not coordinates. The bombs would go through the visual-aiming pipper now dangling downward in my HUD, like a pendulum.

5.3 miles.

Bunting over a little, I lightly touched the stick to put the pipper below the first two helos and pulled the throttle back a notch.

My right thumb hovered above the pickle button on the stick. Out of habit, I held my breath as the little circle with the dot in it kissed the nose of the first helicopter. Mashing down smoothly and firmly, I held my thumb in place. The F-16 rocked as both canisters of CBU-103 cluster bombs kicked off.

Shoving the throttle full-forward, I banked up hard to the left then came back to the right. Twitching my tail, so to speak, to catch any Triple-A or SAMs that might be coming up at me.

But we'd caught them by surprise and, due to the pounding Baghdad had taken, coordination between Iraqi air defense sites was becoming increasingly rare. So the Iraqis that had shot at us earlier hadn't passed any information to these bastards. Flicking my air-to-air radar into the DOGFIGHT mode that would automatically lock onto anything it saw, I came off left toward the west and looked back at the airfield.

Several things happened at once.

The helicopters on the western edge of the concrete pad simply vaporized as my cluster bombs, each containing two hundred softball-size pieces of encased high explosives, detonated.

The other helicopter was untouched. And then every piece of Triple-A on Khan Bani Sad woke up and began shooting.

"ELI One is off . . . west."

Zing's reply was immediate. "ELI Two's in from the east."

Looking back, I could see the smoke drifting south with the wind, which was good. My wingman would have a clear look at the remaining helos.

"Push it up, Two . . . the other copter may bolt outta here."

I damn well would, if several of my buddies had just disappeared in front of me.

"ELI Two . . . thirty seconds."

He must've been cheating on the ten-mile arc. Didn't matter now.

"ELI Two . . . your target is west of the smoke . . . west of the smoke . . . next to the runway. A single Hoplite with its rotor turning." A Hoplite was a Soviet-made Mi-2 helicopter.

"ELI Two is tally the smoke . . . looking."

"And Two . . . I'm gonna arc west of the runway and keep the Triple-A busy. *Don't* come off west."

The mike zippered in reply. I pulled the F-16 up about sixty degrees and rolled sideways to keep the airfield in sight. So, with my nose jacked up, I was now skidding sideways at about 6,000 feet above the northern suburbs. The Triple-A was still firing, but I thought they were having a tough time seeing my gray jet against gray clouds. However, I wanted them to see me and not my wingman, so I'd have to help them with that.

I put out a flare. Then another.

Eyeing the HUD, I let the airspeed bleed off to 400 knots, over-banked, and pulled down toward the ground. Coming all the way over on my back, I glanced to the west, to a bend in the river that looked like a big ear, and saw my bright orange flares drifting slowly to earth. There was also an SA-6 site marked on my map, which supposedly lived there. It was a very nasty SAM nest, so my eyes were everywhere.

But nothing came up at me. Accelerating toward the ground now, I tugged the throttle back a bit and rolled left to see the airfield. My flares had definitely attracted attention, and all the gunfire was arcing west toward me. Most of it was being shot visually, but I saw several Triple-A radar symbols on my threat-warning system. I could live with that. Just no SA-6s. I could die from that.

It was a dangerous game. I was trying to get shot at by what I knew was there, while not sure what else was tracking—or waiting until I got real close before shooting. This was the essence of SAM killing—Wild Weaseling. "You've gotta be shitting me," indeed.

The airspeed made the jet shudder. Raw power. Without taking my eyes off the ground, I blended the roll with a pull back up through the horizon. Straining against the Gs that pressed me into the seat, I stared at the airfield. If the last helo took off before Zing got it, then I'd kill it with a Sidewinder missile. I doubted my air-to-air radar would be able to pick up something so slow against the trucks and tanks moving around down there, so I needed to keep my eyes on them.

I was just about to data-link a position request from him, when the center of the northern taxiway blew up. It looked like someone had placed a giant shotgun a foot off the ground and pulled the trigger.

And the other Hoplite disappeared. I never saw ELI Two and neither did the Iraqis, so maybe my flare-dropping antics kept them busy. In any event, the helicopters were dead. Maybe Saddam, too, I thought.

But I doubted it. That would be too much luck for one day.

"ELI Two's off north."

"Nice job, Two. Arc northeast above six thousand . . . ELI One is in from the southwest."

He zippered a reply. I slammed the throttle forward, yanked the fighter over, and dove down to 5,000 feet while he climbed up above 6,000 feet. This kept us clear of each other and gave the Iraqis headaches.

I swung around in a lazy circle toward the Tigris, the airfield now behind me and most of Baghdad before me. I did this to get some room for my next and last pass on the airfield—and so I wouldn't be belly-up to an SA-6.

Focusing on the river bend, I could see lots of military buildings, straight lines, and revetments, but nothing that looked like a SAM site. I'd take the chance. Now, five miles directly west of the airfield, I rolled the fighter up again and attacked.

No guesswork this time. I knew exactly where to aim. There was one serviceable hangar beside the shredded runway, and I reasoned that if there were spare helos, then that's where they'd be. One more pass with the cannon, and we'd get the fuck out of here.

Suddenly, a string of bright orange balls dropped out of the gray sky. They were going down, not coming up. Flares . . .

I grinned under my oxygen mask. It was Zing doing for me what I'd done for him and trying to attract attention. Good man.

4.1 one miles.

I could plainly see the mess we'd made of the airfield. Fires glowed beneath the oily black smoke that only came from burning machines. Up a bit higher, the smoke changed to a lighter gray and spread out, like a widening ripple on a pond. The entire oblong smear was drifting slowly south.

But there was the runway. I angled a little left, held it a few seconds, and then came back to the right. The hangar was now clear of the smoke and I pushed the throttle up. Switching to the GUN symbology, I lowered the nose and concentrated on aiming. Off to my left were flashes from Triple-A, which had to be from Baqubah, another airfield, about ten miles north of me. A few remaining guns on Khan Bani Sad also opened up, generally in Zing's direction, but I knew he was far enough east to be clear.

At 3.4 miles, I cracked the throttle back a notch, noted that my decoy was transmitting, and lined up the steering cues. I put the pointing cross at the top of the HUD on the center of the runway, and the gun pipper on a road south of the field. Bunting forward, I held the picture and flew straight at the hangar. As I descended, the pipper inexorably moved up toward the long, low rectangle of the hangar.

Three thousand feet.

Almost there . . . I pressed lightly on the stick to adjust the steering and the pipper came up through a row of straggly trees just behind the hangar.

Twenty-six hundred feet. Pipper coming up . . . almost . . . twenty-four hundred feet. The pipper skipped over the trees, touched the base of the hangar doors, and I squeezed the trigger.

"BUURRRPPP."

The jet shuddered violently as the cannon fired. Twenty-millimeter shells spat from the gun port behind my left shoulder and streamed toward the hangar. I released the trigger and began to pull up and right away from the airfield.

"BEEP . . . BEEP . . . BEEP . . ."

My eyes instantly swiveled to the radar warning display.

"6."

Directly behind me and very, very close!

Mother of God . . .

The nose came up through the horizon and I rotated the throttle outboard and shoved it forward. Thirty-six thousand pounds of thrust kicked in with the afterburner, and the fighter leapt forward.

Slapping the chaff button with my left hand, I pulled off left and down. Twisting sideways, I stared behind me for the SAM.

"BEEP . . . BEEP . . . BEEP . . ." The RWR frantically tried to tell me that the missile was close enough for its on-board guidance to take over. Terminal guidance.

I hoped not.

Mouth dry, eyes wide, I twisted back right and brought the jet around with me. Down! down! Yanking the throttle out of afterburner, I slapped out more chaff.

"ELI One . . . defending SA-6 . . . eastbound over the airfield!"

His reply was instantaneous. "ELI Two . . . No joy on the SAM. Blind at 6,000 feet . . ."

So he'd lost sight of me and didn't see the SAM. I was now heading south right off the end of Khan Bani Sad. Bottoming out at 3,000 feet, I yanked the nose up, slammed the burner in again, and rocketed upward.

"ELI Two . . . climb up above ten thousand and head one-five-zero . . . ELI One is passing five thousand."

Staring right, to the west, I forced myself to quarter the sky rather than let my eyes dart back and forth.

Off the wing . . . high . . . low. Check the HUD . . . Between the wing and the tail . . . high . . . low. Check the HUD. Fifty-five hundred feet and 400 knots . . . roll and pull. Inverted now, I looked toward where the SAM must be. Behind me and high.

But there was nothing.

"WARNING . . . WARNING . . ."

I flipped the jet upright and glanced at the display. FUEL . . . FUEL . . . was blinking at me.

Pulling hard with my right hand, I brought the F-16 back to the left. To the northeast, away from the airfield and away from Baghdad. If he was heading 150 degrees southeast, he'd be off my right wing by four or five miles.

Data-linking a position request, I pulled the throttle back to hold 400 knots and continued my left turn around to the south. Before Khan Bani Sad disappeared, I saw fires from my last pass glowing through the haze. I couldn't see the hangar, but that was good. This meant the building, and whatever was inside of it, was burning.

I never did see the SAM. Maybe it hadn't really launched. Or maybe I'd reacted quickly enough to send it off into space. As I spiraled upward through a cloud break well east of Baghdad, the data-link came back. Zing was also alive and well, cruising about three miles behind me and to the west.

Breaking through the clouds, the sunlight hit my face, and I blinked for a long, happy moment before lowering the tinted visor. Still several hundred miles deep inside enemy territory, I didn't relax. But I felt the familiar rush of gratitude that always came on after an intense combat mission. Later on, lying on my cot in the darkness, I'd think of what could've happened. But for now, as the salty sweat dried on my face and the chaffing dampness under my harness cooled, I was grateful to be living and breathing.

Gently banking the F-16 to the left, I noticed my chaff dispenser said EMPTY, and the decoy had been shot off. *Wonder when that had happened?* So there had been a SAM, after all. That was a chilling thought—I decided not to think about it.

As my breathing returned to normal, I caught a flash of sunlight on metal and saw the other F-16 shoot up through the clouds. The friendly radar symbol appeared on my radar warning display, and I knew Zing had locked onto me. Staying well clear of Baghdad, we kept climbing in order to put some altitude between us and the clouds. Clouds hid SAMs and Triple-A.

And I'd had enough of that for one birthday.

12

ENDGAME

IT LOOKED LIKE A GIRAFFE.

I blinked.

Then blinked again and raised my visor. Rolling up on one wing, I skirted along at 400 knots just over the Baghdad rooftops and stared at the thing loping across the road below me.

It *was* a giraffe. No shit.

This was the morning of April 8 and I'd just crossed the Tigris River in southern Baghdad and was heading north toward the al-Quds district to kill tanks. The river made a huge, thumb-shaped loop near Dora Farms and the old Baghdad Muthenna airport. Just above it lay the Baghdad Zoo, from which the animal had evidently escaped.

Grunting against the Gs, I reefed the fighter into a hard level turn back toward the west. Below me was a huge, semicircular complex dedicated to Saddam's megalomania. At the far end lay a wide boulevard with arches at both ends. Letting up on the Gs, I realized the arches were actually enormous arms, each grasping a sword.

Saddam's Arches of Victory.

Smirking a bit at the irony, I reversed the turn and came back around, heading northeast toward the Tigris. Arches of Victory—well, there wouldn't be much of that for Hussein, since infidels like me were buzzing overhead and wild animals were running loose in the street.

Just ahead, the sluggish, seaweed-green river cut startlingly through the browns and grays of Baghdad. There were a half-dozen bridges I wanted to scope out, because enemy troops were using the northern suburbs as a safe haven. If they tried to come south to fight, they'd have to cross those bridges. Two of them, the Sinak and Jumhuriya, were right at the center of the action.

This particular morning, the Gamblers had three two-ships roaming about looking for trouble. We each took different kill-boxes and flew around trying to draw fire. When we found some-one dumb enough to shoot, we'd mark the position and figure the best way to attack. This would depend on the battlefield, how many weapons we had remaining, and the terrain. Environmental factors were actually a big part of a Weasel attack. Like overfly-ing water to avoid ground threats and using the sun's position to interfere with enemy optical trackers. Some tactics hadn't changed since World War I.

But urban Weaseling was tough. Too many hiding places for SAMs and mobile Triple-A, and the potential for fratricide of friendly units was disconcertingly high. To complicate things, sometimes our own grunts would shoot at us, unable to distinguish between Iraqi and U.S. aircraft. Moreover, ever since the Marines and Army had entered Baghdad, there'd been heavy street-fighting for days.

In fact, we were over Baghdad because just ten minutes earlier my two-ship had answered an emergency call for close air-support. FACING 43, an A-10 Warthog, had been hit by a shoulder-launched SAM. He had the dubious choice of landing at the newly liberated international airport or trying to limp back to a forward airstrip like Tallil—not surprisingly, he chose Tallil. But the jet couldn't make it, and the poor guy ejected over Baghdad. Luckily for him, some 3rd Infantry Division combat engineers watched him float down and sent a squad to rescue him.

The pilot, Major Jim Ewald, quite rightly assumed everything around him was hostile until the grunts shouted, "Hey pilot dude . . . come on out. We're Americans."

It was all over by the time we got there, which is how I ended up stalking giraffes. "LAPEL . . . this is CHIEFTAIN."

"Go ahead." CHIEFTAIN controlled fighter activity for the Navy and Marines. Theoretically.

"Ah . . . we've got AROMA 31, two Hornets, inbound your sector at Angels ten and SNOOP 23 inbound at seven thousand."

"LAPEL copies, we'll stay west of the river."

"Copy. KARMA is trying to reach you on Strike Prime."

"Got it. Thanks."

KARMA was the AWACS today, and he couldn't talk to me because I was too low. That suited me fine. I sighed and pulled up over Muthenna airport in central Baghdad. No doubt he wanted to know my shoe size or some other vital bit of information.

In fact, he didn't. KARMA ordered us up north about thirty miles to a suspected chemical-weapons facility. We found an entire complex guarded by tanks and armored personnel carriers. The other Gambler flights joined us, and we had a regular shooting gallery. I destroyed two tanks with CBUs and strafed a truck that made a break for the highway. He didn't make it.

ELI 21 and TOXIC 25 both took turns bombing and strafing. Between the six of us, we accounted for seven tanks and four trucks. Storm'n Norman, who was ELI 21, also had a 20-mm round explode in his own gun barrel.

TWO DAYS LATER, ON APRIL 10, WE WERE BACK UP NORTH again, looking for mobile SAMs. Six CeeJays, divided into three flights of two, had started the day north of Baghdad hunting RO-LANDs. This missile system was originally a joint Franco-German project and, with the history of love and cooperation between those two nations, you can imagine how that panned out.

However, it was fielded eventually, and Saddam bought about a hundred of the ROLAND II version back in the early 1980s. It's an all-weather, short-range system with its own Pulse Doppler radar and optical tracker. Very quick and mounted on trucks, all-terrain vehicles, or tank chassis, the ROLAND was extremely hard to see visually or electronically. Iraqis would hide behind buildings or under overpasses to escape detection. They'd get target information from their own system, spotters, or air traffic control radars, then scoot out, lock and shoot, then scuttle back into hiding, like hermit crabs. Iraqi ROLANDs had killed a few Iranian jets, several British Tornado fighters, and at least one American A-10.

We'd put a Killer element (of the Hunter Killers) over the area at about 15,000 feet. Their job was to listen to the Hunters, develop a "picture" of the situation, and be ready to attack. The Hunters would then take turns flying low over suspected locations to draw fire. We called this "slapping the bull." If a ROLAND, or any target, could be provoked into firing then, while the Hunters evaded the missiles, the Killers got a visual on the SAM and would swoop in to attack.

This was best done with six aircraft, called a Six-Pack, with the extra flight acting as spotters. The spotters would fly between the Hunters and the Killers and watch the ground. This was absolutely critical when hunting SA-6s, SA-8s, or ROLANDs. The spotters would also act as extra Hunters or Killers, if needed. A Six-Pack also gave us lots of flexibility with weapons and extended our time over a target by rotating flights back and forth to the tanker.

The communications involved were the simple "attacking-defending-shooting" contracts we'd used against the SA-3s on April 6. This was almost always done on a clear frequency, using plain English. Weasels don't usually have the luxury of convoluted code words—and the delay inherent in using secure radios could be fatal. So we just talked. And it usually worked.

But not today.

"FABLE 33 . . . this is ELI 63 on your Victor." Storm'n had been leading the first six-pack that morning, and I assumed he wanted to pass a situation report.

The aerial refueling tracks had moved north now that southern Iraq was more or less subdued. I'd just come out of the track and was headed north toward the Alpha Sierra series of killboxes north of Baghdad.

"Go."

"Two Dogs . . . found aircraft up at Balad, and we took out at least nine of them. We're off target now, and I think you'd better come up here and see if we missed anything."

Damn it. I frowned and shook my head in disgust. I was sure that Storm'n hadn't left anything behind. Sighing, I replied, "Roger that . . . fifteen mikes."

Nine aircraft. Targets were getting harder to find these days. I looked out at the now-familiar gray-and-black clouds that perpetually hung over Baghdad these days. Hussein and his psychopathic sons had fled the city, and no one knew where they were hiding. However, all bets were on his hometown of Tikrit, so the threats had to be cleared for the grunts to advance farther north. As a result, the Weasels were roaming up and down the 89 series killboxes along Highway 1. Balad was the biggest MiG base in Iraq, and it lay between the highway and the Tigris River about thirty miles north of the capital. We'd showed up there on April 2 and I'd destroyed seven aircraft that the Iraqi Air Force had left lying around. Apparently, Storm'n and the boys found some more.

Eighteen minutes after leaving the refueling track, I keyed the mike. "FABLE Two . . . Balad is right two o'clock low, twelve miles." I then sent a data-link.

My wingman that day was a young captain who'd been brought in to work on the mission-planning team. Called "Chucky"—after the title doll in the horror movies, because he had red hair and tended to become satanic with a few drinks in him—he was a good pilot and had been a great help. As alluded to earlier, mission-planning truly sucked for guys that were used to being *in* the action, not watching it. But it had to be done right, so you grabbed top-notch guys from other squadrons to do it. They all volunteered, because otherwise they'd be left behind, and at least this got them close to the action. Close is usually as good as it got, but the 77th Fighter Squadron commander, Storm'n, permitted these guys to fly, too. This was partly because he was a good man, who knew the value of rewarding performance, and also because our mission-planning products improved drastically after the planners got some current experience.

"FABLE Two . . . contact." He had seen the runway and sounded a bit excited.

But if Storm'n and his Six-Pack had been beating up on the airfield for twenty minutes or so, I figured there wouldn't be much left. Balad was plain to see. There were two big runways that came together in a "V" with the point facing southeast. We'd taken particular pleasure in knocking the crap out of this place, since it had been a thorn in our sides between the wars. I leaned forward, stared at the once-proud fighter base, and grinned.

Not so proud anymore.

Thin columns of black smoke rose from all over the center section of runway. They looked like pillars with no roof to support.

At about eight miles, I zippered the mike and gradually swung around to the north in the standard Weasel arc. Balad lay just west of the Tigris, and the long, gray runways were easy to see against the flood plain. Several of us had been flying with binoculars, so I flipped the autopilot on and stared at the base.

The main area was between the eastern runway and the river. There were lots of buildings, a road network, and housing. I shrugged. Nothing worth sticking my nose down there for. Holding the binoculars with one hand, I reached down and adjusted the autopilot to keep the turn coming. The burned-out fuselages from our last trip here were clearly visible. I smiled. The Iraqi air-defense gunners had been *pissed* off. I always wondered how the Iraqi fighter pilots felt as they peeked out of their shelters at the Gamblers swirling overhead and strafing the shit out of their base. Probably the same way the 363rd Ops Group commander felt when our returning jets would roar overhead and spill his coffee. Impotent.

There'd been so much Triple-A over the airfield that day it looked like a small thunderstorm. But no SAMs, which was strange. Nor any today, I confirmed with a glance at the RWR. *Yet.* No, everything of value looked like it had been smacked hard. Planes were burning bright, hot yellow flames with dark-red edges gave way to the thin plumes of black smoke.

Suddenly, a series of rippling flashes caught my eye, and I dropped the binoculars. Anti-aircraft fire from at least three different pits had found us. Judging by the rapid twinkling, I'd guess it was 57-mm and, a few seconds later, I saw the bursts.

"FABLE 33, Triple-A, Balad," I said calmly. We were about three miles from the base, so I wasn't concerned. However, where there's Triple-A there are usually SAMs.

"FA . . . FABLE Two copies. I see the bursts!" Again, I smiled at his excitement, but it was his first combat mission, and I understood. We were crossing the northern end of both runways looking down the funnel at the point of the "V."

"Two, heads-up for SAMs. We'll continue arcing around to the east."

"FABLE Two copies." He sounded slightly incredulous. We'd said all this on a clear frequency, because it was easier and maybe some intelligence officer down there would understand. He might then get the gunners and SAM guys to shoot at us. I'd certainly hit the Triple-A pits if nothing else showed up but I'd rather bag some bigger game. Like a SAM or more aircraft.

As we crossed the river heading southeast, the visibility got a little better. There were high broken clouds, and narrow beams of sunlight would poke through like fingers reaching for the ground. It wasn't great, but then again it never was. I touched the RWR volume to make certain it was up and watched for missiles.

The big lakes west of Baghdad were gray smudges along the horizon. The city itself was due south of me and lay dark and defeated, quiet for the first time since the war began. Yesterday, Baghdad had been declared an open city, and Hussein's regime was formally over. The Marines famously had pulled down the forty-foot statue in Firdos Square, which had been erected for Saddam's sixty-fifth birthday. Happy birthday, fucker. I'd still seen flashes and tracer fire as we'd overflown the capital, but no Triple-A or SAMs. I sighed again. It meant we'd have to go farther north to hunt.

Looking southeast, I had an idea and unfolded my big tactical map. Glancing at it, I tugged out the latest SAM chart and compared the two. There was an airfield at Baqubah, about six miles at my left ten o'clock, and, as far as I knew, no one had ever hit it.

"FABLE Two, float west." I zippered the mike and reversed slowly to the east, putting Balad behind me. A huge, ambiguously named "military complex" was also marked on my map just outside of town.

"Two . . . look at right two o'clock." I rolled out headed east. "See the town?"

"Affirm."

"Call contact on the east-west running hardball road north of the town."

"Contact."

"Target is the airfield, north of that road and west of the big river bend."

"FABLE Two is visual . . . uh, contact." He corrected himself. Good enough.

Calling up my air-to-ground-weapons symbology, I checked the CBU settings and eyeballed the airfield. Pulling the fighter around to the northeast put the town of Baqubah three miles off my left wing. White puffy Triple-A immediately blossomed and I angled a bit away to the east.

Bringing the power back to hold 450 knots, we dropped through 10,000 feet, paralleling the runway to the northeast. I remembered a story about an F-86 Sabre pilot during the Korean War, who actually did a low approach on an enemy runway. They were so shocked and offended they forgot to shoot for a few moments. When they did open up, the gunners couldn't depress the Triple-A muzzles low enough to kill the insane American. I grinned under the mask. The good old days for sure.

Leveling at about 6,000 feet, I began to count in my head and stared over the canopy rail at the airfield.

Two.

Just a typical bunch of buildings clustered around central hangars and—

There! Immediately slewing the diamond over the center of the parking area, I took a mark.

Three.

Cranking up sideways to the ground, I flicked my wing to the left, then rolled out. FABLE Two obediently pulled over across my tail, and I shoved the throttle forward to mil power. As the nose came through the horizon, I shot up about 500 feet to defeat any Triple-A that might be lining up to shoot. It was all performed subconsciously, as I was still padlocked on the concrete parking area between the big hangars.

We passed the runway headed west at 7,000 feet and 450 knots with Highway 2 directly off the nose. I data-linked the mark point, and when the distance read 4.0 miles, I keyed the mike. "FABLE Two . . . for the attack you'll take the aircraft and hangars on the south side of the apron and One will take the north. Drop on my call."

"Two copies." I zippered the mike, rolled inverted, and sliced back toward the target. Snapping upright at 6,000 feet, I centered the steering and eased the throttle back to hold 450 knots. No. 2 barrel-rolled over me and ended up on my right side about a mile away.

"Triple-A, right two o'clock high," I called out the 57-mm bursts just beyond the city of Baqubah. This had to be where the military complex was located. I'd remember that for follow-on missions. The mike zippered, but Chucky held firm.

At four miles, I could plainly see the parking area west of the runway, with two big hangars on either side. I squinted at the aircraft that was parked there. It was some sort of transport or trainer aircraft, painted white, and I snorted. I'd rather strafe fighters.

However, it was the only game in town at the moment, so I centered the steering and watched the release cue slip down the big vertical line in my HUD. I refined my aim, putting the little dot at the base of the aircraft and saw 2.5 miles on the distance readout. As the release cut began flashing, indicating the target was within range, I pushed up the throttle, mashed the pickle button, and keyed the mike.

"FABLE One . . . Rifle."

Holding steady a moment, I felt the cluster bombs kick off. Glancing over at my wingman, I saw a single CBU drop from under his left wing. Pulling straight up to the horizon, I rolled left to the north and snapped upright. FABLE Two floated past my tail as I twitched to the left. Bunting over, I popped a chaff bundle, came hard right, and stared back at the airfield.

For a second, all was quiet. A typical airfield with tin roofs shining in the weak sun and clusters of brown buildings against the tan dirt of Iraq. But then I saw the ground explode upward in dirty pillars of gravel and metal fragments. The plane, or something flammable, blew up. Red flames shot up through the dust and almost immediately turned into black smoke.

"Cool," a voice said. My wingman, feeling his oats. This was my fifteenth combat mission in this war, and I was too jaded at this point to get excited. However, I did take a professional interest in destruction and noticed a smaller blast a hundred yards east of mine in the dirt next to the runway. He'd pickled late and missed the hangars. I zippered the mike and brought us around heading north.

"Two, at six miles turn back in for your re-attack. One will stay high, arc east, and keep you in sight."

So he did. The other F-16 ramped down in line with the runway as I stayed over the Diyala River and looked out for Triple-A or SAMs. There were none, but I did find three revetments with aircraft. As Number Two came off, he pulled away to the west and began to climb. I continued to arc around the southern end of the runway and watched his CBU impact in the middle of the fire. We rejoined to the south, and my wingman remained high for cover while I dropped in and emptied the gun out after four strafe passes. A pair of aircraft blew up and burned in their revetments. I made a couple passes against the third one but never could get it to blow.

Either it was a decoy, or its tanks were empty, or I missed. Twice. Personally, I'd go with options one or two. Still, anything's possible.

Figuring we'd wrapped it up, Two and I went to the tanker and headed home. Chucky had a good mission, and together we bagged at least three aircraft, a hangar, and probably a bulldozer or two. What a Turkey Shoot. I remember thinking that the war was about over.

Wrong.

APRIL 13 DAWNED CLEAR AND BEAUTIFUL, FOR A CHANGE. NO clouds, light winds, and maybe 200 miles of visibility. As AGNEW 21, I led the last two-ship of the morning Hunter Killer mission. We were originally fragged to work the new Highway of Death between Baghdad and Tikrit, deep in the Salahuddin Province.

With the collapse of Hussein's regime, we were now dealing with die-hard military units and renegade *fedayeen*, sort of urban commandos. In a country that had required National Service and had fought, however badly, an eight-year war with Iran, there were plenty of Iraqis who knew how to handle weapons. In fact, more than a hundred thousand automatic weapons, along with grenades and MANPAD rocket launchers, had been handed out as the ground troops approached Baghdad.

Signs of this threat were everywhere. Off my right wing, dozens of smoky fingers rose for fifty miles up and down Highway 1. Like dead slugs, wrecked and stalled vehicles lay on either side of the roadway as the living crawled slowly north. Running my Maverick missile-seeker head along the pulsating jam, I searched for military trucks or tanks. Unfortunately, all I could see were bongo trucks, cars, carts, and bicycles. Then AWACS called.

"AGNEW 21 this is KARMA."

"Go."

"AGNEW . . . stand by grids."

He passed the coordinates and I stared down at the map. They plotted out in Killbox 91 Alpha Romeo, west of Tikrit and nearly a hundred miles north of my present position. Unlike during Operation Desert Storm in 1991, everything north of Baghdad had been quiet throughout this war. Militia, irregulars, and *fedayeen* tended to vanish back into their villages, but remnants of regular military units were fleeing north to Tikrit, Mosul, and Kirkuk. Anticipating this—or, more likely, to secure the Mosul oil fields—a thousand paratroopers from the 173rd Airborne Brigade parachuted into northern Iraq. Still, there had been no "northern" front to this war, and generally anything beyond the thirty-fourth parallel was a Special Forces playland.

"AGNEW . . . say ETA and playtime."

I looked at the estimated time of arrival readout in the HUD, my fuel, and did some quick math in my head. "Twelve minutes with a twenty mike playtime. If I hit the tanker first, I'll be on station in forty-five minutes with a forty-five-minute playtime."

"KARMA copies. You're cleared to the DOG track at two-six-zero and contact TOGA 40. Contact KARMA when refueling is complete."

I zippered the mike and peeled away left back to the south. This had become normal these days, as our planned missions were frequently changed in flight to solve whatever problems had come up. For a Weasel, it was no big deal, because we often didn't have hard-and-fast missions anyway—besides killing SAMs, that is. Although the previous day *someone* had tried to get us to fly escort for an unmanned aerial vehicle (UAV). After I finished laughing, I refused and went on with more important business. UAVs were becoming fashionable with the bespectacled computer-screen officers living in fortified operations centers. These little things, called Predators (which was also funny), were singularly useless in any kind of environment with SAMs, MiGs, and anti-aircraft artillery. In other words—a war.

Forty minutes later, my wingman and I slid off the tanker and once again headed north. Angling east of Milk Lake, we flew directly over Habbaniyah airfield about thirty miles west of Baghdad. There were still supposed to be five active SA-3 sites in this area, and we'd been trying to provoke them for several days. I think they were in heavy self-preservation mode, or just deserted, by this point. Think about it: if everyone you knew and everyone in your chain of command refused to communicate and/or disappeared, would you be motivated to fight?

Nothing showed itself, and we continued north up the east shore of Tartar Lake. KARMA passed us off to another controller, and we were given a holding point and altitude in the stack west of Tikrit. The city itself looked like a disturbed beehive. Fighters were everywhere, swirling, diving, and attacking. F-16s dropped like flashing darts and swept over the battered town. Distinctive, cruciform-shaped A-10s wheeled back and forth with their deadly cannons, spitting out shells as big as my forearm. Mushroom clouds blossomed every few minutes as a new target was destroyed.

"MUSKET 65 . . . SAM in the air! SAM in . . . over Tikrit!"

"MUSKET Two defending."

I woke up and stared out at the city. We were about ten miles due west at 20,000 feet, and fortunately the sun was almost directly overhead.

"STAB 74 . . . second missile airborne and heading west. Heads-up, MUSKET!"

The Hogs were scattering as the missile shot up in the middle of their wheel. A third smoke trail shot up and headed east, so there were at least two active launchers down there. I supposed at least one Iraqi SAM crew had had enough of us. Maybe their women were watching. It was going to cost them their lives.

"KARMA, KARMA . . . AGNEW 21 is tally the SAM site."

"AGNEW . . . can you attack?"

Can I attack? What else am I here for? I slewed my MARK diamond over the launch point and took the position.

"Affirmative. Clear all friendlies out to fifteen miles and above fifteen K. AGNEW is descending over the lake."

"AGNEW One . . . this is MUSKET One."

"Go."

"There's light Triple-A in addition to the SA-3."

It was actually an SA-2, but he was trying to be helpful. "Posit?"

"AGNEW, call contact on the pond east of town."

"Contact."

"Go one pond length due west to the city."

"Continue."

"Intersection of a north-south hard ball road and an east-west road with a curve in it. Movers and trucks."

"Contact. Thanks," I added.

As KARMA cleared everyone out of our way, we dropped smoothly down to 10,000 feet and headed south over Tartar Lake. On Victor, I said, "Two . . . FENCE, green it up, check AGM power."

I glanced out at the big Mavericks under my wings. These were H-model missiles, newly arrived and perfect for this sort of Weaseling. Eight feet long, about half of its 700-pound weight was the warhead. This variant used electro-optical guidance (think television camera) and was improved specifically for use in the desert. The picture was so good that we used it like a targeting pod. Although still in testing when the war began, Kanga Rew had moved heaven and earth to get a limited number of them here.

I checked my fuel and looked over at my wingman. "AGNEW One is 8.7."

"AGNEW Two is 9.5. Power on."

I saw a gray puff beneath his left wing as the Maverick's dome-shaped cover blew off. This was a thin, fragile coating that protected the seeker head and was generally left in place until the missile was ready to fire. Sunlight glinted off metal, and I looked up. Four F-16s passed overhead several thousand feet above me, and the leader rocked his wings. Returning the greeting, I pushed the nose down farther, tugged back the throttle, and we glided down over the gunmetal-gray lake water.

Leveling at 5,000 feet, I held 400 knots and stared past the left wing. The Tigris snaked southward like a dirty green ribbon before disappearing into the Baghdad suburbs. I zippered the mike, pulled the F-16 around, and headed for the river.

"MUSKET One . . . this is AGNEW. Any friendlies down there?"

"Ah . . . negative on that, AGNEW. No friendlies."

I'd trust battlefield intel from an A-10 pilot. He'd have the latest and greatest information. "Copy that. We're in from the south. Two minutes."

I pylon-turned over the river and looked down at a town on the east bank. "Two . . . see that walled compound on the northern edge of the city off the left wing?"

"AGNEW Two . . . uh . . . contact."

"That's our rejoin point. Evens and odds below fifteen K."

"Two copies."

"Evens and odds" meant he'd always go to an even-numbered altitude, like six or ten thousand feet. Plain to see through the Maverick's seeker was a huge building shaped like a crescent roll. Beyond it, stretching back to the rivers, were miles of ruins. As it vanished beneath my wingtip, I realized that this place was ancient Samarra and the big structure was the Great Mosque.

Leaning forward, I peered through the HUD at the tiny diamond that designated my mark point. Close enough to start with, I thought, and data-linked it.

"AGNEW Two, capture," my wingman replied immediately, meaning he'd received the data-link. He was hanging off my right wing two miles away and slightly high. Juice, as we called him, was one of the quiet guys who never stuck out for any reason in peacetime. Good kid, just low-key. Juice, however, became an icy little killer in combat—proving, once again, that you never really know about a guy till he sees the Elephant.

"AGNEW Two, call contact on the pond in the river bend."

We were directly over the Tigris, heading north with Tikrit off the nose. Smoke columns from Highway 1 still rose off to our right and Tartar Lake shimmered along the western horizon.

"Contact."

"Go one pond length west along a light-colored road to the intersection of the north-south hardball road."

"Does the lighter road have a curve in it?"

"Affirm."

"Contact on both."

"One of the launch sites is at that intersection. My target. You'll remain above five K and arc east to north. Heads-up for a second launch site along the pond and for Triple-A."

"AGNEW Two copies."

I let the nose drop a few degrees and focused on the Maverick video in my right MFD. Being heads-down was the one big drawback to using this missile. But I scanned, looked up and around, then scanned again.

"One is Walking the Dog." I thumbed out a decoy, turned my RWR volume up, and stared down at the intersection.

"AGNEW Two, same."

Juice peeled away to my right as I dropped farther toward the city. The Maverick video was amazingly clear, and I shook my head. What I wouldn't have given for one of these things a few weeks ago. A weird-shaped ravine came off the pond to the west. Like a dancing pig with a long snout. Following the curved road, I walked the missile-seeker head along toward the intersection, and there it was!

"SA-2 site a hundred meters east of the intersection on the south side of the road."

"AGNEW 21, KARMA . . . say again?"

Ignoring AWACS, I glanced outside again. Juice was watching as well, but I'd lived too long doing this to get assholed by the SAM I didn't see. A long, dirty strip of concrete ran along the west side of the river south of town. Tikrit South airfield had been one of Saddam's military fields, and I seemed to recall he had a few palaces here.

At four miles, I could plainly see two launchers with missiles up and ready to fire. There were no revetments, just some military barracks a quarter-mile south across an open field. It looked as if they'd just parked by the road and set up shop. Several transport vehicles, called transloaders, were stopped up by the road, but I couldn't see the FANSONG radar. No matter. If we killed the missiles, the radar was useless.

"AGNEW . . . this is KARMA. Status."

Jackass.

When I had something to say, I'd say it. "KARMA this is MUSKET. AGNEW is inbound for the attack so *stand by*!"

I chuckled. Hog drivers were all right. I zippered the mike for him. At three miles I was passing 2,000 feet, and I walked the throttle back a bit to hold 450 knots. Making tiny corrections with the stick, I aimed the jet and the missile. As the pointing cross settled on the middle launcher, I "designated" the target with my right thumb and released the switch. The Maverick locked on the target, and I moved my thumb to the pickle button. Men were sitting around the missiles smoking cigarettes, and several were squatting against the launcher. I smiled grimly. They had no idea that paradise was thirty seconds away.

"BEEP . . . BEEP . . . BEEP!"

Instantly my eyes swiveled to the RWR and the flashing "2" symbols. Right side, close! There . . . the huge, unmistakable rolling white cloud of an SA-2 launch. Southbound, parallel to my inbound flight path and climbing slowly. I took a mental snapshot of the location and snapped back to the Maverick video. The missile was still locked and the Iraqi shooters were all standing now.

"AGNEW One . . . there's a launch in your vicinity . . . just west of the pond!" At least my wingman was watching. I kept the jet steady, watched the SAM from the corner of my left eye, and mashed the pickle button. There was an instant, hard kick as the Maverick lunged off the rail and nosed over. I immediately went to mil power, pulled hard left into the airborne SA-2, and punched the chaff button.

"AGNEW One . . . Rifle SA-2, Tikrit."

Shoving forward, I floated off the seat and watched the SAM. My own missile was on its own, a true "fire and forget" weapon. Fortunately, the SA-2 was a relatively slow starter and not particularly maneuverable. I could never have hesitated against an SA-6 or a ROLAND.

"AGNEW . . . this is KARMA say again?"

I slapped a few more chaff bundles out, popped the jet upright directly over the Tigris, and stared back at the target area. "AGNEW One, defending . . . northeast over the river bend. Two, posit?"

"Two is due north, five miles . . . tally SAM to your south."

"Mark the launch point."

"Done."

Good kid. I rolled up and flew sideways up the river, watching for Triple-A. Suddenly, there was a tremendously bright flash near the intersection. Billowing up and out, a black mushroom cloud with dirty-brown edges completely obscured the area. As I keyed the mike to speak, flaming orange bits shot from all sides of the clouds. Then a thick, white plume shot up through the middle as one of the spare missiles cooked off. It corkscrewed wildly for a half second, then plowed into the military barracks south of the site.

"Cool," someone said on the radio.

"Good hit AGNEW."

I smiled but didn't take my eyes off the target area. Sure enough, another SAM lifted off from the site that I hadn't seen the first time. This one was headed east in my general direction, so they had an operable radar down there.

Shoving in the afterburner, I punched out more chaff and cranked the fighter over at the SAM site.

"AGNEW One . . . attacking SA-2, Tikrit."

My eyes danced around the cockpit. The decoy was still intact, my jamming pod was transmitting, and the other Maverick was up. Using the HUD, I called up the BORESIGHT cross and simply dove straight at the SAM. As the Tigris disappeared beneath me, I stared across the pond at the launcher. Glancing at the video, men were plainly scrambling, and I blinked. They were swiveling the missile around *by hand* on its launcher. Maybe the motor had burned out or they'd lost power. I shrugged, refined my aim, and locked the base of the launcher. It wouldn't matter in about forty seconds; as the missile swung around toward me, I hit the pickle button again.

The right-hand Maverick leaped off the rail, and I instantly pulled up and over to the right in a kind of half-barrel roll. More chaff . . . and I knife-edged over the pond on my left wing. For a

long second, I saw the whole picture, and realized why we hadn't
seen this junk before. It was all concealed in the ravine. Launchers,
transloaders, trucks, and missiles. They were hiding here until they
were ready to fire—then they'd scoot out, let the missiles fly, and
scuttle back into the ditch. That's why there'd been no revetments.
They weren't needed, and, in fact, the Iraqis had figured out those
were dead giveaways.

"AGNEW One . . . Rifle SA-2."

Zipping past an island in the Tigris, I headed west over the
town at a thousand feet and 500 knots. As I screamed over the outskirts of Tikrit and zoomed up in a left-hand climb, my missile hit.
There were several explosions and lots of tracer fire. Must've hit an
ammo dump, too, I thought, and pulled the power back. Leveling
at 6,000 feet and 425 knots, I checked my gas and gauges and sent
a data-link.

"AGNEW Two . . . request."

"Go ahead."

"Two would like to attack from the north. Tally a transloader
at the eastern edge of the ravine."

I looked at the MFD. He was about six miles northwest of the
target.

"Say gas."

"8.2."

"AGNEW Two . . . cleared hot."

He zippered the mike, and I took a deep breath. A couple good
hits from two successful H-model Mavericks. Kanga would get a
woody over this. There were a dozen brownish crop circles about
six miles west of town, so I slowed down more and began an easy
orbit. There might be other sites down there, and I wanted to watch
Juice's attack. Slewing the radar off to my right, I was rewarded
with a lock.

And there he was. The F-16 was over the Tigris, heading south, and I began a gentle right turn to keep him in sight. Even though he was about eight miles from me, I plainly saw the Maverick launch beneath his wing. I caught a brief glimpse of his belly as Juice racked the jet up and away across the river to the east.

"AGNEW Two . . . Rifle . . . Tikrit."

As I orbited, I saw his missile impact. It wasn't a huge explosion, but the amount of smoke and fire suggested he'd hit one of the big transport trucks. He must've seen it, too, because he almost immediately said, "AGNEW Two, request a reattack to strafe."

"On what?"

"Two is visual . . . uh . . . tally some missiles on a truck. At the far north corner near the road. I think they're trying to pull out."

"Cleared."

"AGNEW Two's in from the northeast."

There wasn't time to go back out and hit it with his last Maverick. The kid had good eyes. This should be interesting. There was now a lot of smoke over the target area from our previous attacks, and I never saw him come back in. To my horror, I saw a long, burning trail of fire smear itself across the ground where my wingman was attacking.

No . . . *no*. It couldn't be.

Swallowing, I keyed the mike and watched the flaming mess spread out. Whatever was at the front was pointed and moving very, very fast.

"AGNEW Two . . . status?"

Nothing.

Ah, shit. I brought the Viper around just east of the road and stared through the smoke. He'd hit the ground. He'd fucked up his strafe pass and hit the ground. My eyes flickered up above the smoke, looking for a parachute. Maybe he'd ejected just before impact. Maybe—

"AGNEW Two is off west. Didja see that?"

I exhaled and squeezed my eyes shut for a second. Rolling back out heading south, I replied, "Good hit."

Shaking my head, I managed a weak grin. I'd tell him about *that* later. We loitered around for ten more minutes while I strafed my cannon empty. I destroyed another truck that was trying to escape and got the FANSONG trailer.

"MUSKET, STAB . . . AGNEW flight is off for the tanker. SA-2 site south of the city is dead. Happy hunting."

"AGNEW from MUSKET One . . . great work guys. And thanks!"

Zooming up above the burning city, we headed south. Passing 20,000 feet, I glanced back at the black fingers of smoke that rose, twisting and fading, from the brown desert far below. My wingman seemed motionless against the clear, blue sky as he hung in perfect formation off my left wing. Rocking him into close formation, I watched as he slid from side to side checking my jet for holes. I dropped the sweaty oxygen mask, took a long pull of warm, plastic-tasting water, and gazed down at Baghdad.

APRIL 13, 2003, WAS MY LAST COMBAT MISSION OF THIS WAR. In fact, my last combat mission as a military officer and fighter pilot. Baghdad had fallen on April 9 and, though I didn't know it at the time, all major military operations would end tomorrow, on April 14.

During this war, 20,228 fighter sorties had been flown to employ 19,000 guided munitions along with 9,200 dumb bombs and CBUs. In a big, raised middle finger to those who'd believed strafing was obsolete (space clowns and UAV-lovers), we used 328,498 rounds of 20- and 30-millimeter ammunition. Flights over Iraq consumed an astonishing 612,891,043 pounds (90,131,035 gallons) of jet fuel. Sadly, some of this was used to drop 31,800,000 silly propaganda leaflets with more than eighty different messages. So many leaflets, in fact, that you could make a paper highway from Texas to Alaska out of them. (I remember a leaflet from the first Gulf War that said "SURRENDER AND DIE" instead of "SURRENDER OR DIE." A PsyOps weenie actually wanted us to fly back to Baghdad to drop the corrected version.) Someone thought there was more value added to this than, say, Weasels getting H-model Mavericks. Makes you wonder.

More than sixteen hundred SAMs were launched during the Iraq War. Yet only one fixed-wing fighter and six helicopters were brought down. Just twelve years earlier, during Desert Storm air operations, we'd lost thirty-nine fixed-wing fighters and five helicopters. Better aircraft, training, and countermeasures all contributed to this success, but I believe there are other reasons: Iraqi confusion and tactics aside, Desert Storm tended to focus on jamming and suppression. Both are necessary but are basically defensive in nature.

By the Iraq War, the offensive, hard-kill mentality of some of the Wild Weasel squadrons made the difference. We went after critical command-and-control nodes, radars, and SAM sites with hard ordnance right from the beginning. HARMs were used to maybe make the Iraqis duck a bit, but the threats were killed with precision munitions and cluster bombs—not suppressed. We were allowed to do this by officers in leadership positions who didn't presume to dictate weapons and tactics to us. All they wanted were results, and how we got them was up to us.

The 77th Fighter Squadron alone *killed* more than fifty SAMs and vital air-defense components with hard bombs, CBUs, Mavericks, and the cannon. These included SA-2s, SA-3s, SA-6s, and ROLANDs. Twenty-eight radars, thirty-seven Triple-A pits, and eight surface-to-surface missiles were also knocked off. Of course, we did other things, too. Forty-six aircraft and helicopters were destroyed on the ground along with sixty-five tanks, trucks, and armored personnel-carriers. So, if we'd succumbed to the HARM suppression-only mind-set advocated by some, how many friendly aircraft might have been lost? Amazingly, there were several Cee-Jay units that hadn't embraced the concept of destruction of enemy air defense. They largely spent their war thirty miles from the action, at 30,000 feet, and brought their HARM missiles home each day.

No, thanks.

A MONTH LATER, THE GAMBLERS LEFT PRINCE SULTAN AND never returned. On the way home, we stopped over for a night at Lajes Air Base in the Azores Islands off the Portuguese coast. The Air Force support folks and their families gave us a real American cookout—hamburgers, hot dogs, and margaritas. It was heaven. We ate and drank, thrilled to be alive and happy to be going all the way home the next day.

I'd survived another war.

I knew that, occasionally, in later years, paths would cross again, and those of us who knew the Elephant could talk about it. The combat bond is like no other, and there's really no way to explain it. But for now, I knew, all was well. So, as an afternoon rain squall popped over the rolling green hills, I lay down in the cool grass, let the rain fall on my face, and smiled.

Endgame.

EPILOGUE

SEVEN MONTHS AFTER THE GAMBLERS WENT HOME, SADDAM Hussein was pulled from a filthy spider hole on a farm outside Tikrit. It wasn't even a mile from the SAM we killed on April 13, and when I heard the news, I wondered if he'd been there at the time and seen the action. His two barbaric sons and a grandson were killed that July, and Saddam followed them on December 30, 2006. Hung up by his scrawny neck until his eyes bulged, his bowels let go, and he died.

Winning that war was a foregone conclusion. When the American military is turned loose and allowed to fight, we prevail. Yet it would take eight more years before the last American combat troops came home. There were no more MiGs or SAMs to contend with, no Iraqi armor or set-piece battles; but it remained a war—and a particularly nasty one at that. Caught between vacillating peacetime leadership and ambiguous, shifting political goals, the U.S. forces still adapted, overcame, and rolled out of Iraq with their banners flying at the end of 2011.

As for the Weasels, the battle continues. While the Air Force shrinks under budget cuts, and as the tremendous cost of the F-22 and F-35 programs seek justification, there is a continuous push to combine missions. Think of it as a one-size-fits-all approach. Now don't get me wrong, I believe single-mission aircraft are a ridiculous waste of resources. However, just as absurd is the notion that plinking away at map coordinates with smart munitions is Weaseling.

Then there's the problem of mentality. With a decade of permissive skies over Afghanistan and Iraq, some flawed conclusions are being reached. The love affair with stand-off weapons and unmanned aerial vehicles are perfect examples. Once again, those who are too old or who were never good enough for combat continue to advocate the replacement of manned aircraft. These are the same guys who said we'd never strafe and we'd never drop bombs on SAM sites. But combat pilots know that as long as ground troops are fighting, they'll need close air-support and Weasels.

Ask any infantryman.

I also know that UAVs, in their present form, would never survive in any threatening environment with MiGs or SAMs or Triple-A. When generals began insisting that fighters fly escort for the things, then we were at the edge of the abyss. We went over into the abyss when the Air Force made a noncombat officer the Chief of Staff.

Not too long ago, a Predator "pilot" tried to write himself up for an Air Medal —it didn't happen, but a lot of fine fighter pilots threw up at the thought. What's next? A Purple Heart for carpal tunnel syndrome?

Be that as it may, I'm not opposed to any solution that kills SAMs. Fixed sites are relatively easy. Naval bombardment, cruise missiles, or even Special Forces teams with satchel charges are all options for killing those types of SAMs. Wild Weaseling, to most of us, is a special mission done on the fly against unknown and unplanned mobile SAMs. Often reactive, it's over very quickly. Too rapidly to be coordinated through the net-centric, space-based, convoluted virtual world promoted by cyber desk-jockeys. That doesn't work, since the threat has killed and moved by that time. There will always be a critical need for an aggressive, lethal Wild Weasel right up front in the action. The point is, we won against Iraq because we were prepared to do battle with a superpower. I fervently hope we don't train in the future to fight a lesser threat and get whacked by a well-armed China or Russia.

AFTER OUR STOPOVER IN THE AZORES, WE ARRIVED HOME AT Shaw AFB in the late afternoon, and despite the fatigue of the flight, we joined together as four-ships to fly overhead in close formation. Pitching out, I remember looking down at the green fields of South Carolina and the crowd waiting for us on the flight line. I knew it was my last war, and I was content. I was happy to be alive and it was good to be home. Home is the best of things to a man in combat. More than just a safe haven, it symbolizes a place where good things happen. Where you don't wake up drenched in sweat from a nightmare or roll into a ditch because mortars are falling on your head. Home is safe.

Weeks later, after the flags were put away and decorations received, we tried to reconnect as best we could. Of course, the lessons were put into briefings, all the numbers quantified and lectures presented, but nothing really changed. Pilots moved on to other assignments. Several became generals, some left for airline jobs, the National Guard, and some, like me, retired. I always wanted to try island living, so I went off to the Caribbean and bought a big sailboat. Several men who I thought would never get married now have wives and kids. Others, who had perfect families, seemed like they would never split up—and they did just that. At least two are now dead, killed in another war on another continent. Regardless of how my brothers ended up, they're frozen in my memory as I last saw them, and in that sense, they'll live forever.

The summer following the war, I met a middle-aged woman during a Fourth of July parade. Her son, a young Marine, had been killed in Nasiriyah on March 24, 2003. I could see her gamely trying to take some meaning away from the fireworks, the band, and all the uniforms. We quietly talked for a few minutes as the parade passed by, and I told her about that day as I'd seen it. I think she was grateful to see someone who had physically been nearby when her boy died. I don't do platitudes and couldn't attach significance to her loss, but I did tell her that the Iraqis lost that battle and that I'd made them bleed for her son. I don't know if it was the right thing to say, but she smiled through her tears as she walked away.

IT WAS TIME FOR THIS STORY. NO GRAND DESIGNS OR PHILO-sophical fluff—just an honest view of life and war from one fighter cockpit. The modern military would have you believe that everyone is a warrior. That everyone is out there fighting enemies, taking chances, and killing threats. But it's just not so. The Air Force alone deployed about 65,000 people for the second Gulf War, and there were only 450 active, flying fighter pilots. That's a 144:1 ratio of support personnel to shooters. Most military folks serve a vital purpose, and fighter pilots wouldn't get far without them, but the vast majority are not fighting men. That's simply the way it is. The Air Force, in particular, needs to remember that and keep labels like "warrior" in their proper place.

Fighter operations, and especially Hunter Killer missions, are not a series of logistical challenges. It's a violent form of combat moving along at hundreds of feet per second with just fractions of moments to react or die. It's also solitary. There may be other jets flying with you, but in the end, you're alone. No armored fighting vehicles and no platoon of heavily armed buddies to watch your back. Most of my 151 combat missions were so deep into enemy territory I had no hope of rescue if I was to go down.

Combat is not the ultimate test, but it is one of them. Men have been tried this way since the dawn of time, and many have failed. There is no way to prepare for it. You can be trained to fight, to handle weapons and sophisticated equipment. You can be taught to survive, to resist interrogation, and to kill. But you never really *know* until you're there. And in the end, you either have it or you don't. If a man can't cut it, then I believe he bears a terrible burden the rest of his days. Thankfully, this is a weight I won't carry.

I made a difference. I could see the Hunter Killer version of the Viper way back in 1992. I *knew* it was right and I saw what was needed. Despite the skeptics, everything we pushed for eventually came to fruition. When F-16CJs are in the news today, and I see the pods and weapons slung under their wings, I grin. I helped make it happen, and no one can take that away.

I LOVED BEING A FIGHTER PILOT, BUT EVENTUALLY YOU HAVE to stop. Physically, anyway, if not mentally. I repaid the Air Force for the skills I'd been taught and the opportunities I'd been given. I paid back those who'd believed in me. I wanted to go out as I'd lived my career—on my own terms. And I did. Perhaps if the Air Force was made up of guys like MooMan, Kanga, and Storm'n, I would've stayed.

Perhaps not.

No one really ever comes back from war. Not all the way.

Memories can be compartmentalized, put away in a dark place, and rarely, if ever, visited. Some men are better at this than others. I never killed a noncombatant or a child. Those whose lives I ended were trying to kill me, and they had their chance to do the same. At least we faced off like men and took our best shots. They missed, I didn't.

Like many fighting men, I was comfortable in combat. Not that it's a nice place to be, but I could deal with it. In a way quite unlike everyday life, it made sense, and I knew what I was doing. Combat is simple—you live or die. It's life that's complicated, and you either cross your own Rubicon and get to the other side someday or you do not.

After twenty years of tactical flying and several wars, it's impossible not to have proud memories—and a few regrets. In the end, each man must decide for himself what to keep and what to let go. In my case, I'll always be able to look at myself in the mirror and know that when it counted, I flew honorably with brave men.

I flew with the Wild Weasels.

ACKNOWLEDGMENTS

No one writes a book alone, and this is certainly no exception. I need to especially acknowledge those who believed in me, taught me, and waited for me to grow up somewhat, to become the officer and fighter pilot in this book.

The story itself would never have been possible without the men, named and unnamed, who were part of this over the years; my brother fighter pilots who possess the extraordinary flying skills, courage, and aggressiveness that win wars. None of us would have gotten to the fight without the dedication and long-suffering professionalism of the support folks and aircraft maintainers who put us there. They have my lifelong thanks for handling the million details required to put fighter jets in the air. Special thanks to the 99 ABW/PA and the 57th FW Viper AMU, Nellis AFB, for their time and the loan of a jet for the ebook filming of *Viper Pilot*.

Sincere appreciation goes to my agent, Jeff Herman, and everyone at William Morrow/HarperCollins who assisted with this effort. True professionals, they politely pushed, chopped, corrected, and ultimately brought this book to publication. This especially applies to my editor, Peter Hubbard, for his many insights, unfailing enthusiasm, and calm direction throughout this endeavor.

GLOSSARY

ACC: Air Combat Command. The major command containing all stateside fighter units.

ACT: Air Combat Training. Generally, as one or two pairs against an unknown number of adversaries.

ANGELS: Altitude in thousands of feet. Technically, only used for friendly aircraft.

AOR: Area of Responsibility. Places like Iraq, Afghanistan, etc.

BFM: Basic Fighter Maneuvers. 1 v. 1 dogfighting.

BINGO: A preset amount of fuel that, when reached, results in mission termination. Influenced by weather, threats, availability of air refueling tankers etc. . . .

BLIND: Lost visual on a friendly flight member.

BLOCK 50: A type of F-16. Block designations are for different specific capabilities. Block 50 includes the HARM Targeting System pod and associated avionics.

BOARDS: Slang for speed brakes.

BURNER: Afterburner.

CBU: Cluster Bomb Unit.

CEEJAY: F-16CJ. Also a Block 50.

COMPANY GRADE OFFICER: Junior officers. A second lieutenant, first lieutenant, or captain.

DEFENDING: Technically, a defensive reaction against a SAM or anti-aircraft artillery. Usually accompanied by the type of threat, if known, and a direction for the maneuver.

EAGLE: F-15C.

EOR: End of Runway. This area is directly to the side of the runway and used for arming/de-arming.

EWO: Electronic Warfare Officer. A specialist in signals analysis. Not a pilot.

FIELD-GRADE OFFICER: A major, lieutenant colonel, and colonel.

FIGHTING WING: A fluid, loose formation that puts a wingman on about a one-mile string behind his leader. Think of a water skier behind a boat.

FINGERTIP: Close formation. Usually about three feet from wingtip to wingtip.

FOX ONE/TWO/THREE: Air-to-air missile shots. "Fox One" is an older radar-guided AIM-7 Sparrow. "Fox Two" is a close-range, infrared Sidewinder, and "Fox Three" is the advanced medium-range air-to-air missile (AMRAAM).

FRAG: Fragments from an explosion. Also a "fragmentary order"—a squadron's piece of the larger air-tasking order detailing missions, targets, and weapons.

FWIC: Fighter Weapons Instructor Course.

GRUNT: Slang for an infantryman. Friendly ground forces.

HARM: High Speed Anti Radiation Missile.

HOG: Slang for A-10 Thunderbolt II.

HORNET: Slang for the F/A-18 multi-role fighter.

HOTAS: Hands On Throttle And Stick. Technology that permits the activation of weapons, aircraft systems, and cockpit displays from multifunction switches on the control stick and throttle.

HTS: HARM Targeting System Pod.

HUD: Heads Up Display. A transparent plastic rectangle mounted on the glare shield with superimposed flying symbology and weapon attack cues.

IFF: Identification Friend or Foe. An electronic code that can be read by other friendly aircraft.

ILS: Instrument Landing System.

KILLBOX: A thirty-mile square piece of airspace. Given an alphanumeric identifier, killboxes are used for deconfliction between flights of fighters.

KLICK: A "kilometer." A little over one half of a mile.

LANTIRN: Low Altitude Navigation Targeting InfraRed Night. An older, specialized system used on Block 40 F-16s for low-level night-strike missions.

LOOSE DEUCE: A wider, more flexible form of Fighting Wing. A two-mile string.

MAGNUM: Warning call made to indicate a HARM firing.

MFD: Multi Function Display.

MiG: An abbreviation for *Mikoyan Gurevich,* a prominent Soviet/ Russian aircraft manufacturer. Sometimes is generically applied to any enemy fighter.

MIKE: Microphone. Also denotes "millimeter," as in *twenty mike mike* (20-mm cannon). Can also mean "minutes."

MIL POWER: Full non-afterburning power.

NO JOY: Lost visual. Should be used only for enemy aircraft. Often used in place of "blind."

NVG: Night-Vision Goggles.

PADLOCKED: Brevity communication for "my eyes are locked and if I look away I'll lose sight."

PATCHWEARER: Graduate of the USAF Fighter Weapons School. Also called "Target Arm."

RIFLE: Brevity comm for a Maverick missile shot. Used now for any guided munition.

ROE: Rules of Engagement. Specific conditions that permit the use of deadly force.

ROUTE: A wider, more relaxed version of fingertip formation.

RTB: Return to Base.

RTU: Replacement Training Unit.

RWR: Radar Warning Receiver. Tells the pilot which radar system has locked him.

SHOE CLERK: A rear-echelon type. Noncombat personnel.

SLAPSHOT: A quick-reaction HARM shot along a line of bearing to a threat.

SMS: Stores Management System. Onboard computer that accounts for all weapons ballistics and aiming symbology.

TACAN: TACtical Air Navigation system. Provides bearing and range to a selected channel that can be located at a ground station or between other aircraft.

TALLY HO: Visual sighting of an enemy aircraft. Sometimes used to indicate sighting any aircraft.

TARGET ARM: A graduate of the USAF Fighter Weapons School. Also called a Patchwearer.

TD BOX: Target Designator Box which is put around anything locked onto by the F-16 radar.

TOC: Tactical Operations Center.

TOT: Time Over Target.

UNIFORM: UHF radio.

VICTOR: VHF radio.

VIPER: Slang for the F-16 multi-role fighter.

VISUAL: Sighting of a friendly aircraft.

VUL: Short for "Vulnerability" time. This is the fragged, or allotted, time that fighter is given in a target area.

WALKING THE DOG: Streaming an activated towed decoy.

WILCO: "Will Comply." A military way of saying "I'll do it!"

WSO: Weapons System Officer who controlled the radar in older fighters, like the F-14 and F-4. Not a pilot.

ZAP: A data-link.

ZIPPER: Clicking the mike several times by way of an affirmative reply.

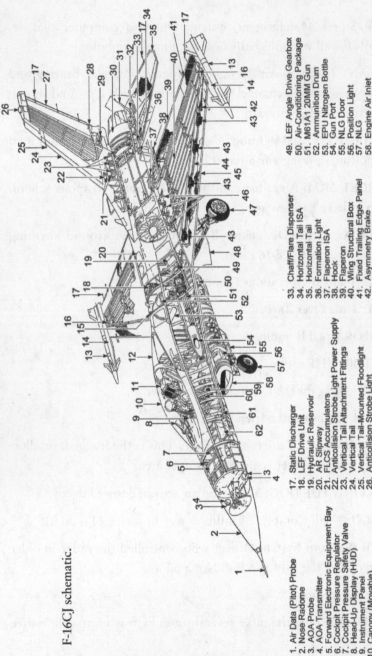

F-16CJ schematic.

1. Air Data (Pitot) Probe
2. Nose Radome
3. AOA Probe
4. AOA Transmitter
5. Forward Electronic Equipment Bay
6. Cockpit Pressure Regulator
7. Cockpit Pressure Safety Valve
8. Head-Up Display (HUD)
9. Instrument Panel
10. Canopy (Movable)
11. Ejection Seat
12. Canopy (Fixed)
13. AIM-9 Missile
14. Missile Launcher
15. AR and Formation Light
16. Position/Formation Light

17. Static Discharger
18. LEF Drive Unit
19. Hydraulic Reservoir
20. AR Slipway
21. FLCS Accumulators
22. Anticollision Strobe Light Power Supply
23. Vertical Tail Attachment Fittings
24. Vertical Tail
25. Vertical Tail-Mounted Floodlight
26. Anticollision Strobe Light
27. Rudder
28. Position Light
29. Rudder ISA
30. Turbofan Engine
31. Speedbrake
32. Speedbrake Actuator

33. Chaff/Flare Dispenser
34. Horizontal Tail ISA
35. Horizontal Tail
36. Formation Light
37. Flaperon ISA
38. Flaperon
39. Hook
40. Wing Structural Box
41. Fixed Trailing Edge Panel
42. Asymmetry Brake
43. LEF Rotary Actuator
44. LEF Torque Shaft
45. LEF
46. Wing Attachment Fittings
47. MLG
48. MLG Door

49. LEF Angle Drive Gearbox
50. Air-Conditioning Package
51. M61A1 20MM Gun
52. Ammunition Drum
53. EPU Nitrogen Bottle
54. Gun Port
55. NLG Door
56. Position Light
57. NLG
58. Engine Air Inlet
59. Left Console
60. Throttle
61. Strake
62. Lower Equipment Compartment

MAP OF IRAQ

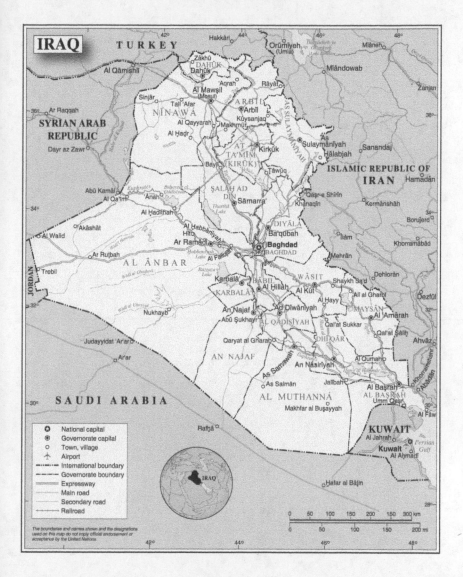

INDEX

Read on for an exclusive excerpt from

THE MERCENARY,

an e-original novel of air combat

by the *New York Times* bestselling author of

VIPER PILOT

ONE

BLURRY CURTAINS OF RAIN DROPPED FROM THE SKY AND OB-
scured everything around the airfield. Layers of oily gray clouds
tore away from the overcast and rolled heavily toward the nearby
coast. Beyond the coast lay the sea. Blown flat by the wind, only the
white crests of the breaker line flickered through the night.

From the shadows on the far north side of the airfield a dark
shape slowly crept forward. A big twin-tailed jet fighter taxied deliberately through the rain and slid to a stop at the end of the long
runway. Showing no lights, the aircraft swung around and crouched
on the concrete. Vapor wafted upward from the hot tail section and
rain streamed from its gray metal body. Inside the warm, dimly lit
cockpit the pilot barely spared the shining wet runway and black
night a thought. It was a terrible night to fly by most standards but
that was one reason he was doing it. Weather and bad conditions
were just variables to him. Not obstacles.

This was his business.

He yawned and glanced again at the three big multicolored
displays before him. Adjusting the brightness on the fire control
radar, he was pleased to see the damn thing appeared to be working. A Russian design manufactured by the Chinese—could that
be any worse? Finishing the built-in tests, or BITS, on the air-to-air
missiles, he noticed that one had failed. Not that it mattered. Tonight wasn't about air combat. In any event, no one was going to

intercept him and force a dogfight. He rechecked the weapons and attack display, called the WAD, to verify that the six cluster bombs beneath the wings were configured correctly. They were.

Looking up, he squinted through the pelting rain at the fuzzy outline of the control tower and then glanced at the time readout on the Heads Up Display. He was early by a few minutes. Reaching around to the side console, the pilot pulled out a pair of night-vision goggles. Removing his helmet, he ignored the whining of the engines and attached the goggles to the mounting bracket. Replacing the helmet, he lowered the goggles, switched them on, and stared again at the control tower.

Much better. Not daylight exactly, but green twilight was certainly better than black sludge. He made several small adjustments to the focus, then flipped the gogs back up to see the cockpit gauges. Russian and Chinese pilots didn't fly with NVGs so the instrument and display lighting inside the cockpit wasn't compatible. But the pilot wasn't about to do what he'd come for without goggles.

This jet was a big bastard, he thought, and glanced around the cockpit again. The SU-27SK was called a FLANKER by U.S. and NATO pilots, and a J11 by the Chinese. It was probably the best multi-role fighter ever produced by the old Soviet Union and more than a match for all but the latest American fighters. With weapons hardpoints for ten air-to-air missiles and more than 20,000 pounds of fuel, it was a dangerous adversary. He smiled slightly. Flown, that is, by the right man.

A flicker caught his eye and the pilot looked up to see a green light blinking dimly through the thick haze. It was the "prepare to launch" signal from the control tower. There would be no radio calls tonight. At least not to him. He flipped the small handle by his left knee to arm the ejection seat, then put his hand on the throttles. Rotating the night-vision goggles down over his eyes, the pilot stared at the other parallel runway a mile to the right. The flashing anti-collision beacons of two other FLANKERS were plainly visible. He knew they were to take off precisely at 2145 hours and that they would do just that. They would fly a two-hour practice mission inland over the Qilan mountain range here in eastern China and then return to land shortly before midnight.

He also knew that they knew nothing about him.

Suddenly a pair of huge orange flames lanced through the darkness as the lead FLANKER lit his afterburners. Starting slowly, they sped down the runway and smoothly rotated upward. Orange changed to blue and then abruptly vanished, leaving only the disembodied strobe light climbing away into the clouds. Then the second FLANKER lit off and sped down the runway after its leader.

Across the airfield, the pilot waited until the second jet began to climb and then pushed his own throttles forward. He felt his shoulders hit the back of the ejection seat as the fighter surged down the runway. Straining against the tremendously powerful Lyulka turbofan engines, the pilot leaned forward and stared at the ribbon of glistening runway before him.

The FLANKER picked up speed fast as the burners kicked in. Without lights the pilot could only use the wet gleam from the center stripe to keep himself on the runway. At 170 knots he eased the stick back and braced his right forearm against his thigh. The big fighter's nose lifted and the wings wobbled as the jet tried to fly. Left hand locked on the throttles, the pilot pulled the stick back a bit farther and felt the wings bite into the moist, heavy air. One bounce . . . another . . . then the main wheels left the runway and the FLANKER was airborne.

Ignoring the HUD, he used the old-fashioned attitude indicator to keep the nose exactly ten degrees above the horizon. Rocketing upward into the dark drizzle, he pulled the throttles out of afterburner and slapped up the landing gear. He wished the burners hadn't been needed but the jet was so heavy there hadn't been a choice. The two other fighters would mask his noise and hopefully distract anyone who might be watching.

That had been the point of launching them. But fifty-foot flames from his engines would be impossible to hide. On the other hand, Luqiao Air Base was hardly a metropolis, and in China *no one* questioned military affairs. Except the military. He shrugged under the shoulder harness. Nothing to be done about it now. In any event, it was too late to stop him.

Two hundred feet . . . five hundred feet . . . the altimeter spun upward and he smoothly bunted the nose over to hold one thousand feet, then gently walked the throttles back to hold 400 knots. That was fast enough for the moment.

Damn the metric system. Translating it was a nuisance and all the indicators and instruments were metric. He frowned under the mask and brought the FLANKER around in a smooth, gradual left turn to avoid the mountains south of Luqiao. This was his third flight in the SU-27 and he was glad he'd taken the other two. Despite the risk of discovery, he could at least now fly the thing and use the weapons systems. A simulator was fine, and he'd spent five days flying that too, courtesy of the Chinese government. But nothing took the place of air under your ass.

He knew the other two FLANKERS had turned right and circled above him before heading off to the west. Steadying up on an easterly heading, the pilot flipped the NVGs down, nudged the fighter over, and descended back through the clouds. At 500 feet he started paying attention again. Letting his eyes flicker between the altimeter and the blackness beyond the canopy, he forced his fingers to relax around the stick. Flying tense was never good.

Three hundred feet . . . one hundred fifty feet . . .

Easing the fighter still lower, he didn't think about the absurdity of flying an unfamiliar jet over unknown terrain at night in the rain. It was simply an obstacle that he had overcome with skill and experience. The darkness shredded apart a bit as he came down out of the clouds. Eyes out now, he instantly found the ground and flew visually.

There!

A pale ribbon of sand stretched out north and south as far as he could see. The beach. The coast.

Holding the jet rock steady at 100 feet, he switched on the autopilot and felt a slight tug as it engaged. Exhaling slowly, he relaxed his hold on the controls until only his fingertips were resting on the stick. Ignoring the sweat dripping down his cheek, the pilot focused intently upon the autopilot for a few long, skeptical moments. He then called up the navigation data and checked the route timing.

Converting kilometers in his head, he read 107 miles to the air traffic reporting point of SALMI. This was a point, called a fix, which commercial airliners crossed on their way over the East China Sea, and it was his first destination. Walking the throttles forward an inch to hold 500 knots, he again glanced at the time display for his arrival at SALMI: 2204 . . . four minutes past ten P.M., and a little more than fifteen minutes from now. He disconnected one side of his oxygen mask and let it drop.

Perfect.

He smiled then, white teeth against his dark face, and shifted back against the ejection seat. With a roar lost in the thundering surf, the fighter streaked over the rainswept beach and disappeared out to sea.

Go behind the scenes with Dan Hampton in the enhanced eBook!

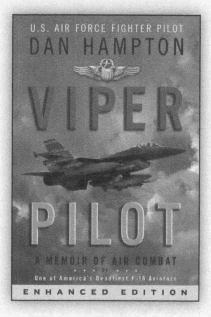

Get inside the cockpit with Dan Hampton, one of the military's most decorated F-16 pilots, in this enhanced e-book edition of *Viper Pilot*. Exclusive to this edition are:

- Eleven video interviews, where Hampton talks candidly about his time as a Wild Weasel and about the fighter jet that kept him alive through so many dangerous skirmishes.

- An interactive "first-person" cockpit diagram lets you get deeper into the action, providing a visual companion to the book that leaves you feeling like you're sitting in the iconic F-16 itself.